SPIES FOR THE BLUE AND GRAY

BOOKS BY HARNETT T. KANE

LOUISIANA HAYRIDE
THE AMERICAN REHEARSAL FOR DICTATORSHIP

BAYOUS OF LOUISIANA

DEEP DELTA COUNTRY
(IN THE AMERICAN FOLKWAYS SERIES)

PLANTATION PARADE
THE GRAND MANNER IN LOUISIANA

NEW ORLEANS WOMAN
BIOGRAPHICAL NOVEL OF MYRA CLARK GAINES

NATCHEZ ON THE MISSISSIPPPI

BRIDE OF FORTUNE
NOVEL BASED ON THE LIFE OF MRS. JEFFERSON DAVIS

QUEEN NEW ORLEANS, CITY BY THE RIVER

PATHWAY TO THE STARS
NOVEL BASED ON THE LIFE OF JOHN MCDONOGH

THE SCANDALOUS MRS. BLACKFORD
NOVEL BASED ON THE LIFE OF HARRIET BLACKFORD
(In Collaboration with Victor Leclerc)

GENTLEMEN, SWORDS AND PISTOLS

DEAR DOROTHY DIX
THE STORY OF A COMPASSIONATE WOMAN
(In Collaboration with Ella Bentley Arthur)

THE LADY OF ARLINGTON
NOVEL BASED ON THE LIFE OF MRS. ROBERT E. LEE

SPIES FOR THE BLUE AND GRAY

Property of
Mrs. H. A. Fagan
2728 Brookdale Ave-
Oakland 2-
Calif.

SPIES for the Blue and Gray

★

by Harnett T. Kane

HANOVER HOUSE
GARDEN CITY • NEW YORK

Library of Congress Catalog Card Number 54–10780

Printed in the United States
At the Country Life Press, Garden City, N.Y.
FIRST EDITION

To Judy

Contents

Introduction

The Ladies Came First

Agents for the Blue and the Gray . . . In an era of hydrogen bombs, guided missiles, and germ warfare, the subject may have an Arcadian sound, the ring of a simpler, more romantic time. But in that respect, as in others, the conflict of North and South was a paradox, a combination of paradoxes.

That war of almost a century ago produced the nation's first mass armies, and a brutality and mechanized slaughter that shocked the sensibilities of the day. It had aircraft—balloons that floated over the lines—submarines, ironclad warships, automatic guns, trenches, a military draft—and the first organized espionage that the country ever knew. On both sides the spying involved treachery, filching of official secrets, the skillful seduction of loyalty. This war between Americans probably saw more espionage, involving more people, than any in our history.

It has been called the first of the modern conflicts; it was also the last of the romantic ones. In its spying, the generation that thrilled in admiration of Sir Walter Scott usually observed "rules" of knightly, or at least gentlemanly, conduct. Had that not been true, had Northern and Southern leaders not played *Ivanhoe* on endless occasions, scores of undercover agents would never have survived to tell their stories.

It was a spy-conscious war, and sometimes it seemed that everybody was spying on everybody else and talking volubly on the subject, in newspapers, parlors, bars, and at street corners. Nevertheless, few officials did anything to stop the enemy's espionage. The present-day reader may be astonished at the ease with which agents made their way across the lines and through opposition territory. Repeatedly they presented themselves to civilian and military officials, pumped them of information, and rode off with a bright good-by.

The nature of the war made espionage easy to carry on and difficult to stop. A Tennesseean looked and acted much like a Pennsylvanian, a Texan like an Ohioan; if he simply paid attention to regional accents, an agent had little trouble. Repeatedly Southern and Northern commands turned apoplectic on discovering that the man whom they had escorted proudly over their fortifications was a spy for the other side. By that time he was usually well on his way to his home base.

Yet by and large these agents for the Blue and Gray played an amateur's game. Espionage had not yet become a high art or achieved the status to which Continental masters soon elevated it. The American spies improvised, experimented, and what they lacked in finesse they made up in energy and determination. They broke rules usually because they had never heard of them. They were a mixed crew, gentle and flamboyant, earnest and brazen, ingenious or crafty. They ranged from shoe clerks to young plantation owners, lawyers to *grandes dames,* actresses to plump housewives.

The ladies were terrific. In this war they made their American debut in espionage, and never since have the nation's women taken such an active part as spies. No matter how raging a partisan a man might be, his wife or sister was probably still more impassioned. They became the best recruiting sergeants; they were "not at home" to those who lagged in enlisting, and they sent such friends white feathers or boxes containing dresses. They connived endlessly, they took great risks, and they pushed through to success in ways impossible to simple males. They showed again that the female is not only the deadlier of the sexes, but also the livelier.

In the eighteen-sixties the double standard prevailed in spying as in other matters, and to the ladies' benefit. Neither side did a great deal about it, even when the identities of women agents were well established. As the war grew slowly more bitter, men operatives were hanged, one by one. The women received threats, or perhaps a prison term, and then freedom to try again. That war saw no Ethel Rosenbergs, and no Edith Cavells. After all, a lady was a lady. . . . A gentleman could not bring himself to order her shot or swung from a gallows.

In part this is a tale of two cities, Washington and Richmond, with scenes in Louisville and New Orleans, Nashville and St. Louis and Baltimore. By an accident of geography the capitals of North and South lay only a hundred miles apart. Their proximity made them obvious targets for rival armies and no less for rival spies.

At the war's beginning neither Union nor Confederacy had a security organization nor a secret service; the nation had never known one. The general war effort started as an exercise of amateurs. Struggling to create a colossal military machine of a kind that the country had not previously visualized, each side floundered. In no field was the process of trial and error more pronounced than in espionage.

In Richmond and Washington roughly organized intelligence units gradually emerged. Inconspicuously located in the Richmond War Department was an office halfway between that of Jefferson Davis and the War Secretary's. Most Richmonders considered the Signal Bureau only the headquarters of that newfangled branch of operations which used "flag-floppers." Confederates teased the dapper young men who carried blue and scarlet cloths: "Mister, is the flies a-botherin' of you?"

The Signal Bureau, however, had special functions. Its offices carried on an unending correspondence in cipher with Confederate agents in Washington, Baltimore, and other key points in Union territory. Early in the war the North tried to establish "land blockades" to cut off communication as well as thousands of items not available in the nonmanufacturing South. But representatives of the Confederate Signal Bureau managed to run courier lines in all directions over land and water.

Several offices beside the Signal Bureau involved themselves in Southern espionage—that of Jefferson Davis, the successive War Secretaries, the provost marshal. So many had a part, in fact, that the effort suffered; responsibilities were scattered, confused, and Union spies appeared to slip in and out of the Confederacy like fish through a wide-meshed net.

The North stumbled on in its own way. Arriving for his inauguration, in the face of threats against his life, Abraham Lincoln lacked even an official bodyguard. In the early months of the war Southern agents had a field day, working almost without hindrance. The first Federal defeat brought an awakening, a shake-up, and the North's first secret service bureau.

Authority over the new service was transient. The State Department supervised intelligence matters in the beginning; then they went over to the War office, and as in Richmond the provost marshal and other officials had a finger in the pie. Sometimes Washington spies seemed to be spying on other spies. But then, if only because of the war's course, which brightened steadily for the North, the Union system became more expert than the Confederacy's, boasting some rare feats of espionage.

Early and late, spies for both sides had a superb asset—the almost unbelievable carelessness of officialdom and citizenry alike. Little or no effort was made to check clacking tongues, and casual gossip told all an enemy needed to know about an impending advance or a strategic installation. A man had an "open face," so he *must* be on our side, you understand.

Another aid to spying lay in the newspaper situation. In Dixie as in the North the press blandly printed vital information. Preparing for the Battle of Chickamauga in Tennessee, Confederate General Braxton Bragg received a New York *Times* clipping which explained precisely how the Unionists would fool him into a shift of position. Bragg stayed put. Near Vicksburg a Northern spy brought his superior a newspaper story in which a correspondent described in full the Federal plans for a "secret canal" behind the Mississippi. The project had to be dropped.

More than perhaps any other Southern general, Robert E. Lee used secret agents to supply him with every available Northern newspaper. The Virginian studied them by the hour, noting, comparing, questioning. A Southern spy with a copy of the Philadelphia *Inquirer* provided information of a withdrawal by McClellan; as a result, Lee shifted thousands of troops. The Southerner's military shrewdness kept him from accepting false stories planted for his benefit, and Lee himself once inserted a fake in Confederate papers.

The complete story of American espionage of 1861–65 will, of course, never be known. Much of it was never committed to paper; countless incidents were understood by only three or four people, who never gave out the facts. Innumerable agents died obscure deaths, shot down on a dark road or succumbing to exposure.

When Richmond fell, one of the last acts of Judah Benjamin was reportedly the burning of most of the South's secret service papers. Years later Jefferson Davis discouraged attempts to give out details of Confederate spying. On the Union side General Grenville Dodge similarly opposed efforts to reveal names and activities. Too many people might be hurt.

Nevertheless, a great deal of data is available from a variety of sources. In the Official Records of both armies were recorded thousands of pages of correspondence, orders of inquiry and arrest, some of them carrying evidence of all too human rage and puzzlement over the episodes.

These episodes chiefly concern civilian spies, though related work of military scouts is involved at some points. The story is at times bizarre, almost unbelievable. A plotmaker concerned with credibility would hesitate to let his characters do some of the things these spies did in real life.

H. T. K.

Part One

Chapter 1

Within Rifle Range of the White House

The Widow Greenhow's narrow brick house on fashionable Sixteenth Street, a few blocks from the White House, appeared, in the words of a contemporary, "somewhat on the quiet side." Which, he might have added, was not exactly what neighbors said about the widow herself.

Those neighbors of the late 1850s would have been blind—and less than human—had they failed to notice the number of times a well-identified carriage drew up at Rose O'Neal Greenhow's door. There was no reason why the affable, stocky Mr. Buchanan should not call; he was a bachelor, and thousands of Washingtonians would have leaped to accept an invitation from the beautiful and elegant Madame Greenhow. But narrow-minded residents in the vicinity of Sixteenth and I streets, staring through the meshes of their lace curtains, whispered about the late hours at which Mr. Buchanan called, the length of his visits, and the dubious part the lady played in national affairs. For James Buchanan was President of the United States.

The widow received other male visitors: young, handsome ones in uniform; older and obviously more important individuals—heads of congressional committees, judges, Cabinet members. Few gossips, however, would have dared to say anything openly against the leading hostess of the powerful Democratic administration, for she boasted family connections with several reigning American clans. She was, moreover, described as "the most persuasive woman ever known in Washington," and as "a woman of almost irresistible seductive powers."

Whatever charms and powers she possessed, physical and mental, Rose Greenhow was eventually to use them against the wartime government of the United States. Most of her life she had worked from sheer love of power to win a unique position for herself in Washington. With the approach of conflict, it seemed as if all those years had been a preparation for the adept and daring espionage that she carried on for the Confederate government. Behind a barricade of power and influential connections, Mrs. Greenhow ran a spy ring unprecedented in America.

Rose O'Neal Greenhow worked her way upward by strenuous effort to the glamor and adventure of her wartime activity. She was born in 1817 in Montgomery County, Maryland, a country girl of very modest means. She was related, however, to the families of social importance—Lees and Randolphs and Calverts. Her father died early, and the young O'Neals grew up in the settlement of Rockville, fifteen miles from Washington.

When she reached her early teens the family sent the dark, pretty Rose to the capital to stay with her aunt, Mrs. Hill, who kept the Congressional Boarding House in the Old Capitol Building. With Rose went her equally good-looking sister, Ellen Elizabeth. A boarding place patronized by dashing young men, transient bachelors, and politicians might not have appeared an ideal environment for the O'Neal girls. But they conducted themselves with discretion.

Rose, however, became a pet of the guests of that many-windowed building, with its fan-lighted, multipaneled doorway. The great brick structure was to have a curious, recurring part in her life. One contemporary recalled her as "a bright, handsome but illiterate country girl." It was doubtful that she was ever really illiterate, and in Washington she learned quickly—names, places, subjects—and she forgot nothing.

A man much older than she, the fierce-eyed John Calhoun of South Carolina, who held court in her aunt's lodginghouse, was a major influence in Rose's life. He patted her head while she listened entranced to his talk of Dixie's grievances. From him she absorbed a profound identification with the South. As she said later: "I am a Southern woman, born with revolutionary blood in my veins, and my first crude ideas on State and Federal matters received consistency and shape from the best and wisest man of this century." Catching the zealot's fervor, she spoke hotly of the South's need to strike out for its rights.

She had vigor and emotion to spare, and it was said that "her fresh charm drew many admirers." "The Wild Rose," a young man called her, and the title clung. Long-legged, slim-waisted, she had olive skin and eyes that looked brown in tranquil moments, black when anger swept her. Many commented on the whiteness of her teeth when the full lips parted. Her brows were heavy, and her sleek black hair was pulled back almost severely. Despite her lack of education, this young Rose was certainly noticed, especially by men.

When she was about seventeen she attracted the attention of the first important figure with whom her name would be connected—Cave Johnson of Tennessee, who eventually became Postmaster General. He introduced Miss O'Neal to Washington society; on his arm she gained entree to one drawing room after another. Some people inquired pointedly who *that* might be, and then snubbed her. Rose only smiled; she survived the snubs because she had to. After a time she came into conflict with a young woman no less ambitious than she, Senator Tom Benton's daughter Jessie. They got along like oil and a lighted match.

That fresh, engaging air must, however, have won over most of those who met Rose. She was a good conversationalist and she also listened well. Her partners received the most flattering of tributes, an interested silence. And many testified later to her kindness, her generous acts of friendship.

For some time the dowagers expected her to marry gallant Cave Johnson, but other escorts appeared and suddenly Rose was seen riding beside a Virginian of Virginians—gentlemanly Robert Greenhow, onetime doctor, writer, and linguist. For several years Rose went to cotillions and receptions with Dr. Greenhow. With such an escort she was accepted without question. Seventeen years her senior, Dr. Greenhow had position, a handsome home, an impressive background in Richmond. How much love Rose felt for him no one knows. Hers was a fervent nature, but her head governed her heart, in this case at least. At twenty-six, Rose married the scholarly Dr. Greenhow.

About the same time her sister Ellen also made a rich match, with James Madison Cutts, Dolly Madison's nephew, allied with the George Washington clan. The Misses O'Neal had done more than well for themselves. In a handsome establishment on F Street Mrs. Greenhow began to dominate a widening circle of friends, and also, it is indicated, her indulgent husband. She enjoyed Washington politics and its mixed population of soft-mannered Marylanders, affable Georgians, Westerners with nasal accents. She delighted in the maneuverings for position, in which she took her part, in the gaslighted balls, in the continual conflict and change.

Robert Greenhow wrote an authoritative history of Tripoli, and another of Oregon and California, while he served as translator for the State Department. Happily Rose found herself increasingly thrown with her old friend Calhoun. Her husband established a Virginia newspaper in support of the South Carolinian, and Calhoun stayed for months with the Greenhows. More and more the girl from the country felt the warming certainty that she was "in" with the best people.

Those best people were chiefly Southerners. Founded only sixty years earlier along the Virginia and Maryland border, Washington had the air and manner of Dixie—the slow, casual pace, the hot, humid climate, slaves on the streets, auction pens, and, not least, heavy Southern accents heard in Willard's Hotel and the many boardinghouses. The men of the Old Dominion, the Carolinas, and the lower South maintained a tradition of rule. Southern officeholders and their wives controlled the lively social life of the city, the stately dances in the glittering ballrooms, the diplomatic dinners and official gatherings. Europeans were amused by the contrasts of Washington life. With its intermittent glitter and sophistication, the place remained an unfinished city, with mudholes in most of its unpaved streets.

During the 1840s Madame Greenhow became an outstanding social figure, a woman of wit, with a touch of the dramatic in voice and manner, her silks billowing as she stepped out of her carriage on Pennsylvania Avenue. A few Washingtonians who had once merely tolerated her now recognized Rose as "a leader, famous for her beauty, the brilliance of her conversation, her aptitude for intrigue, the royal dignity of her manners, and the unscrupulous perseverance with which she accomplishes whatever she sets her heart upon." The tone of this observer is unfriendly, but the description is a shrewd one.

The Greenhows produced four children, all daughters, and on them Rose poured out a warm and possessive affection; at least one, her namesake, was as spirited and vigorous as her mother. Dr. Greenhow, never very strong, suffered a number of illnesses. During one siege he and Rose became guests at the home of a particular friend, James (Old Buck) Buchanan, the important senator from Pennsylvania, who became Minister to England in 1845. It was said that Buchanan's slightly crossed eyes did not conceal their interest in the lustrous Mrs. Greenhow.

For years Rose had close ties with members of Washington's diplomatic corps, particularly the English and the French, and one or two critics remarked bitterly on these connections. In her private records the hostile Jessie Benton, who had become the wife of the explorer Frémont, wrote an acid paragraph about her. Jessie had helped translate messages received by her senator father from a confidential Mexican agent regarding British maneuverings in the Southwest. Ordinarily, Jessie declared, such notes would have gone to Greenhow, the State Department's translator. "But his wife was in the pay of the British legation as a spy, and our [the Bentons'] private information reached them through her." And so, Jessie concluded, officials diverted the messages from Dr. Greenhow. Whatever the basis of this accusation, Rose had found in Jessie a strong personal enemy.

Early in 1850 Mrs. Greenhow suffered a loss from which she was slow to recover. One chilly night an urgent message brought her carriage clattering to the doorway of her aunt's old boardinghouse, where her patron Calhoun lay dying. For hours she sat ministering to the sick man, and heard his last gloomy predictions of the dissolution of the Union. She would never forget them. . . .

That same year, her husband saw a great opportunity on the West Coast; in California he became law officer for the United States Land Commission. Rose found the change painful, yet she followed him to San Francisco. Four years later, in March of 1854, Dr. Greenhow met with a serious accident, falling six feet off an elevated sidewalk. Probably as a result of this mishap, he died soon afterward. Always one to look after her own rights, Rose sued San Francisco and won a judgment, although the damages awarded were not large.

Robert Greenhow had left one or two properties, a few securities, but no great wealth. With four children to support, the thirty-seven-year-old widow took up life again in Washington. In that swiftly changing town she needed all her dark beauty, all her charm, to regain her old position. She had, of course, her friends and connections, and before long her niece and namesake, Rose Cutts, made a brilliant match. She became the second wife of Senator Stephen A. Douglas. Everyone thought that Douglas, the Democrats' "Little Giant," would become President.

Yet Rose knew that she must depend primarily on herself. Her best asset was her extraordinary ability to influence others, and that she used to the utmost. She became what would today be called a "fixer," a lady who could obtain favors from legislators, army officials, and government workers. Her correspondence (eventually seized by the government) has a remarkable range, and almost a present-day ring. A New Yorker wrote her that his brother-in-law wanted to be a post-office architect. A Virginian told her that in suggesting his name to the President for appointment to the Supreme Court she had put him under obligations he would never forget. A San Franciscan hoped she could get copies of two legal opinions, "you being pretty much the only person really to be relied on when things are to be done up *brown*." Another man regretted she had not received "that $190 as early as I had promised."

Mrs. Greenhow helped army officers to get promotions; she called on senators; she arranged meetings between interested parties, and more and more often the meetings took place in her new small house on Sixteenth Street. Despite her limited funds, she had made it very attractive. She had kept her fine chairs and carved sofas, oil paintings, statuary, and, always her special pride, a "rosewood pianoforte with pearl keys."

For a time she was seen frequently in the company of Joseph E. Lane of Oregon, a senator whose easygoing manner concealed from nobody his ambition for the presidency. Contemporary diarists wrote that the widow "entertained" for him at suppers and receptions, where she made certain that Lane did well for himself. Their letters indicate not only their mutual interest in politics, but also a more personal interest. In one note Lane complained that he found her "always surrounded by admirers," but would be back at nine that evening. Apparently when he returned he learned that she had gone out. "I could not sit long alone, naturally impatient, restless and almost reckless," he complained in another message. "Please answer–Your Lane."

Rose was never one to be taken for granted; rarely did a man walk up that short flight of stairs with the certainty that Madame was his to command. Nearly always, it would seem, there was at least one gentleman in the double parlors who cursed secretly at the others and wished they would get the devil out of there. It had become clear, too, that the widow had the ability to fascinate younger men; the house on Sixteenth Street was frequently as tense as a battleground.

The year 1856 brought to the presidency Rose's friend Buchanan. In her memoirs she wrote casually of tête-à-têtes with the Chief Executive. As Major Doster, later provost marshal of Washington, declared: "There was much gossip at this time arising from the intimacy between Mrs. Greenhow and the President."

Buchanan's niece was his official hostess, but whatever that prim maiden thought, the presidential carriage often rolled down the short route from the White House to the residence on Sixteenth Street. "Queen" of the administration, one hostile newspaper called Rose. Her friendly rooms were known as "headquarters" of the regime. In spite of the exaggeration, the comment reflected a widely held opinion. Certainly the lady could perform wonders when she wished.

President Buchanan went serenely about his duties, his squinting eye no better with the years. Big, pink-faced, and ponderous, he liked parties. He also believed in moderation. The clouds were gathering, but Buchanan worked to mitigate the furious conflict over slavery's extension to the new territories. He placated, he shifted, yet he generally favored the South. Rose approved of Old Buck's administration; he approved of Rose.

While the South was most strongly represented at her soirées, the Widow Greenhow's invitation list was long and varied. Some of her best friends were the emerging Republicans, despite their crusading fervor on the slavery issue. Among them, more and more often, appeared Senator Henry Wilson of Massachusetts, plump and unpolished and scowling. His fellow guests might frown at Wilson as the blackest of abolitionists, but, after all, he was a member of the vital Military Affairs Committee. Soon he was its chairman, and eventually became Vice-President of the United States, but "they" said that Rose had reasons other than his rising political star for her great interest in the man. . . .

In the same drawing room, wearing his habitually suave smile, there often stood the powerful New Yorker, William H. Seward, who, as most people thought, would be the Republican candidate for Chief Executive. (No matter who became the next President, the widow would have her well-shod foot in the door!) And there was also a gentleman who carried himself with a certain tense dignity, Jefferson Davis of Mississippi. Everybody went to Madame Greenhow's!

In the spring of 1858 she was written up in the New York *Times* for her role at a masquerade ball. Rose made a bow as "a most comely Housekeeper of the Old School; and although her costume was not as showy as some, yet the *esprit* of the wearer made her 'glorious as a diamond richly set.' "

The following year brought the startling raid on nearby Harper's Ferry by the bearded fanatic, John Brown. The South cried out in its fear of mass uprisings, burning, pillage; the North hailed Brown as a martyr to the cause of human liberty. People everywhere were sick with the realization that the nation was truly and deeply divided. Rose made Washington social history at this time with an oddly mixed and fashionable dinner party. Into a circle of Southerners she introduced Congressman and Mrs. Charles Francis Adams of Massachusetts.

Over the hum of table talk, Mrs. Adams suddenly spoke out for John Brown. An embarrassed silence followed, and then Madame Greenhow lashed out at her guest. The party ended early and icily, and within an hour the story was all over the capital. When President Buchanan mentioned the subject, Rose had a peppery answer: "Do you keep spies in my household?" He placated her, saying he admired her independence.

Scenes similar to the one at the Greenhow dinner party were taking place all over America. Men rose in Congress to shake their fists and swear at their opponents; with unprecedented daring several members brought guns to the Chamber. In the South, over breakfast coffee, over punch bowls, on street corners, men and women talked of cutting all ties with the Yankees and forming their own nation. Early in 1860 Lieutenant Colonel Keyes, secretary to Commanding General Scott of the Army, joined a party at the Stephen Douglases', where he expressed "great delight with the Southern damsels, and even some of the matrons, notwithstanding the incandescence of their treason."

The ladies at that party felt certain there would be fighting between North and South; they talked openly of it. Rose Greenhow went to work on the fatuous Keyes. "After expatiating on the injustice of the North," the lady tried "to persuade me not to take part in the war." Later, reflecting on the efforts of Rose and her friends, the colonel remarked on "how often I was lured to the brink of the precipice." For months Madame Greenhow tried to draw the waverers over that precipice. She watched intently as the Democratic party split. In the fateful election in November of 1860 the Republicans won, and the elements hostile to Lincoln swore that they would not live in a nation run by such a man.

Before Christmas, South Carolina flung down the gauntlet,

and seceded from the Union. As Buchanan delayed and hoped, and did little, Mississippi followed, and then Florida, Alabama, Georgia, Louisiana, and Texas. While Washington reverberated with talk of plots and predictions of disaster, Lincoln arrived in March and took the oath to serve a broken nation. Old time Southerners said good-by to the capital, riding away with their Negro servants to join the new Confederate government. The city and the nation were in flux. What would happen next? At Fort Sumter in Charleston Harbor, the question was answered.

Among those who did not leave Washington with the change in administration was Rose Greenhow. Her pro-Southern sentiments had grown stronger and more definite. Northerners were "mudsills," a race apart, barbarians and worse, but she stayed on among them. Eventually she thanked God in the presence of a Union commissioner that "no drop of Yankee blood ever polluted my veins." For Rose there were also family griefs and tensions. One of her daughters died, and she went into deep mourning; two of the others married, and, though she liked the sons-in-law, one who had joined the army chose to remain with the Union.

Rose kept a good many of her Northern friends, and she still held her sensitive fingers on the pulse of the capital—with a purpose. Early in the course of secession, she had decided to do what she could for her South. In the spring of 1861 fortune sent her an opportunity in the person of a handsome fellow one or two years her junior. He was Thomas Jordan of Virginia, soldier, journalist, man about town. Tom Jordan moved on at least the outer fringe of Mrs. Greenhow's wide social circle. The bright-eyed army lieutenant had organizing ability; he also had imagination. Preparing to quit the Union, he set to work in advance to help his side by laying the groundwork of an espionage system.

Incidental notes are the only remaining evidence of Jordan's activities. He met pretty matrons, lawyers, doctors, clerks, housewives, and, as the currents of war swept closer, he enlisted them all into service. Tom Jordan must have felt, however, that his major conquest was the famous lady of Sixteenth Street. For hours he and the Widow Greenhow analyzed the situation and, we gather, no other callers interrupted. Jordan made it clear that what was needed was quick, dependable information about troop movements, army supplies, relations among government and army officials.

Rose understood; she had ways to get such data, she thought. Before Lincoln's arrival in Washington, she had "employed every capacity with which God has endowed me, and the result was far more successful than my hopes could have flattered me to expect." Lieutenant Jordan gave her a simple cipher system that he had devised, and with it his spy name, Thomas J. Rayford. Then on April 13 Fort Sumter fell into Confederate hands, and war was a black certainty. From the White House went Lincoln's first call for seventy-five thousand troops. On May 21 Lieutenant Jordan, like scores of others, left the Union. Soon he was ranked as lieutenant colonel of Virginia troops and chief of staff for the Louisiana Creole, Beauregard, hero of Sumter.

As Washingtonians reacted to the situation in confusion and alarm, Rose Greenhow rode about town as calmly as ever, calling on Mr. Seward, now Lincoln's Secretary of State, issuing invitations, meeting friends. She once explained that she could move through Washington "as the Indian savage in the trackless forest, with an enemy behind every bush."

She admitted—rather, boasted—that "without scruple" she led Federal men to provide information, which she "at once communicated with pride and pleasure" to her Confederate connections. In a confidential message to the Secretary of War of the Confederacy, Judah Benjamin, Jordon told how he had originally wondered about Rose's true faith in the South. Receiving her messages with caution, he at first "communicated nothing to her." She swiftly convinced him not only of her good faith but also of her amazing access to the sources of important facts.

General Beauregard spoke warmly of the espionage arrangements that netted him the "most accurate information, of which politicians high in council, as well as War department clerks, were the unconscious ducts." With tact and persistence the glamorous widow worked on her men; she asked cleverly, she listened well.

Some of her informants were not entirely unconscious of the help they gave her. There were young government employees in strategic positions whom she chose for their Southern inclinations, their resentment against Union plans, or their simple appreciation of Rose's feminine appeal. As one federal official noted, she obtained facts and figures "that could have been found nowhere else but in the national archives." And he added: "She has not used her powers in vain among the officers of the Army, not a few of whom she has robbed of patriotic hearts. . . ."

She was now forty-four, and her wild, fresh charm had been replaced by a softened loveliness, a great elegance. Rose's figure remained excellent. Her dark hair, parted in the center, was still drawn tightly back, giving her a slightly Spanish look. Uncurled despite the current style of ringlets and swirls, it had a sprinkling of gray that she did not try to hide. And her warm lips smiled more than ever on those from whom she wanted military information.

Her private papers reveal her methods. In one case a captain assigned to a vital battle area near Washington did not visit her as he had promised. Rose thanked him for "thinking of me at all amidst the battle of camp life." Sweetly she continued:

> Of course I looked for you and stayed at home all through the day and was disappointed as women generally are when they wish for anything. But I knew that "circumstances over which you had *no control*" must alone have made you disap-

point a real true friend. . . . I never dreamed that you intended to neglect, or do any other *disagreeable* thing. So you see I have faith unbounded in *those* I call *friend*. . . . I only wish that you even sometimes avail yourself of a room which I will always have ready for you.

In frightened, overcrowded Washington of 1861 Rose Greenhow's spy ring grew in size and strength. Close to her in her operations was a shadowy younger woman, Miss Lillie Mackall. Wispy, lackluster, Miss Lillie had no personality, but she would have leaped off the top of the unfinished Capitol if Rose had asked it. Lillie carried messages, listened in halls outside government offices, and made contact with housewifely types like Mrs. Betty Hassler, another of their helpers.

There was the banker, William Smithson, who maintained good social connections while he led a double life as one Charles Cables. There were the popular dentist, Dr. Aaron Van Camp, who started by attending to Rose's teeth and went on to transmitting her cipher messages; young Messrs. Walker and Rennehan of the government offices; many nameless lawyers, merchants, and men about town. Before long, as a Federal detective later reported in annoyance, Rose kept for her convenience a long list of available aides, with "alphabets, numbers, ciphers and various other not-mentioned ways of holding intercourse . . . unknown to any but themselves." Among them slipped her pert daughter Rose, then about ten, who could curse a Yankee with the best of them.

The Greenhow ring was ready for its greatest services. As the summer of 1861 began, Washington thronged with Union men who marched about the dusty streets, filled the bars and brothels, camped on the outskirts, and wondered how soon they could end the war and go home. It was a concentration of people unprecedented in American history. At the same time, however, nearby Virginia thronged with men in gray, taking positions at strategic points.

Which force was superior? Nobody could be sure. At the railroad center of Manassas Junction, thirty miles west of the capital, General Beauregard of Louisiana had the largest Southern force, with an outpost thrust to within fifteen miles of Washington itself at Fairfax Court House. Sixty miles away, General Joe Johnston of Virginia had an army about half as large. In all, counting soldiers at one or two other points, the Confederacy had perhaps thirty-four thousand men. Could they be knit together in time to meet a strong Union threat?

The Union Army rolls showed a great superiority in numbers. Opposite Johnston at Winchester they had eighteen thousand men. In Washington itself, on the front closest to Beauregard, Commanding General Irving McDowell had thirty-five thousand. Nevertheless, McDowell had trouble in concealing his uneasiness. But while he wondered about the quality of his troops, Union confidence was returning and rising high—too high.

For months Washingtonians had watched the raw recruits idling at the corners, getting into brawls, eating up government money. Why didn't McDowell get under way? One real pounding, and the whole secesh crew would be on the run, tails between their scurvy legs, and the war would be over in a day!

"On to Richmond, on to Richmond," was the cry. Rose Greenhow and her friends heard it and redoubled their efforts. McDowell was unready; his raw forces needed discipline, seasoning, drill. The harassed general complained gloomily to a friend: "This is not an Army. It will take a long time to make an Army." He was not given the time. July Fourth saw a grand review, banners flapping in the breeze, flowers tossed at grinning privates, fireworks, bands, the sound of fife and drum. The patriots shouted louder: "By God, hit the Rebs, hit 'em *now!*"

At the house on Sixteenth Street Mrs. Greenhow saw unmistakable signs that Union men were preparing for the war's first great battle. Drilled or undrilled, the Northern forces had so many more men. If only the South knew the route they would take, and when . . . That information was precisely what the widow provided.

On July 10 she drew one of her agents, a quiet, dark-haired girl, Betty Duvall, into her hallway for a private talk. Miss Duvall reached out for a small rectangle of black silk; inside it lay a thin sheet of paper with a cipher message. The girl fastened the cloth in the ropes of her hair, tightened her chignon, and left unobtrusively. A wagon awaited her in the street, and Betty, wearing the rough gray dress of a marketman's daughter, rode out of the city without challenge. Continuing down the Union side of the Potomac, she reached an area of Southern sympathizers. She stayed overnight at a friend's residence, that of Commodore Jones.

In the morning, wearing a neat riding habit and accompanied by a cousin, Betty mounted a horse and rode off again. Crossing the river at Dumfries, she sped toward Fairfax Court House, Beauregard's advance post. When a sentry stopped her, she lost time in arguing her way in. Sixteen years later the commander, aging General M. L. Bonham of South Carolina, well remembered the incident.

As Bonham's provost marshal announced Betty's arrival, the general hesitated. He had just ordered all females kept away from the lines; too many Yankee women had been going through on secret errands, pretending to be Confederates. Yet Betty had said she must talk to Bonham in person about a "vastly important" matter.

Finally he agreed. When she entered, the general recognized "a beautiful young lady, a brunette with sparkling black eyes, perfect features, glossy black hair," whom he had seen once and clearly not forgotten. Betty spoke hastily: unless Bonham would send on her message to Beauregard and at once, she wanted permission to ride forward with it. On the general's assurance that he would dispatch it, "she took out her tucking comb and let fall the longest and most beautiful roll of hair that I have ever seen on human head." The man in gray was full of admiration. "Flushed from the morning's ride, with the flow of patriotic devotion beaming from her bright face, she looked to the Confederate General radiantly beautiful." A few minutes later the letter had started toward Beauregard.

It read: "McDowell has certainly been ordered to advance on the sixteenth. R.O.G." Beauregard lost no time in sending his aide to Jefferson Davis in Richmond. . . . On July 16, preceded by ambulance, wagon trains, and other advance vehicles, the Federal Army ground into Virginia. But the day before, Rose Greenhow and her helpers had provided even more important data. At Manassas, Colonel Tom Jordan talked with a stolid individual, G. Donellan, who had just come over to join the Confederates. Until then Donellan had been a clerk in the Union's Interior Department. Jordan had a task for the recruit—to make contact with Mrs. Greenhow at the first possible moment.

At dark on July 15, at a spot near Alexandria, a Confederate sympathizer rowed Donellan over the Potomac. From there he rode slowly to Washington in a buggy. Early on the sixteenth, Donellan's vehicle moved with difficulty past the rumbling traffic of Federal Army units on the way from the capital. An hour or so afterward he talked briskly to the Greenhow maid, who aroused Mrs. Greenhow.

Who had sent him? Rose demanded.

"Mr. Rayford of Virginia."

She asked for credentials, and Donellan handed her a paper with a cipher message: "Trust bearer."

Now Mrs. Greenhow was fully awake and she spoke urgently: she had news, and he must take it right away! Her maid Lizzie gave the emissary breakfast while Rose scratched out a note. A little later Donellan, a man whom few would notice in a crowd, rode out of Washington. Clattering down the eastern bank of the Potomac, he changed horses from time to time. As he approached a ferry landing in Charles County, a cavalryman, awaiting him by prearrangement, snatched up the letter and pounded on toward Manassas. By dark Beauregard and his spy director Jordan stared at Rose's words:

McDowell, with 55,000 men, will advance this day from Arlington Heights and Alexandria on to Manassas via Fairfax Court House and on to Centreville.

This was what the Confederate general had needed most to know. Shifting batteries, he deployed his men to meet the oncoming Federal troops. He ordered Bonham to pull back from his advance position at Fairfax Court House. And to Jefferson Davis in Richmond, Beauregard rushed a message urging that General Johnston's army be sent on to supplement his own. After a short delay, as the Unionists marched slowly on, Davis acted. Because of Rose Greenhow's work, the battle picture changed: the South was able to use two armies instead of one against the Union forces.

Meanwhile Jordan set his underground to work again, directing G. Donellan back to Washington. Madame Greenhow was ready with a third message: the Union planned to cut the Manassas Gap railroad in an effort to hold off Johnston's movement. . . . Beauregard could boast later that he was "almost as well advised of the strength of the hostile army in my front as its commander!"

As Washington's Unionists were shouting their certainty of triumph, Rose suddenly went to New York. One of her married daughters was sailing for California; if the Confederate spy had other reasons for spending that critical July 21 at the Astor House, she never gave them. . . . For the Northern forces the battle day started well. The Union army moved steadily along the route Rose had outlined so well–Fairfax

Court House, Centreville, and beyond. This prelude to bloody tragedy was played against a background of musical comedy. Carriages rolled from Washington toward Manassas carrying senators curious to watch the battle from a safe distance. Breathless ladies held fashionable opera glasses to their eyes; clerks clutched sandwich baskets; and a madam took her stable of girls for a day off.

The gay onlookers, in holiday mood, found points of vantage, gesticulated toward the smoke, put fingers in their ears when cannon fire pounded nearby. A Federal commander made a blunder, exposed his men unnecessarily near Bull Run, and drew back, badly rattled. The Confederates had their own troubles. Johnston succeeded in evading the Union general opposite him, but his arrival at Manassas was delayed, almost fatally. He came on at last, just in time, and the Southern reenforcements held.

All at once, in midafternoon, the spectators' eager interest turned to terror. Union forces began withdrawing, slowly at first, then in a rout; the Confederates sent them reeling. An army had turned into a mob, every man for himself, and to hell with anything except his own salvation. Infuriated commanders were powerless to check the confusion on both sides. Now the Northern soldiers were retreating madly to the Potomac, and over Washington there fell a deathly silence.

Exhausted men in uniform staggered toward the capital, leaving dead comrades in the roads with the wrecks of wagons and ambulances. Reaching town, hundreds of them sat dazed on the curbs. In the White House Lincoln was calmer than his advisers, who feared that the Confederates might plunge into Washington itself. . . . Rose Greenhow, at her New York hotel, heard the news with delight; she had been certain the Southerners would do precisely what they had done. New York was no longer the place for *her*.

Home in early morning, she received an excited report from

Miss Lillie Mackall, and then from others of her aides. With her daughter Rose watching, she read Tom Jordan's tribute, brought to her by special messenger:

Our President and our General direct me to thank you. We rely upon you for further information. The Confederacy owes you a debt.

Mrs. Greenhow would never forget that accolade in the troubled years to come. Once again Beauregard was to recognize the important services of this "lady who lived within easy rifle range of the White House," and others credited her as the agent who made possible the South's vital victory at Manassas.

While Unionists of Washington were asking one another if all were lost, Rose Greenhow talked with the man whom she still treated as her friend, Secretary of State Seward. He assured her that "there was nothing serious the matter"; everything would be over in sixty days. The Union was preparing for the expected Confederate attack. His confidence was not shared by others, according to Mrs. Greenhow. "Everything about the national capital betokened the panic of the administration," she wrote. At the first warning of invasion three guns would roar and every church bell would peal.

Her agents moved about the city, and Rose arranged to have the "principal officer in charge" take her around the capital's fortifications. She obtained, moreover, a full set of blueprints and a detailed statement of military strength, with pages of figures: forts, size and number of fieldpieces, undefended points, descriptions of ammunition and its condition. She was also given estimates of morale and the political leanings of officers—what certain ones had said about the Union prospects, and which ones might yet shift to the Southern side!

And if the Confederates approached, Rose and her helpers, male and female, would play their part in a well-planned sabotage scheme. In the inevitable panic they were to cut telegraph wires connecting the forts and other defenses, and they would try to spike the guns. They had plans galore.

The Southern army never arrived, and the first Confederate prisoners trudged wearily into Washington. They were spat upon, threatened with shooting as they passed furious civilians who believed tales of Southern atrocities and mutilations. The Unionists marched the captives to a place long familiar to Rose Greenhow. Her aunt's former boardinghouse had now become the Old Capitol Prison, and Mrs. Greenhow headed there at once. With her helper, Miss Mackall, she carried baskets of food, clothes, and supplies to the prisoners.

As she walked into the yard, Superintendent Wood was addressing the dispirited men, demanding that they take the oath of allegiance; if they did not, he shouted, they would regret it. When he had finished Rose went from one group to another, talking earnestly. They must take no such oath. If the North injured them in any way, the Confederacy had prisoners "100 to 1" to retaliate. As she and Lillie Mackall swept off, the men cheered and the superintendent gave her a long, glowering look. That night Rose used a courier to send the prisoners' names to the South.

When she called again, the prison doors were closed to her. Indignantly she wrote to officials and received a pass permitting her to leave clothes at the entrance. It was not enough, and she made another appeal, one intended to be disarming: if she could visit again, she would give her "parole of honor" not to say or do anything of which the Union disapproved. Though she still did not get in, she sent food to the prisoners through others and continued to forward information about them and from them to her Confederate superiors.

She kept scrawled messages that told of her generous help. "Mrs. Greenhow: Basket containing articles for prisoners all received in good order, for which receive our grateful thanks."

"Sergeant T. Jeff Bates, compliments to Mrs. Greenhow; he has received the articles she so kindly sent."

Obviously as a blind for her real interests, she then wrote to the Federals, offering suggestions to help *their* army. After Manassas she had had a bright thought. Why not protect the men from Southern bullets with "shoulder shields"? Politely a Northern army official declined the recommendation.

About this time Rose scribbled a note, a kind of memorandum to herself, which she left in her desk:

There is a feeling of the heart,
A dreary sense of coming evil
That bars all mirthful thoughts
And sends enjoyment to the d—l.

To the rhyme she added: "No misfortune of my life but has been foreshadowed by a presentiment—its warnings oft times disregarded, but ever recurring, when the thunderbolt has fallen. . . ." July of 1861 had given way to August. Drastic changes were occurring in Washington, and Rose's "thunderbolt" was about to fall from the hands of the Union's first spy catcher. His name was Allan Pinkerton.

Chapter 2

The Lady and the Detective

The Widow Greenhow was now to meet a worthy antagonist, one as emotionally involved in the conflict as the lady herself. Like Rose, Allan Pinkerton had known drab early days; like her, he had succeeded by his own efforts. But there any resemblance ended. It would have been hard to find an opponent whose temperament differed more strikingly from hers. It was the gifted amateur against the professional.

Pinkerton was suspicious by nature, and he showed a lively ingenuity in probing the acts and motives of men under investigation. He saw life as a melodrama, and he acted accordingly. A short, plump-faced American of Scottish descent, forty-one years old, with sharp eyes that revealed nothing and a beard that helped conceal his expression, Pinkerton had acquired a great deal of assorted information as he knocked about the world. His father, a Glasgow police sergeant, died of injuries suffered in a workman's riot. Growing up as a cooper's apprentice, the boy joined the "other side," the militant workers' movement.

Learning about violence from personal experience, young Pinkerton had to leave Scotland to escape jail. Now he shifted roles. In America he became one of the earliest detectives on the Chicago police force, then established one of the nation's first private investigating agencies. Despite his toughness, the ambitious, persevering man never lost a certain crusading feeling. Sympathizing with John Brown in his raid, he hoped for a time to rescue the doomed zealot at Harper's Ferry. And as war loomed in 1861, Pinkerton's was 100 per cent pro-Union.

He began his spying in an indirect way, before hostilities started, even before Abraham Lincoln assumed the presidency. A year or two earlier, Pinkerton had accepted an assignment for the Philadelphia, Wilmington and Baltimore Railroad; in January of 1861 the head of the line summoned him. Officials had been tipped off that secessionists of Maryland planned to wreck bridges, ferry boats, and other railway property. Baltimore was disputed territory, a badly divided town. The route was one of the country's most heavily traveled, the main line between New York and Washington, and the results might be disastrous.

In Baltimore, Pinkerton learned a great deal. Assuming the role of a Charleston broker, he talked amiably and listened carefully. One of his staff maneuvered himself into a secessionist militia organization with secret projects. Another, a polished New Orleans Creole, joined a hard-drinking group of planter sympathizers. Weeks later they picked up details of a plot to murder Lincoln as he went through Baltimore on his way to his inauguration.

Lincoln had already started on his slow progress to the capital. As Pinkerton revealed the plot to government officials, an organization of Maryland hotspurs was drawing ballots for the murderous task. On the given night street fighters would divert attention from the President-elect, and eight men would strike simultaneously at the man from Illinois. Pinkerton insisted he knew what he was talking about; his agents had seen the very drawing of the ballots!

The detective went to Lincoln himself with this information. The President-elect hesitated, until his friend Seward and old General Winfield Scott sent separate reports that seemed to corroborate the scheme. Reluctantly Lincoln changed plans; at Harrisburg, Pennsylvania, he and several of his party entered a closed carriage that took them to a darkened train. All traffic had been cleared from the express track to Philadelphia. Telegraph lines were cut, and with as many safeguards as could be devised, the President-elect began a run designed to elude his enemies.

At Philadelphia an official used a ruse to hold up the regular night express to Washington. A second dark carriage took Lincoln on a twisting route to the new station. There a Pinkerton woman operative had reserved the last three sections of the sleeping car for her "ailing brother" and friends. Lincoln dropped into a seat behind the curtains and the detective, gun ready, kept watch as the train sped on. He had been warned of danger at specific points; at each one he peered out, and an assistant signaled with a lantern—two beams, all well so far.

At 3:30 in the morning the presidential train reached the most hazardous spot, Baltimore. There it was necessary for the party to be taken to the station across town by means of creaking horsecars. Tense and alert, Pinkerton and his crew stared into the darkness and listened. Had Lincoln's enemies learned of his secret arrival and changed their plans accordingly? At the second station they found that the connecting train would be two hours late—two long hours of anxiety. . . . For Abraham Lincoln this could not have been an easy interlude, and yet he did not let the pervading gloom envelop him. He passed the time telling funny stories.

Slowly the pressure of fear lessened. Dawn had arrived when the train rolled into the embattled capital, and Lincoln stretched his long legs in relief. "Well, boys, thank God this prayer meeting is over!" Thus ended the Baltimore Plot of 1861, an incident over which historians would wrangle in subsequent years. Out of it there emerged before long the first secret service organization in the nation's history.

For several months early in the war, Allan Pinkerton served an old friend and patron, General George B. McClellan, commander of the Department of the Ohio. With the young officer, one of his former railroad employers, the detective had formed a spy ring to gather information in the Ohio region. Immediately after the Union's disaster at First Manassas, the North called Little Mac to Washington to take command, and McClellan in turn summoned Pinkerton.

Necessity had brought a new attitude, a new spirit to Washington. Gone was the early listlessness and the overconfidence. The conviction had grown that this would be a hard, disrupting war—a grinding and bloody effort that might yet end in a Northern defeat. Some people realized that part of the Union's peril lay in the mixed loyalties inside the capital.

Pinkerton received his assignment, to discover "secret traitorous organizations" and put an end to the spying in and around Washington. He took the name of Major E. J. Allen, one of several that he used. He gathered almost his full organization in the capital, and promptly found many leaks in the Union's vital communication centers. Southern officials, he discovered, knew the position of "every regiment and brigade and the contemplated movements of the commanders and the time of proposed action. . . . Indeed it was openly boasted that the secret information given to the rebel generals had been mainly the cause of the defeat of our armies at Bull Run and Manassas."

In July of 1861, less than a week after Manassas, official Union attention was drawn to the house at Sixteenth and I streets. The secret service organization was only a few days old when Thomas A. Scott, Assistant War Secretary, paid Pinkerton a visit. The administration wished him to "watch a lady whose movements had excited suspicion. . . ." This lady was Mrs. Greenhow. At last Rose's friend Mr. Seward had realized he must do something about her.

The spy had been far from idle. Crowing a bit, she once

noted that she might "almost be said to have assisted at Lincoln's Cabinet councils, from the facilities I enjoyed, having *verbatim* reports of them as well as of the Republican caucus." After McClellan's arrival she could speak "ex cathedra" about him, as she obtained "minutes of McClellan's private consultations, and often extracts from his notes!"

The new commander found it disastrous to talk even guardedly of his plans. The Prince de Joinville, who served temporarily on the general's staff, tells how McClellan was once forced to explain his intentions at a war council, "and the next day they were known to the enemy. Informed no doubt by one of those thousand female spies who keep up his communications into the domestic circles of the Federal army, Johnston evacuated Manassas at once. . . ."

From then on the administration stationed a guard near Rose's home. Every person entering or leaving must be investigated, and if any of them tried to cross enemy lines they were to be arrested. The government wished daily reports; though Pinkerton does not say so, it also wished caution. With Rose's influential connections, a false step might cause the War Department considerable grief. . . . Nevertheless, Allan Pinkerton plunged delightedly into the assignment. The lady liked to plot; he liked to pry.

For days he kept a discreet guard near the Greenhow house. Then, acting on a good lead, the detective discovered late one afternoon that the shutters were all tightly closed. A heavy rain lashed the city, and with two specially picked assistants Pinkerton took shelter under the trees across the street. After a while he made out slits of light on the first floor. The three men darted over, the aides stood side by side, and Pinkerton, kicking off his boots, stood on their shoulders. Noiselessly he peered through the slats of a shutter into Rose's parlor.

"Somebody coming!" The trio hid, as a stranger came down the street, mounted the steps, and entered the house. Pinkerton then resumed his role of Peeping Tom. As the caller stepped into the gaslight of the parlor, the detective recognized him—an infantry captain in charge of a provost marshal's station. The tall, good-looking officer seemed nervous, but he relaxed when Rose came in with a cordial smile. They sat at a table, and Pinkerton's eyes bulged as they bent over a large map of Washington's fortifications.

The watchful detective could hear the captain talk at length about the defenses. Then, so he recorded in his report, the couple, holding hands, disappeared from view. An hour later they returned to the parlor and said good-by at the door, with a sound the detective thought was a kiss. The officer started off, and Pinkerton trotted noiselessly behind him in the rain, having left his shoes in the grass under the window.

Pinkerton was followed by one of his helpers, and for some distance the three traveled in a single file. Once the captain halted, and the detective feared he had been seen by the officer. Turning at Pennsylvania Avenue, the officer vanished into a doorway. Four soldiers rushed out with bayonets and seized Pinkerton and his aide. The hunted had trapped the hunters! The building was a barracks, and now the angry captain asked his captives several questions. Pinkerton would say only that his name was E. J. Allen.

The Union spy chief spent a glum night in a dark cell. Wet, miserable, and still without shoes, he nevertheless managed to win the guard's favor and send out a message. Quietly released in the morning, Pinkerton reported to the War Department and the captain was arrested. Accounts of the sequel differ; some give the officer's name as Ellison, others as Elwood. General Doster, by then provost marshal, gives a circumstantial description of the way the hapless Elwood landed in prison, where he was confined for more than a year.

Pinkerton had determined to get the whole story. For months Elwood remained sealed off from the world; even the attendant who took in food could not talk to him. The captain had a single caller, a detective who grilled him again and again and made him admit "all sorts of things." Finally officials found Elwood on the floor of his cell, "his throat cut by his penknife. . . ." No formal charges had ever been filed against him.

Long before that, however, Pinkerton acted against the principal in *l'affaire Greenhow.* As his men continued the watch over her home, the "fascinating widow" received a series of prominent men, including "earnest" senators and representatives who were "perhaps in entire ignorance of the lady's true character." According to Mrs. Greenhow, she had known for some time that certain individuals were suspicious of her, checking on her guests' and her own movements. It made her more wary, but it did not halt her work. She and Miss Mackall, she recorded, eluded their pursuers from time to time and laughed about it afterwards. Even when she learned that the investigators might arrest her, she did not stop her work.

When one of McClellan's officers whispered to a Georgetown woman friend that Madame Greenhow and a prominent pro-Confederate of Washington were on the "dangerous" list, Rose shrugged it off. She informed the man under suspicion, William Preston, former United States Minister to Spain, and he fled to the Confederacy; she went right on with her spying. Perhaps she thought her family standing made her immune, or that she could outwit any Yankee. Though she received strong hints that one of her own spy ring had gone to the Union general with a dispatch from Jordan, she did not lose her head. Behind her closed shutters Rose calmly burned many of her private papers.

On the morning of August 23, as she was taking a leisurely stroll, she met a diplomat acquaintance, and they continued together to a neighbor's house. The diplomat bowed good-by, and a moment later another friend passed Rose with a whispered word. Several men seemed to be standing on the street ahead of her watching her every movement.

With a careful smile Mrs. Greenhow remained stock-still for a few minutes. In her pocket she crumpled a scrap of paper that held her cipher, put it into her mouth, and swallowed it. She was carrying a bulkier note, equally important, but it would have to wait. A second member of the Greenhow ring passed and Rose murmured: "Watch from the corner. If they arrest me, I'll raise my handkerchief."

Very casually, the widow walked to her house, and her nemesis, Pinkerton, stepped up. "You're Mrs. Greenhow?"

She stared contemptuously. "Yes. Who are you? What do you want here?"

"I've come to arrest you."

She demanded that he prove his authority, and he told her he could—from both the State and War departments. While the detective spoke, Rose touched her handkerchief to her lips, and her agent caught the signal. She turned on Pinkerton in a cold rage: "I can't stop you, but if I were in my house I'd have killed one of you before I'd have submitted to this." The detective merely motioned her toward the door, and she entered.

Immediately, she recalled later, "the house became filled. . . . Men rushed with frantic haste into my chamber, into every sanctuary. Beds, drawers, wardrobes, soiled linen—search was made everywhere!" As Pinkerton directed his men, Rose felt "the calmness of desperation." They expected her to commit some "womanly indiscretion"; instead, she would "test the truth of the old saying that 'the devil is no match for a clever woman.'"

Frantic scenes followed. Although the Federal men clustered inside, no guard was stationed before the door, for Pinkerton hoped to net some bigger fish. He had forgotten about little Rose, who scrambled through the doorway and cried out:

"Mother's been arrested, Mother's been arrested!"

When the detectives ran after her, Rose's daughter climbed a tree and continued to call the news to the world. By the time the detectives had pulled her down, the girl had served Mother well. . . . Mother had another concern, the dangerous paper still in her pocket. Pleading the heat, she told one of the guards she must change her dress. Reluctantly he agreed and she quickly went upstairs to her boudoir, shutting the door.

As she pulled out a hidden paper the guard, sensing his mistake, quietly opened the door. He stood just out of sight and Rose says she pulled out the gun she kept handy, ready to shoot him if he entered. But he did not enter, and Rose quickly chewed up the paper. A moment later "a female operative" bustled into the room, but not before Rose had hidden the gun in the boudoir. The woman detective searched her "to her linen."

Downstairs, Rose's most trusted assistant, Lillie Mackall, walked in with her sister, and they were soon followed by a former Greenhow servant and Mrs. Mackall. Allowed to talk together, Rose and Lillie remembered a batch of dangerous papers in the library—several of Colonel Tom Jordan's letters and a dispatch of Rose's own—which they had been about to send off. (Obviously she had been less careful than she thought.) Now she had to get them, or, in her own words, she would have to burn down the house during the night.

But there were other problems even more immediate. Through the window she saw two friends coming down the street toward her house. She made a frantic signal at the window and a detective seized her, injuring her arm. The two Confederates retreated hastily.

The next time friends approached, luck was against her. Into the detectives' grasp walked two neatly dressed men, William Walker and F. Rennehan, government clerks who admitted their identities. They explained that they were only friends paying a social call. The Assistant Secretary of War came to join Pinkerton in questioning them. After a time the detectives took them away.

Pinkerton also left, "on some other errand of mischief," Rose declared. After the house was quiet, several Union attendants reached into her brandy cabinet. She welcomed their drinking, for she might have a better chance to get at the papers in the library. She and Lillie went to her room. When their guard disappeared for a few minutes, Rose tiptoed to the library, took a book off the shelf, and removed the incriminating sheets. By the time the guard came back, Rose lay beside Lillie on the bed.

Should she tear up the papers? In spite of the detective standing at the open door, Rose daringly decided to get the dispatch through to Jordan. She slipped the paper under the sheet to Lillie. "Keep it in your stocking," she told her, remembering that when the woman attendant searched her she had not bothered about shoes and stockings. It was worth a try.

At 3:30 A.M. the detectives decided that Lillie could leave. She descended the stairs with last instructions from Mrs. Greenhow. If it appeared that she was to be examined carefully, Lillie was to burst into tears and say that she really could not leave her good friend. . . . But Lillie escaped with only a cursory inspection and, despite the fact that Union men trailed her, succeeded in forwarding the message to the Confederates.

The next day Washington buzzed with the news of the first widespread attack on Southern agents and sympathizers. Many had been caught, including some outstanding Washington figures—Mayor Berret, and the wife of the former Alabama congressman, her two daughters, and her sister. Apparently Rose was associated with some of them; yet none of them admitted anything. . . . For Mrs. Greenhow the week was full of anger and concern. As the search through her house intensified, Pinkerton's agents took down beds to test footboards and headboards, knocked apart chairs and tables, and one man methodically lifted pictures out of their frames. Mrs. Chesnut's famous diary reports:

For eight days she was kept in full sight of men, her rooms wide open, and sleepless sentinels watching by day and by night. Soldiers, tramping by, looked in at her by way of amusement. Beautiful as she is, even at her time of life, few women like all the mysteries of their toilette laid bare to the public eye. She says she was worse used than Marie Antoinette, when they snatched a letter from the poor queen's bosom.

If the Union men gazed at the widow with interest, they had an excuse. On the night when she had torn dozens of records to bits and thrown them into the fire, Rose had neglected to make sure that everything burned. The detectives had fished out damaging evidence, strips of paper filled with cipher messages, bits of letters with military information. She claimed they were her daughter's "unlettered scribblings"; alas for Rose, they were easily proved to be far more than that.

Among them was a group of spicy love notes, tied together with a string and marked: "Letters from H., not to be opened —but burned in case of death or accident." Though only one was dated, they had been written very recently. They were from a man high in government affairs, with access to information that Rose wanted badly—a man infatuated. If anyone had given the widow secrets, it would have been "H." The course of their love had been stormy with pleading and reproaches. A message written on congressional stationery and dated January 30, 1861, after the secession movement was well started, told of "spies" who watched them and their need for secrecy:

Your note is rec'd. Believe me or not, you cannot be more wretched than I am. I cannot now explain. Let it suffice until we meet that for the last few days *every* movement and act of mine have been watched with Hawkeyed vigilance. For your sake more than my own I have been compelled to be cautious. But tomorrow at 10 A.M. I will see you at all hazards.

There were others:

You will know I love you–and will sacrifice anything on my own account. I have feared bringing you into trouble–for I repeat to you that spies are put upon me, but I will try to elude them tonight, and once more we can have a happy hour in spite of fate. H. . . . I am happy to say that I feel *particularly* well this morning; and can well account for the favorable change. We are in the act of entering on the consideration of the Pacific Railroad Bill. I will not fail you tonight, and will bring you the thing of which we spoke last night. Bless you always, Yours, H. . . . You know that I *do love* you. I am suffering this morning; in fact I am sick physically and mentally, and know nothing that would sooth me so much as an hour with you. And tonight, at whatever cost I will see you.

I am in receipt of your note. If you knew how much I suffered last night, and am still suffering, you could find it in your heart to forgive me. . . . But sick or not, I *will* be with you tonight, and then I will tell you again and again that I love you. . . . Ever your H.

In the National Archives the notes were originally labeled: "Love letters from Henry Wilson, U.S. Senator from Massachusetts." Later a precautionary "supposed to be" was inserted. Experts believe the writing is not Wilson's. In *Reveille in Washington* Margaret Leech speculated that, although she destroyed much correspondence, Rose "carefully preserved" these letters, even if Wilson did not write them, hoping that they would appear to have been written by the chairman of the Senate Military Affairs Committee.

Still, Mrs. Greenhow was certainly far less careful with her papers than she should have been, and the possibility remains that these letters were copies rather than originals. In her memoirs Rose referred often to Wilson in friendly terms, and quoted him as telling her of White House incidents about which only he could have known. She mentioned a Cabinet meeting at which she was discussed, with several Republican officials called in—including Wilson, "as being implicated by my information."

Nine years later Secretary of State Hamilton Fish wrote in his diary of a story recounted by the Confederate Tom Jordan, Rose's spy supervisor, to a diplomat publisher. By this account, Jordan had learned at the war's start of an "intimacy" between Mrs. Greenhow and Senator Wilson. Then Jordan had become friendly with Rose and "induced her to get from Wilson all the information she could." It was from Wilson, said Rose's colleague, that she discovered McDowell's orders to advance on Bull Run "within a few hours after the orders were given." One observer has commented kindly that, whoever "H" might be, he might not have been guilty of conscious betrayal of secrets, but merely "let a lady's glamor blind him to her politics."

In any case, for weeks following its seizure by Pinkerton, many Unionists shivered as they wondered what Rose's correspondence would reveal. It told a great deal, even in shredded pages, about the considerable volume of data she had handed to the South. One note said:

Dear Mrs. Greenhow: I heard from a good source that a large force was to have been sent to Acquia Creek and under the protection. . . . and take possession. . . . I think I heard Wednesday mentioned. Please make a note out——

Another declared:

31st July. All is activity. . . . A troop of cavalry will start from here this morning to Harper's Ferry for reorganizing.

Another, with cipher characters interspersed, said:

This may be brought to you by a gentlemen / / / . . . will take it at. . . . Alexandria. But / / /. . . . be able to. . . . / / / the railroads. . . .

Pinkerton also found a copy of one of Rose's cipher letters to Jordan. It gave the name of Dr. Van Camp, the dentist, and the papers in her fireplace mentioned Walker and Rennehan, the clerks seized at her house. Pinkerton's men went to work on each name. . . . Delightedly they pounced on a note from G. Donellan, the agent who had taken the news to Manassas. This was a letter introducing to Rose a man of strong Southern interests, Colonel Michael Thompson of South Carolina. Picking up his trail, the detectives learned that he kept close contact with Smithson, the banker, and also Van Camp. Pinkerton still waited; he was giving them all the time they needed to trap themselves.

Meanwhile Miss Mackall returned to the house to begin voluntary imprisonment with Rose. (Lillie was probably the only spy messenger on either side who asked to be taken into custody!) From then on, said Rose, they were "like the Siamese twins, inseparable." Under Union eyes, the mild-looking Lillie served Mrs. Greenhow well. One day, as the detectives labored assiduously over the papers, Lillie noticed a blotter and nudged her friend. Rose caught her breath, for she had used the blotter on her dispatch to Jordan at Manassas, and the words were clearly outlined. For once, she admitted, she was frightened; but not for long. Her "Siamese twin" deftly removed it.

So the days passed, and Pinkerton tried varying tactics. Some of his men hinted that they would be happy to take letters from Rose to anyone outside, but she rejected the kind offers. A "burly Irishman" courted her maid on sentimental walks, and Lizzie, who had also chosen to stay with Madame, used this chance to perform confidential errands for her. But the more the Unionists read of Rose's early correspondence the more disturbed they grew. Her drawings of Northern fortifications proved full and accurate, "as well they might be," she commented, considering their source.

She received word that she might be tried for treason. "Let it come," she responded. They could prove nothing, she still felt sure, and in any event, "there will be rich revelations." A number of Unionists lost sleep over that possibility. However, as Carl Sandburg and others have noted, the federal government might have hanged her under its espionage laws.

Company arrived at the house on Sixteenth Street: a group of women were brought in under guard, and Rose discovered that her home would be turned into a "female prison." In spite of her protests, she, her maid, Lillie, and little Rose were shut into two rooms, her parlors stripped, doors nailed, and chambers made into cells.

She winced when detectives put their dirty shoes up on delicately carved sofas, broke vases, and spat on her floors; the clink of muskets sounded as guards took up their posts. "My castle had become my prison." When she heard weeping, she learned it was Mrs. Hassler, another of her messengers. Betrayed by one of their associates, Applegate, Mrs. Hassler had been held for days in a cell with straw for a bed. She had been "most infamously used," her nervous system shattered. Now Rose tried to reach Mrs. Hassler's room in vain. Hours later Lillie Mackall succeeded in getting to the distraught woman and telling her she must deny knowledge of Rose. It was too late; Mrs. Hassler had already confessed to a great deal, and Pinkerton was tightening his net.

Rose did not worry for long; she had new business to concern her. She went steadily on, helping the South under the eyes and in the hearing of the Unionists. Federal authorities have testified angrily to her skill in sending out messages. In her record of this period Mrs. Greenhow referred to "*peculiar, square*" dispatches to Jefferson Davis, and to a "bird" that flew to Confederate territory, although it once took refuge in "the dovecote of the enemy." Also, "I was at this time seized with a taste for tapestry work. Colors needed came through the provost marshal's office. . . . I had made a vocabulary of colors, which though not a very prolific language, served my purpose."

Rose was now a greater celebrity than ever, as the first great spy of the war. Crowds passed the house hoping for a glimpse of the lady, and thousands talked of the new prison—"Fort Greenhow." An official assured her he could have made a great deal of money by charging the public ten dollars for each peep at her. She was inspiring other Confederates to espionage, and thousands of Unionists to resentment. The New York *Times* declared that she should have been sent South at once, and there would have been no more talk of "heroic deeds of Secesh women, which she has made the fashion."

The provost marshal testified that Rose used a variety of weapons to undermine prison authority: some of her captors she smiled at and flattered, and others she withered with scorn. She made a number of friends among the jailers, who remembered her happily and spoke of her only with kindness in later years. While Pinkerton maintained his official interest, the detectives now withdrew, being replaced by a detachment of McClellan's bodyguard, the Sturgis Rifles. Among them the widow saw material for conquest in a new man, young and personable.

Before long Lieutenant N. W. Sheldon was giving her privileges—privacy, writing paper, protection against annoyance. He sided with her when she fell into a running fight with the prison doctor, Brigade Surgeon Stewart. Plump and loud, Dr. Stewart wore "enough gold lace for three field marshals," in Rose's words, and basked in his own importance. When he announced he was to make a daily inspection of her "sanitary condition," the lady ordered him out. He asked: "Is there anything *materia medica* can do for you today?" She asked "Materia Medica" what this intrusion meant. Tactfully Dr. Stewart answered that if a Union man called on a secessionist, it was a favor, not an intrusion. She pounded for her lieutenant friend, Sheldon, and had the doctor removed.

At first Mrs. Greenhow's lively daughter almost enjoyed her home prison. Little Rose tossed balls back and forth with the guards and became a pet of the men. Then the girl caught "camp measles," and her mother wrote to the provost marshal for the right to have her own doctor in attendance. Instead, her bristling enemy, Stewart, arrived, and Rose played the scene for drama. She leaped forward: "At your peril but touch my child! You're a coward and no gentleman, thus to insult a woman." The pudgy surgeon shouted, Rose beat on the floor for help, and he "slunk away." The daughter recovered.

"Fort Greenhow" received a new inmate, Miss Poole, who acted as stool pigeon against Mrs. Greenhow and, of all people, the junior Rose as well. For some weeks the child played games on the sidewalk, with a guard nearby. Seeking favor, Miss Poole told authorities that little Miss Greenhow was giving and taking messages for Mama; thereafter the child had to stay indoors.

As weeks became months Rose spied as much as she could, though in some ways she proved less adroit than she thought she was. Official records make it evident that the government intercepted several of her papers, and, while she continued blissfully confident that her cipher could not be broken, Pinkerton's experts mastered it.

The detective had one of her notes copied, with incorrect information inserted, and forwarded it to the South. Jefferson Davis relayed it to Rose's employer, Jordan, who explained to the Confederate President that he no longer used that cipher. However, Jordan commented, Rose had for some time communicated with him in another way. She had reported a new Union attack point at Smithville, and neither Pinkerton nor the Federal Army could keep her from sending out a copy of the very map that McClellan was employing. It had come to her through a clerk attached to the Senate Military Affairs Committee.

Through an emissary she next forwarded news that McClellan would march on the South within ten days. In this case stone walls obviously did not a prison make! On the day after Christmas she advised the Confederates:

> In a day or two 1200 cavalry supported by four batteries of artillery will cross the river above to get behind Manassas and cut off railroad and other communications with our army whilst an attack is made in front. For God's sake heed this. It is positive. They are obliged to give up. . . . They find me a hard bargain, and I shall be, I think, released in a few days without condition but to go South. . . .

She had sent the word to Jordan through Smithson, the banker, despite the fact that Smithson was already under surveillance by the Union. An accompanying note said the source of at least some of Rose's news had been "one of McClellan's aides" and Assistant Secretary of the Navy Fox! Those two had called on her to discuss her possible release, and apparently she had wheedled information from them.

The McClellan aide was Colonel Thomas Key, who paid her several visits. Mrs. Greenhow was not impressed: "He was, or affected to be, very deaf, as an excuse for approaching very near. . . . He attempted to take my hand, as he said, 'to find out whether I had ever done any work.' " Rose bridled; she let him know she worked with her head, not her hands. After hesitating, Colonel Key told her she sorely puzzled the government. Its only solution might be to do what England did with certain Irishmen—banish her. To what terms, he asked, would she agree?

Mrs. Greenhow had her answer ready: unconditional release,

indemnity for all losses, return of her papers. And she would never take the oath they generally asked, pledging herself not to work against the Union; she would make no promise of any kind. With a sigh Colonel Key departed. . . .

By this time the government realized how well Rose's "Siamese twin," Lillie Mackall, had served in transmitting her messages, and Miss Lillie received orders to leave her prison. Lillie protested; she wanted to stay right on with Mrs. Greenhow. Nevertheless, she was forced to go.

Lillie continued to work for her mistress throughout the icy winter weather. She caught a severe cold and was ordered to bed, and one of the Mackalls soon brought Rose the news that Lillie had died. Rose asked her onetime friend, Secretary of War Seward, if she could not attend the funeral. In a note to the provost marshal, Seward gave a remarkable testimonial to the spy's skill: her "correspondence with the commanding general of the Army besieging the capital renders improper all interference in her behalf. . . ."

Rose's son-in-law had become an outstanding Union officer, winning promotion for his service against the South. Captain Moore wrote her about the way in which he had led a Union party in the West and stamped out an organization that would have turned the territory over to "the so-called Southern Confederacy." Meeting up with a doctor active in behalf of the South, he tried hard to send the doctor to prison. Rose was shocked and dispirited.

And then she heard disturbing and strange rumors. It is hard to believe that anyone would have accused the fervent Rose of anything except devotion to Dixie, yet certain hotspurs claimed she really spied for the North, on the pretext of helping the Confederacy. Mary Chesnut gossiped in her diary: "Some say Mrs. Greenhow had herself confined and persecuted so that we might trust her the more. The Manassas men swear she was our good angel, but the Washington women say she was up for sale to the highest bidder, always—and they have the money on us!"

Rose herself wrote bitterly of her own sister's attitude and that of her niece, the now-widowed Mrs. Stephen A. Douglas. She described people who thought "family escutcheons tarnished by the misguided members who advocated the Southern cause. . . . No one suffered in this respect more than myself, for many members of my immediate family sided with the despot and held high official position." Nevertheless, her relatives and friends did what they could for her. They did enough, in fact, to make Detective Pinkerton write a long plea against a plan to release her. To save the lives of Union soldiers, he insisted, the lady must be kept under guard.

Nearly every week the indefatigable Mrs. Greenhow managed to give the fascinated country a new headline. Opening a cake sent to her, "Fort Greenhow" officials found it filled with treasury notes—evidence, they asserted, of a plot to help Rose buy her way out. To the consternation of her Unionist (and very correct) niece, Mrs. Douglas, newspapers linked *her* with the scheme.

Pinkerton moved in again to crush the very heart of Rose's spy organization. By a stroke of fortune, Union forces captured a blockade runner with incriminating letters, including a note from Colonel Tom Jordan to a Colonel Empty. Pinkerton discovered that this meant Colonel *M*ichael *T*hompson, whose name had already been discovered in Rose's correspondence. Other notes in the batch were signed by Charles Cables, and concerned Federal troop movements. Pinkerton knew that "Cables" meant Smithson, the banker. Also involved in the letters was the dentist, Van Camp, who scurried in and out of Washington on Southern errands.

At the same time a doctor trying to quit the Union Army and escape to the Confederacy fell into Pinkerton's hands. He told how Van Camp had assisted him and provided the buggy he used. Everything added up, and the detective arrested all these men. At "Fort Greenhow" the watch tightened around Rose. Every item of laundry must be examined; a guard received a biting reprimand when he did not inspect a sprig of jessamine left for her.

But was Madame Spy stopped? She was not. She still managed somehow to have information passed in and out of her prison. To Secretary of War Seward she addressed a daring letter. In long, closely reasoned pages she demanded he tell her by what law she had been arrested without a warrant, kept a captive in her own house, her property seized. She showed that she understood American law, and she asked a series of highly embarrassing questions. To make sure the world would know about it, she or her friends forwarded a copy of the letter to Richmond, where newspapers published it in full, to Seward's red-faced indignation.

The government ordered new precautions; guards searched her rooms, took away her writing paper, nailed up the windows. Newspapers were denied her; nobody was to talk with her, even tell her what the headlines said. Her friend Lieutenant Sheldon was suspect for a time, receiving orders to have no "personal communication" with Madame Greenhow. Several newspapers became bitterly opposed to the suggestion that she be sent South. The New York *Herald* announced that if the Union freed this "spirited, dashing, active and fearless female politician . . . this dangerous agent of a hostile army besieging our national capital," it might as well "abolish our armies."

Colonel Key, the McClellan aide whom she later accused of hand holding, brought her news of an interesting turn of events. The authorities now thought it might be inexpedient to release her, because she knew too much! Rose acted immediately in a way that aroused fresh Federal indignation. Secretary Seward had not recovered from her much-publicized letter to him when she wrote a second, its contents even more inflammatory—and again she published it in Southern papers.

This was too much. On January 18, 1862, Rose Greenhow received two-hour notice that she would be taken from her home prison to a much more spy-proof place, the Old Capitol Prison. Soldiers formed a guard outside, and rumors flashed through Washington that something was going on at "Fort Greenhow." Crowds gathered, stood on carriages, gaped from the adjacent church steps. While her daughter cried and threw her arms around Lieutenant Sheldon's neck, Mrs. Greenhow bade a stately good-by to all. "The next time," Rose informed the soldiers, "I hope you have a more honorable duty." She still had the last word!

Newspapermen scrambled into Rose's house to inspect her quarters, to ask hundreds of questions about the glamorous agent. Artists drew pictures of the scene for the newspapers. Behind her she had left two bottles of "fluid" supposedly used for invisible writing. (She said she put them there as a blind, to fool her captors.) And Lieutenant Sheldon commented wistfully that she had been "the most ladylike of his prisoners, the best educated, and though at times severe in speech, after all the possessor of 'a woman's heart.' "

Rose had not in fact been an amenable prisoner, but stories in even the most hostile journals indicate that she had made many friends at "Fort Greenhow." As she neared the grimy, lice-infested Old Capitol Prison, Rose must have been very gloomy. She had lived there for years in her aunt's boardinghouse days; she had returned there to care for the dying Calhoun. Now, ironically, she was to have the room in which Calhoun predicted to her the dissolution of the Union. Another crowd was waiting to get a glimpse of the famous female, but this time her daughter Rose stole the show, when she said to the superintendent: "You've got one of the darnedest little rebels here that you ever saw!"

Mrs. Greenhow promptly went back to her letter writing, and she still found ways to get her notes out. One contained a copy of a confidential dispatch from McClellan, begging Washington for reinforcements. But her spying had become much less effective, and when this note reached Baltimore it fell at once into Northern hands. She kept on trying, however.

Rose had now passed six months in Federal custody, and she continued to make life exciting for her captors. They accused her of signaling to outsiders by using lighted candles to convey messages from the windows. She laughed at their suspicions and claimed that they never fathomed her methods. For weeks she was locked in her cell, but when she was granted freedom of the yard the widow immediately caused a flurry of apprehension by leaping into a cart and crying, "I'm off for Dixie," while the men prisoners pulled her around. The officials acted, she said, as if they thought she would really escape in that way.

In the Old Capitol Prison there were other women agents who had been connected with Colonel Jordan, and some women held merely on vague suspicion. One was Mrs. Augusta Morris, pretty and friendly to everybody, "a second Mrs. Greenhow," who let people understand she was French and spoke with a Gallic accent. She was really a baker's daughter from Alexandria, Virginia. Augusta had a son with temperament to match that of Rose's daughter; he kicked on doors and shouted: "Let me out, you damned Yankees!" And Mrs. Morris joked with the guards and "worried" pompous Brigade Surgeon Stewart, Rose's favorite enemy, by pretending to be undressed when he approached.

Between Rose and this rival, feelings were strained. Jordan had made use of the attractive young matron in his spying, but wisely kept her work separate from Mrs. Greenhow's. Augusta wrote angrily that "Greenhow enjoys herself immensely. . . . She is drowned by mean ambition of being known [as the only one] in the good work. . . ." Rose countered by mentioning printed stories which told how Augusta approached Federal authorities with an offer: for $10,000 she would give them the Confederate Army signals. When she had no takers, it was said, the lady turned pro-Southern again!

As the months passed, General McClellan and Pinkerton reportedly insisted that Mrs. Greenhow must remain in custody, if only because McClellan had to "change his plans four times" as a result of her espionage. Then, in late March of 1862, Federal policy shifted. Following protests that civil liberties were being violated, Rose and other suspected spies received hearings before a special commission. One of the members turned out to be, to his embarrassment, General John Dix, one of Rose's old party friends.

Rose called the proceedings a "mock trial," and acted accordingly. She informed her judges that the government had made another mistake; it had picked gentlemen for this hearing. And she gave them no help at all. To some questions she simply answered, "That's my secret." As to the source of her military data, Rose asked: "If Mr. Lincoln's friends will pour into my ears such important information, am I to be held responsible?" She assured the judges that she would send her President, Jefferson Davis, a full report, and she underscored the remark with an emphatic nod.

Despite her bravado, long confinement had told on Rose. She had been in prison almost a year; to her increasing dismay she heard that she would be kept there for the rest of the war. "A feeling of lassitude was stealing over me, and a nervous excitability which prevented me from sleeping. . . . This was the gloomiest period of my life." Her passionate nature might have stood anything better than the confinement and silence of a cell.

Late in May the government decided how to dispose of Rose and the other women prisoners: they would be forwarded to Dixie. With her daughter on her arm, Mrs. Greenhow walked out of jail into a cheering crowd. On the way to Richmond men lifted their hats to her, crying women waved handkerchiefs, and secesh children shook their fists at her Yankee guards.

In the Confederate capital Rose was richly rewarded when her friend Jefferson Davis paid a formal call and assured her: "But for you, there would have been no Bull Run." The words made everything she had suffered worth while. Life again had a fresh, rosy look. Mr. Davis wrote his wife Varina that "Madame looks much changed, and has the air of one whose nerves are shaken by mental torture." But Rose soon regained her health; several accounts indicate that all sorts of men continued to admire her.

Her letters of this period glow with happiness. General Beauregard reminded everyone what she had done for his army, and young girls asked if she could teach them how to be spies. On President Davis' instructions, Secretary Judah Benjamin sent her a 2500-dollar check out of Davis' secret service funds, for her "valuable and patriotic services." Rose needed money badly; it was doubtful she could ever regain her Washington property. With the new funds she bought cotton and launched a number of financial ventures.

She continued to serve the Confederacy, too. Traveling about the South, Mrs. Greenhow wrote a series of letters to Jefferson Davis, filling them with military data and appraisals of Federal intentions. That summer of 1862 she received a Confederate assignment in England, its exact nature never revealed. Going to Charleston, and then to Wilmington, North Carolina, Rose waited to run the blockade, and en route sent back some of her most interesting letters. She reported minutely and intelligently on the Confederate situation, adding stories that disclosed civilian morale and the antagonism between certain Southern officials. She made her own concrete suggestions for improving affairs. Governors, legislators, and generals entertained her, and General Beauregard took her over Fort Sumter.

Rose finally arrived in Bermuda and again wrote Jefferson Davis an informative letter. A British vessel took her to France, where she had letters of introduction which gave entree to the offices of Southern agents and the homes of diplomats. She had conferences with Confederate representatives and through them met Napoleon III at the Tuileries. This was the life!

Proceeding to London, she met leading British figures, and Queen Victoria received her with interest. To Englishmen, Mrs. Greenhow spoke dramatically of her spying and still more dramatically of her Union enemies. As always, she was witty, and she knew her way about a drawing room. She became an increasingly skillful propagandist for her cause, according to several admiring British accounts.

From prison Rose had written one of her daughters that she intended some day to write a book about her experiences. Now she had an important publisher, and the volume appeared in November of 1863, creating something of a stir in England as well as in America. Various Unionists became apprehensive as they read what she had said of them; a few had to deny hints that they betrayed their country for her. In London a newspaper expressed astonishment that Madame Greenhow had been allowed to do so much against the Union; "many will wonder, not that she was treated with such severity, but that she got off so well." Nevertheless, the passion in her writing, the facts that she had gathered to support her position, had a strong effect in many places.

Because of her personality, the widow was a real success in London; fashionable Mayfair homes were open to this piquant American. One or two noblewomen sponsored her, and she attended week-end parties at the homes of Lady Franklin and Lady Gray. Thomas Carlyle met her and was said to have been impressed. In a letter to America, Rose recounted a long conversation with the Englishman about Jefferson Davis' determined character. "Carlyle asked me to describe him. His remark was 'God has made the situation for the man.'" Another Englishman, a member of the nobility, was still more impressed, and there is a story that Rose became engaged to him.

Yet, as she wrote to friends at home, her thoughts were "always of the war and my friends." She prayed endlessly for Confederate success, and was depressed by the reports of Northern successes in the field. Also, she felt hopelessly out of touch with America. "It is important that I should have news," she observed, "as I have the means of placing it in proper quarters." At another time she said: "How anxiously I look for letters from home, it would be impossible for me to tell you. . . ."

In time she saw an opportunity for another service to the Confederacy, and perhaps a way to pay her debts. A number of sources describe Rose's financial operations with British interests—blockade running, cotton selling, shipping.

Receiving orders to return to America with dispatches and funds, Rose said good-by temporarily to her fiancé. She placed the beloved little Rose in the Convent of the Sacred Heart in Paris, and boarded the blockade runner *Condor* in September of 1864.

The trip westward was uneventful. Rose carried more than two thousand dollars in gold, some of it royalties from her sensational book. The *Condor*, a speedy, three-funneled steamer, made good time; after dark on September 30 she fought heavy gales as she cut toward Cape Fear River near Wilmington, North Carolina. Suddenly, just after midnight, a Union gunboat spied her, and a chase was on.

Rose Greenhow was frightened. If the Yankees caught her again, and under these circumstances, she might have a really hard time. The *Condor's* captain ordered full speed ahead, and the ship careened on through the wild night, all sails set. The gunboat pressed closer and closer, and Rose's desperation was like a hand at her throat.

It was nearly three o'clock when the blockade runner approached the river mouth; once they were inside, they would be safe. Then in the dim light the captain made out a vague, grayish shape which turned out to be the wreckage of another blockade runner. The *Condor* came about quickly to avoid the wreck and ran aground on New Inlet bar.

Nearby, like a shark in dark waters, a second Federal ship moved slowly toward the trapped vessel. At Confederate Fort Fisher, a short distance off, the commander realized the *Condor's* plight and shouted an order: fire at the Yankees, keep 'em back! Yet the gunboats moved gradually closer. In a few minutes the *Condor* shifted and listed badly on the bar.

Below deck, Rose and several other passengers, including another important Southern agent, were debating their plight. She made up her mind and forced her way to the captain's side. Her face white, black skirts flapping about her in the wind, Mrs. Greenhow told him that he had to lower a boat, he *had* to do it for them! The captain shook his head; it was very risky. She shouted her demand; she was ready to take her chance. Two men joined her, and reluctantly the captain agreed.

With the other two passengers, Rose clung to the side of the boat as it was lowered toward the rough water. The little vessel bobbed like a cork. The men's oars dug deep, then hung in the air as the boat spun about. Shore lay only two hundred yards or so away. Rose Greenhow, drenched, clutching her dispatches and her gold, tried to believe they would reach it.

Suddenly the life boat lifted high, sank into a low trough of water, and overturned. Struggling against the undertow, Rose and the two men fought their way toward shore. When at last the men lay there, spent, breathless, they realized that Rose was not with them. Long after dawn a soldier stumbled upon her body; she had been drowned by the weight of her costume and her load of gold sovereigns.

Even in death Rose Greenhow produced turmoil and intrigue. The soldier stared at the small bag of treasure, ripped it from her, and shoved the body into the water again. Later that day it was washed in again, hands stretching toward the land. Crying his guilt, the terrified soldier ran to headquarters to give up her gold.

Word of Rose's death spread quickly. When a steamer brought her body to the Wilmington wharf, many women lined up to receive it. "A hundred houses," we are told, were available for the funeral, but at a meeting the people concluded it best to have the ceremonial "as public as possible." The townsmen laid her out in state, wrapped in a Confederate flag, and one who saw her thought her even then "a remarkably handsome woman . . . with features that showed much character."

On October 1 of 1864 the cortege passed slowly through Wilmington's streets. A minister spoke of "the quiet sleeper, who after many storms and a tumultuous and checkered life, came to peace and rest at last." As the casket was lowered soldiers fired a salute.

In recognition of her services, her beloved South raised a monument which commemorated "the deeds of Mrs. Rose Greenhow, a bearer of dispatches to the Confederate government." She had died in service, in a last defiance of her enemies.

Chapter 3

"His Lordship" the Spy

Long before the death of Rose Greenhow, her enemy Allan Pinkerton had built his organization into America's first integrated unit of spies and counterspies. Its members were of various ages and backgrounds and of at least two colors; for more than a year its operatives spread over the country on exploits which ranged from mysterious to perilous to slightly ludicrous. At times they failed, with disastrous results; often they achieved success, by ability, luck, or a combination of the two. Male or female, they had at least one quality in common; they were all good actors.

Pinkerton's secret service required specialists endowed with talents for use on particular occasions; though not among his "stars," they performed well, then slipped back into anonymity. There was, for instance, "Stuttering Dave," who made an art of acting like a fool. Pinkerton shrewdly spotted him in the army, recognizing a good thing when he saw it. At a camp near Washington the detective came upon a circle of laughing soldiers clustered around a heavy-framed, awkward fellow in his late twenties, who was having extraordinary trouble in speaking. The man stammered for minutes at a time, squinting his eyes, contorting his face with the effort.

Dropping his faked impediment, he gave Pinkerton his name —Stuttering Dave Graham of the 21st New York Infantry. Yes, sir, he knew a lot about the Virginia countryside; he'd lived there for some time. And he'd done some military scouting for the Army. . . . The more Pinkerton learned about Graham, the more pleased he became. The new agent had rare common sense as well as a comic gift; and he possessed at least one other asset. Dave could throw a superb fit. His epileptic seizure could be assumed at a moment's notice and ended just as promptly; nevertheless, it could mislead even a suspicious doctor.

Graham joined the Pinkerton service and was sent out repeatedly as a humble civilian, a peddler of notions. His destinations were army camps near points of military importance, crossroads settlements, small towns filled with new recruits. A butternut suit, a broad-brimmed hat, a stick and pack over his shoulder, and Stuttering Dave was ready to play the moron salesman, the fool of nature. His special skill served him unexpectedly now and then; once a Confederate recruiting officer appraised Graham's husky frame as he trudged along, and brought him in, determined to add him to the Southern forces. Only a timely fit saved the Union agent.

Stuttering Dave made frequent and always successful trips into Southern areas. Pinkerton said that, as far as he could learn, Dave's identity was never suspected. At least once Graham added an act of sabotage to his deeds. Strolling about a Confederate camp, he made out a train of wagons loaded with heavy ammunition. For an hour or more, as he sold his wares, the peddler surveyed the grounds. That night he went to sleep behind a tree, his pack under his head, but only after he had managed to get hold of a small amount of powder and pieced together rags with a trail of explosive inside.

About midnight the stutterer slipped past two sleeping guards (his enemies' criminal carelessness was a stroke of luck) and stretched the improvised fuse to a point a short way off. There he lit a match to it and scurried into the woods, where he witnessed a series of explosions followed by a fire that destroyed great quantities of powder, wagons, and supplies. Pinkerton was full of admiration for Dave's "peculiar and independent" method of warfare, but ordered him not to risk himself in such incendiary work.

Then there was the widow, Mrs. E. H. Baker, who scored a coup because of two special advantages. Mild and unspectacular in appearance, she had a manner that allowed her easily to assume the character of a woman of means who was faintly bored with life. Also, she had once lived in Richmond. In the fall of 1861, Northern officials heard vague rumors that strange machines shaped like torpedoes, capable of movement under water, were being constructed at the Confederate capital and were, perhaps, nearly ready for action. Mrs. Baker's assignment was to get inside the workshops and yards where the devices were being made, an area which had never been penetrated by Yankee agents.

She remembered Richmond friends, especially a Captain and Mrs. Atwater. In Washington she wrote a letter which Pinkerton forwarded to Chicago for mailing. It explained that she felt restless and believed she might be diverted if she saw Virginia again. The Confederate captain and his wife responded, as she expected, with an invitation to visit their home. Early in November, after a roundabout trip to avert suspicion, the well-to-do Mrs. Baker arrived in Richmond, renewed old friendships, and made new ones. She appeared ready to enjoy herself; those who had known her before considered her especially charming at this time.

A list had been prepared of specific points about which the widow was to show a casual interest. The major one was the Tredegar Iron Works, Richmond's massive munitions factory. At the mouth of the James River the Federal blockading fleet was performing a vital function. Pinkerton and his superiors must have all possible information about the projected "infernal machines" that might lead to the destruction of that fleet.

At first Mrs. Baker avoided all talk of war. She accepted most of the invitations she received, and went to parties, receptions, and on sightseeing trips. Before long those trips included views of Richmond's earthworks and fortifications and attendance at army drills and demonstrations. A judicious word now and then of general Southern sentiment established her firmly with her friends.

One afternoon her host, Captain Atwater, mentioned the Tredegar Works, and Mrs. Baker remarked that she had sometimes wondered what they were like. "I'll be glad to take you tomorrow," the captain volunteered. But no, he frowned. He'd forgotten, he was due downriver to watch tests of a submarine battery. . . . Submarine battery? Mrs. Baker thought that sounded like fun, provided there was no danger. There'd be none, the captain assured her; several officers' wives would go, and she could accompany the party.

The next day Mrs. Baker lost her last traces of ennui as she stood on a windy bank and stared at a big scow which, towed into mid-river, lay a considerable distance from an odd, dun-hued object, rather like an oversized cigar—the submarine. Three youths in strange armor lowered themselves into the "infernal machine," which sank slowly under water. Captain Atwater handed his guest a pair of field glasses: "Watch that." He indicated a small float, painted the color of the water and designed to escape detection, explaining that it led to the submarine beneath and provided air for the men.

As Mrs. Baker and the others watched in intent silence, the float slid slowly forward, approached the scow, remained stationary for a few minutes, then moved off. The captain whispered: The men in the submarine had attached a powder magazine under the water. It contained a half bushel of explosives and was connected to the submarine by a long wire. By now the men must be ready to fire the fuse. . . . A streak of light flashed before them, a booming explosion shook the ground, and the broken scow shot high in the air.

Cries of excitement rose around her. "It worked, it worked!" Mrs. Baker heard frenzied predictions: with these machines the South would break the blockade, send its cotton to England, smash the hold of the New England moneygrubbers!

In every way the experience had alarmed and frightened the spy. On the way back to the Atwater home she learned that a much larger submarine approached completion at the Tredegar Works. The captain himself remembered her wish to see the factory, and a day or two later he escorted her there.

At Tredegar, Mrs. Baker peered at the equipment and devices, listened, and allowed herself a few questions. Returning to her room, she pleaded a headache and labored for hours over notes and sketches, putting down everything she could recall, trivial or important-sounding, clearly or only vaguely understood. Eventually Pinkerton reported that, unprofessional though Mrs. Baker was, she had done a fair job. Her rough plans of the machine were specific enough to be of great help to an expert.

The restless lady soon developed a desire to go home. Richmond had been delightful, everybody was so kind, and still, it would be pleasant to see her family again. . . . Captain Atwater made application for her pass, sped up the process of approval, and Mrs. Baker left for Fredericksburg on her way to Washington. There, with Pinkerton looking on, she reached into the crown of her embroidered bonnet and ripped out the closely written pages of data on the submarine.

Pinkerton raced to Navy officials and to his superior, General McClellan. They sent this intelligence to Union squadron commanders, and the detective stated that, as a result, Northern forces ultimately discovered a float near the blockade fleet off the James. They disabled it, fouled the air tubes leading to the submarine, and apparently drowned the crew.

Mrs. Baker had been the right woman in the right place.

One of the Pinkerton organization's most spectacular feats was made possible by an accident of birth and breeding of another secret service operator. With Pinkerton on the day he played Peeping Tom at Rose Greenhow's were two helpers whom he had called in for an earlier exploit in western Virginia. Most spies work hard to be inconspicuous. Pinkerton chose the opposite method when he sent an "English lord" and his "manservant" into disputed territory.

The least likely figure to be found in the remote western section of the Old Dominion would be a British nobleman on a sightseeing jaunt. To add to the improbability of the picture the agent wore a stovepipe hat, carried objects with a stagy "crest" and cases of champagne, and rode around with a footman whose "Your Lordships" made rural Americans gape.

It would seem a bit too much of a stunt, and yet the masquerade met the test; it worked. Not, however, until after the pair missed exposure by the narrowest of margins. Several times both "lord" and "man" felt the hair rise at the back of their necks as suspicious eyes focused on their regalia and natives pondered their elaborate stories.

Not yet thirty, Pryce Lewis had, when he wished to adopt it, an air that gave people the impression he was definitely "somebody." His pink and whiskered countenance could best be described as cherubic, with a bland unworldliness that gave him an advantage over persons less shrewd than himself. English-born, Lewis had lived for some time in the United States and lost most of his accent, but he was able, of course, to reassume and accentuate it.

As a Pinkerton detective, Pryce Lewis had spent several

months on a case in Jackson, Mississippi, and had learned a great deal about Southerners. In June of 1861 he finished this assignment and reported to his superior near Cincinnati, to find a new task awaiting him. Western Virginia, never an area of large farm holdings worked by masses of slaves, had moved to break away from the South and stay in the Union. Confederate forces had swept in, and the situation was badly confused. Before long McClellan would launch his own campaign there, and he required all available information.

Pinkerton and his aides collected stage props. The detective bought an elegant carriage with a British Army trunk strapped on it where few could miss seeing it, and a pair of sturdy horses, their harness mounted with silver. The staff packed the carriage with food so that the spies could subsist if it became necessary to avoid staying in hotels. With the edibles went bottles of champagne and good port. Pinkerton's assistants faked letters of introduction carrying British names and addresses, to be employed if advisable; and Lewis bought a dark suit in the latest, most baggy English mode.

Pryce had once lived not far from a Lord Tracy and he selected the role of a younger son of this man, though whenever possible he was to be vague as to his identity. Pinkerton contributed his own gold watch and diamond ring, and at the last moment someone threw in a "seegar" case with the British lion in ivory—details that would have raised the suspicions of anyone who knew British nobility. Luckily the spies met none who did.

As Lewis' coachman-manservant the detective chose Sam Bridgman, a fifty-year-old Southern native and a Pinkerton employee for a number of years. The spy chief has pictured Sam as shrewd and good-natured; yet Sam, as we shall see, had other characteristics that his employer had not considered. The situation also bore the seeds of disruption. Though much the younger, Pryce was to command this army of two; Sam must be careful to do whatever his lordship ordered—especially in public.

The pair had a quiet trip by river steamer to Guyandotte on the Virginia line, where they disembarked and encountered the first Southern forces, members of the uniformed Home Guard. The sight might have alarmed the travelers, but the guards asked no question. While Lewis remained aloof, Sam went to work to fraternize. He invited the guards to have a drink, and they demonstrated their good will by helping the Yankee spies to get their baggage off the vessel! (Pinkerton's and other accounts are supplemented by "Pryce Lewis," by Dr. Harriet Shoen in the *Davis and Elkins Historical Magazine.*)

At the town's best hotel Lewis hesitated, then registered in his own name. He would not object when others, after hearing Sam, addressed him as "Your Lordship." Let them think he was traveling incognito; if the Confederates ever investigated, the use of his right name would be in his favor. . . . Paying his bill in the morning, the tall-hatted stranger took care not to understand the value of American dollars. He threw down two sovereigns and waved away the change. Outside Sam opened the carriage door, removed his cap, and made a low bow; while a crowd gawked, Pryce signaled him to start.

Hours later they had a meal at a farmhouse. The owner, they were informed, had ten sons in the Southern armies; when Pryce ordered Sam to bring out the wine, the father told where the boys were serving, the names of their commanders, the strength of the troops, and he also repeated reports of impending troop movements. In a long and mellow conversation, Lewis learned a great deal. So far, more than good. As he and Sam rode off, they were dismayed to see several mounted Confederates ride out of a wood up ahead.

Sam called back to his fellow spy: hadn't they better turn around? Lewis shook his head; it was too late now. The first

Southerner stopped them and asked to see their pass, and his lordship gaped in astonishment. A pass, to travel along the public road? The sergeant offered to take him to the commandant, Colonel George S. Patton. (As Dr. Shoen notes, the colonel became a general, and his grandson achieved renown on another battlefield in World War II. Both Pattons were to die in service.)

Patton's headquarters were at a nearby farm, and he proved to be a friendly young officer. While Sam Bridgman watched uneasily, he rose from his desk to shake Lewis' hand, asked several polite questions, and announced that he had no wish, sir, to stop any Englishman on a tour of the region. The traveler's angelic face had done its work; the colonel ordered a pass made out for him and his servant as far as Charleston, Virginia, where another commander would give them permission to proceed. Pryce had expected nothing so easy, and he could scarcely hide his delight.

Walking to the porch, the youthful Confederate offered Lewis a chair. How did his guest think things were going for the South? Casually Pryce took out his glittering cigar case, called to Sam to fetch champagne from the carriage, and began to talk. When the footman almost dropped the bottle, Lewis snapped at him in lordly fashion, and Colonel Patton stared in awe at such haughty grandeur. Nonchalantly, his lordship went on to explain that, though Queen Victoria had decreed neutrality, he had strong leanings toward the South, as had most of his class, you know.

Over the wine the colonel grew even friendlier. Without being asked, he announced that he had six hundred soldiers and held Coal Mouth, at the junction of the Coal and Kanawha rivers, the strategic entranceway to the area. Moreover, he wanted to take his lordship over the fortifications!

The offer sounded too good to be true. Had Patton become suspicious and decided to put him to a test? The spy took a second look; no, he would swear the officer meant what he said. Lewis hesitated, reminding himself that he already knew a great deal; if the Confederates became suspicious and it was found that he had made an inspection . . . No, he answered the colonel, he must really start off again. Besides, as a member of Lord Raglan's staff in the Crimean War, he had seen all too many fortifications.

Lewis had read up on the war, and that was as near as he had ever been to it. Colonel Patton was much intrigued, however, and insisted he stay for supper and tell him about it in detail. The recent and colorful Crimean hostilities fascinated thousands of Americans. During the meal, washed down by Lewis' port, with Bridgman deferentially behind his lordship's chair, Patton asked a score of questions about the Crimea, contrasting British and American army procedures.

The spy answered as precisely as he could, but the subject had its uncomfortable side, and he worked the conversation around to a different topic. As they chatted, the colonel let out some vital new intelligence. He regretted that his band could not entertain them, because it had gone over to Charleston to play for General Wise. Oh, yes, the general had taken command there, just the previous day.

Finally Patton helped the travelers on their way with a note to a friend some distance off, and at the friend's house they spent a restful night. Lewis' spirits were soaring; this was all very rewarding. At Charleston he and Sam again sought the main hotel, which they were delighted to discover was headquarters of the new commander, General Wise. Then suddenly there was trouble.

Charleston was packed with soldiers and crowds of woolshirted mountaineers, with revolvers and bowie knives jutting from their belts. Lewis perspired with nervousness when he heard them drawl that General Wise was arresting dozens of Northerners as secret agents and would pick up anyone he suspected. Catching sight of the scowling general, Pryce felt still more anxious. All at once he remembered that Henry Wise, former Virginia governor, the man who hanged John Brown, was a hothead of hotheads.

In the dining room of the hotel the Union agent found himself practically the only man not in uniform; his stovepipe hat stood out like an accusation. All around him he heard people muttering that spies were hiding everywhere, and the South must not let one escape! A short distance off sat General Wise, as fierce and intent as reputed, surely a hard man with whom to deal. After the meal Lewis waited tensely while a crowd clustered about the officer. There was no one to introduce him, and at last the "Englishman" pushed forward to ask for a private interview.

Wise nodded with no show of cordiality, and led the way upstairs. His room was on the same floor as Pryce's, and the spy could not decide whether that was an advantage or not. Wise received his caller in his office-bedchamber and made him stand. Lewis went quickly into his story about his desire to see White Sulphur Springs, Natural Bridge, and other wonders of quaint Virginia. In his own ears the words had a hollow ring. He received an abrupt refusal. No, sir, no pass. Didn't Mr. Lewis realize they were in a war?

The agent rushed on. There'd been no war when he left England; he'd never understood that the States, which prided themselves as examples of liberty, required passports. He said much more, until, realizing he had made no impression on the crusty officer, he tried another way of dealing with him. Very well, Lewis snapped, he'd still get a pass, regardless of the general. Wise turned coldly polite. How would he do that? By applying to the British consul at Richmond. That was his right, said the general, and the spy stamped out.

Perhaps this had been a foolish move; in any case, Lewis had no choice but to carry out the bluff. In his room he addressed a note to the consul, signing his full name. Joining his "master," Sam Bridgman spoke agitatedly: Pryce mustn't mail any letter to Richmond; it would only cause more serious complications. They would be jumping from the frying pan into a mighty hot fire!

Lewis disagreed. No, the note would be a safeguard. It gave them what they needed most, time, because the Confederates here at Charleston would wait for the reply before taking action. Meanwhile he and Sam would continue to dig up information and at the same time hunt for ways to escape into Union territory if they ever had to run for it. Reluctantly the older agent agreed.

In gingerly fashion the two men went separately around the town, letting others seek them out. Once more Pryce's champagne and choice cigars worked; a group of easygoing officers asked Lewis about the Crimea, and then one spoke up just as had Colonel Patton: wouldn't Mr. Lewis visit a camp with him? Perhaps he could make suggestions to help the South!

The Union spy described his unfriendly meeting with General Wise, and the officers smiled; old Wise was a crank. Anyway, Colonel Patton had been in town the night before and vouched for his English friend. Lewis wavered, and then agreed to go to a camp at four o'clock the next day. This opportunity really could not be passed up.

The next afternoon Pryce witnessed a battalion drill and regimental dress parade; afterward, sitting in the commissary, he lectured on the British rationing system—secure in knowledge gained from some very recent reading. Why, they told him, the Confederacy had simpler methods than *that!* Records were shown to prove that precisely 3500 rations had just been issued.

Lewis' new friends took him to other camps, and he found data on practically everything he wanted to know. But near disaster brushed him again. He had devoted close attention to winning the good will of the hotel proprietor. Pryce believed him to be a secret Union sympathizer, as were many others in that area. The manager called Pryce aside; he thought he should tell Mr. Lewis that his man Sam had returned drunk the previous evening, insulted Southern officers, and talked dangerously. If they didn't watch out, both of them would be in a bad spot.

Furious and frightened, the spy summoned his helper. Didn't Sam understand his peril if they were arrested? Lewis might possibly get off as an Englishman, but Sam, an American, would surely swing! Sam contritely promised it would not happen again. . . . It did, however, and this time Lewis sternly threatened and Sam pledged himself not to drink at all.

Pryce kept an eye on his assistant, who now stayed away from the bars, but he worried, knowing that the older man might give in to temptation at any time. Part of the difficulty, it would seem, lay in "his lordship's" convincing assumption of superior airs. Also, the selection of two such different individuals to work together was probably a mistake. As the days passed, Pryce Lewis sensed that they had better move on North with their valuable information. Suppose General Wise lost patience, or suppose the Richmond consul wrote that he had never heard of any Mr. Lewis?

Yet the spy also wondered if perhaps Wise would throw them both into his well-stocked jail at the first sign of departure. Lewis sat up for hours at night puzzling over the problem. On one of these occasions he heard spurs clank as men stamped down the hall and in and out of the room he knew to be General Wise's. Something important must have happened! As soon as he dared, the agent went to his landlord-confidant, who had real news: Northern forces had just reached Parkersburg, and Wise had been ordered there with most of his troops. Colonel Tompkins had taken over in Charleston; would Mr. Lewis like to meet the colonel?

Mr. Lewis assuredly would. Somewhat to his embarrassment,

the landlord woke up the officer, who was an agreeable fellow, listening politely as he rubbed his eyes. Pryce thought quickly and changed his story to fit a new situation. . . . If he could only get hold of a pass, he told himself, he and Sam would start out for Richmond instead of following their earlier, meandering scenic route. Then they would turn toward Union territory and use the pass to reach the border. . . . With his most cherubic expression, the Englishman explained that he wanted to go to Richmond. The Confederate soldier was reassuring. Why, Mr. Lewis didn't need any pass to get there from Charleston. Just travel the usual roads. . . . Colonel Tompkins outlined the route.

A little hesitantly Lewis tried a bland smile: well, to protect him in case of any trouble, wouldn't the colonel sign a pass?

The Southerner was afraid he had no such authority. . . . For several hours, back in his own room, Pryce debated with himself, and then announced that he would be off for Richmond early in the morning. By dawn he and Sam were already dressed and on their way out of Charleston. At the first opportunity they swung off the Richmond road and headed toward the mountains. Now, if only they could avoid meeting anyone who had known about them in Charleston and who might wonder at the change in their direction!

Twenty-five miles farther on, at Logan Court House, Lewis made out troops in gray. His pulse raced as he inspected them. No, he thanked the Lord, they were not from Charleston. His relief was momentary, however, for now he discovered his horses needed shoeing, and they could not avoid making a stop.

As inconspicuously as possible, Pryce took a hotel room, for they would have to stay overnight. But when he went out on the porch, he immediately sensed fresh danger. A group of men, most of them in rough uniforms, stared suspiciously at him, and a figure in black broadcloth stepped up to ask who he was and what he was doing here? Lewis answered vaguely.

When he saw that he was not satisfying his questioners, he went back into the inn.

In the hallway an older man with an authoritative air caught up with him, and the Englishman realized at once that this was someone of real importance. Acting almost by instinct, Lewis once again modified his story to account for his presence in Logan Court House. He was the son of a British cotton manufacturer who had bought heavily in the South. In hopes of being able to ship the cotton home despite the war, he was headed for Louisville to see the consul there.

The contradictory tales which Lewis told violated the general rules of espionage, but this improvisation worked. The dignitary who questioned Lewis was the justice of the peace, and he believed the spy's explanation. Why, the justice said, he could help him arrange a route across the rough mountains ahead. He would be glad to introduce him to the Confederate commander, who had been a mail contractor over the roads Lewis must travel. In a few minutes the Englishman was shaking hands with the colonel, an elderly fellow in blue jeans, galluses, and checked shirt, who escorted him to his room.

The colonel outlined a long, involved route. Lewis was much impressed with the aging man, who seemed one of the most intelligent individuals he had met on his trip. But Pryce perceived a slight change in the atmosphere when the colonel, giving him a canny look, asked: What did the stranger think about the Southern war?

The Englishman broke into a persuasive monologue. . . . England's mills demanded Southern cotton; Britain must and would go to war with the Yankees in order to keep the staple moving across the ocean. The gallused old soldier was convinced and, happily, Lewis invited him and the justice to his hotel room; he had a single bottle of wine left, and they would share it.

As he glanced from the window, he was horrified to see Sam

Bridgman talking to a group of soldiers. Lewis had had no chance to tell Sam his new version of their trip. If his helper repeated the earlier one, the discrepancy would destroy them! But at the moment he was afraid to go to Bridgman.

He had no time to mull over the problem. The colonel left him for a little while and returned wearing an annoyed frown. A few townspeople still had not been convinced about Mr. Lewis, and were sending representatives to speak to him. In walked a group headed by the bad-mannered fellow who had first given Pryce trouble on the hotel porch. The Union agent could almost feel the hangman's rope.

Assuming an ease that was entirely contrived, Lewis bowed to the new arrivals and launched into a fervent address that intensified everything he had said before: cotton-hungry England would crack down on the damned New Englanders and smash them as they deserved. . . . He, an important agent of British textile interest, knew it for a fact!

His listeners were even more convinced than the colonel. They pounded Lewis' perspiring back and left. The colonel insisted on taking him to dinner downstairs, where the Englishman saw Sam sitting with a large party. Lewis' fears rose once more. Suppose Sam drank too much? . . . His assistant had learned to be discreet, however, and the meal passed without incident.

During dinner Lewis picked up startling news. Two more companies were due, who were to march on the next day to join with General Wise's forces. . . . The colonel was asking if Mr. Lewis wouldn't favor his soldiers with a speech before they left? Lewis squirmed; he and Sam *had* to get out of town by morning with their vital information, and every mention of the hostile Wise made him quake. A single wire from the general in neighboring Charleston could halt them.

He explained that he must start by dawn, and the colonel did not press him. Nevertheless, Pryce had to stand about and talk informally to hundreds of the men; then, despite his objections, he must follow the colonel to a local dance that went on until two o'clock in the morning. He and Sam were due to leave at five and, though both of them were close to exhaustion, the spy made certain they rose in time.

As Lewis stepped into his carriage at dawn, someone grasped his arm firmly. "Come upstairs with me!" The colonel's stern tone certainly meant trouble. Wise must have sent a wire, and the jig was up. . . . His step lagging, Lewis followed his summoner. Inside, the colonel reached into his pocket and drew out —a bottle for a last drink. The Englishman gulped in relief and, after a few minutes, to the cheers of the soldiers and the officers' warm farewells, the carriage rolled off. (As Dr. Harriet Shoen notes, Lewis several times expressed great liking for the colonel and regret that he had fooled him. Spies may also feel remorse, especially when the threat of the gallows fades.)

Now they had to ride like the wind, and always under the threat of a command to halt. The colonel's detailed memorandum of the mountain route was a vast help, as Sam made the carriage almost fly across rough ridges and down into muddy valleys. They didn't dare to stop for any length of time. The first night, fagged as they were, they took only a few hours' rest, and then dashed on. Many hours later, with their horses badly winded, they jolted into Kentucky and made out an American flag. Safe!

Lewis' mind was full of figures, names, and military plans which should be given to the Northern forces at the first possible moment. In order to reach Cincinnati, their starting point, they lost a precious day in waiting for a steamboat. By the time they stumbled into Pinkerton's headquarters, they had spent nineteen days on the trip, and both Lewis and Bridgman had aged nineteen years.

When he had their data, Pinkerton immediately wired General McClellan, then at Cheat Mountain in West Virginia. The delighted Little Mac responded instantly. Send Lewis to Union headquarters on the Kanawha River to give his report directly to General Cox. The weary spy went forth once more, to pour out all of his hard-won information—and to receive one of the shocks of his life. Cox didn't believe him!

The general, a former lawyer and new to the Army, was puzzled by conflicting intelligence reports. He quoted others, strong Union men from the area, who estimated the Southern Army as considerably larger than Lewis indicated. Was Lewis *certain* of his facts? . . . Lewis lost his temper. He'd seen far more than anyone else, and he'd been much closer to the facts. The farther a man got from a military point, he said, the bigger grew the rumored number of Southern troops. He assured General Cox that his forces really did outnumber the Confederates and that in one day they could be in Charleston, with the enemy running before them.

The general held a council of his officers and called Lewis in to repeat his story. The Englishman gave all his facts, answered questions, and left. He had done everything he could. . . . The next day General Cox took the plunge. His army would march according to Lewis' advice.

Pryce Lewis returned to Cincinnati. Two days later he received a telegram: Cox had rolled into Charleston, and General Wise had pulled out in retreat. And Cox, who had hesitated to act on the agent's information, gained greatly in prestige as a result of this success.

McClellan's victories in western Virginia took Little Mac to the military heights, and with him went Pinkerton and his company of helpers, not least among them the angel-faced Mr. Lewis.

Chapter 4

Once Too Often

There comes a time in the life of all men, spies included, when it is wise to stop indulging in risky though rewarding undertakings. Had Timothy Webster realized this fact, before he died in harness, he might be remembered as the most effective of all the war's espionage agents.

Big Tim Webster became a figure rare in the United States—a double spy, the war's first. The Northerner worked for one side and posed as an agent for the other. To the Union he gave minutely accurate vital information; to the Confederacy, harmless facts that looked valuable on the surface. The peril of such a course is obvious. One is not surprised that Webster was eventually captured. The amazing thing is that he remained uncaptured for so long.

Tall and impressive, Timothy had numerous advantages in his work—not least among them good luck, the sort of luck, his friends thought, that only a guardian angel could bring. He was accidentally betrayed in the end by his own partisans, in a blunder so bad that the angel must have flown away. Basically, however, his downfall after glowing successes came about because Tim went once too often to the well—in this case, Richmond.

Like his associate Pryce Lewis, Webster was born in England; in time, unlike Lewis, he adopted American citizenship.

When he was twelve his parents took him to Princeton, New Jersey, where, in the fashion of Pinkerton himself, he started as a mechanic. Tim led a quiet life, working hard during the day and being a good family fellow after hours. A chance to become a New York policeman tempted him and he joined the force and did well. He won an assignment at the World's Crystal Palace Exposition of the 1850s, a dazzling show place of progress, and also an inviting focal point for thieves, swindlers, and strong-arm operators.

There, at thirty-five, Webster met Allan Pinkerton. In the heavy-shouldered younger man who moved with silent confidence, the detective recognized a find. Incidents at the Exposition convinced him that Webster had rare physical endurance and nerveless courage. A superintendent of New York police agreed with this opinion; to him Tim was "the bravest, coolest man, I think, that ever lived."

During the four or five years before the war, Webster served Pinkerton in a variety of places, and soon began to emerge as the agency's star. Tim was a detective hailed by other detectives as an artist, a performer of finesse and perception. Everybody got along with Tim; more accurately, he got along with everybody. He "practically mesmerized you into thinking he was whatever he decided to be," according to one of his associates.

By nature Webster was decidedly reserved. When he assumed a role, a new man stepped forth. He might suddenly become an individual of easy tongue and back-thumping affability, or a zealot with fire in his eyes, or an orator of great persuasiveness. He fitted himself to conditions as they arose. His strong nose, high forehead, light and unflinching grayish eyes gave him an "air of trust." That air served Tim well when Pinkerton gave him an especially touchy assignment in connection with the Baltimore Plot against Lincoln; he wormed his way into the hostile Maryland cavalry which supposedly had designs against the railroad bridges.

He worked adroitly in that episode, and then in April of 1861 Pinkerton summoned him to Ohio for his first wartime spying, a survey of munitions, armed forces, and general attitudes in the South. Webster was to go first to Louisville, in Union territory, and then head for Tennessee. That started a full year in which Webster was to live always within a finger's reach of ruin.

At Clarksville, Tennessee, Webster demonstrated his skill at entering a strange town and quickly making friends. A chance acquaintance took him to a gathering, and there he met others who introduced him to Confederate officers who escorted him to a camp where he met a general who told him his supply troubles. The spy spoke warmly of the Southern cause in Baltimore; from his own experiences he described street fighting and "Lincoln outrages." When Tim left Clarksville, a delegation of uniformed men and civilians accompanied him to the depot, urging him to return.

His success worked against him, however. The scene at the station caught the attention of a civilian who, as Webster found out later, could have had him put on trial within an hour. Riding on to Memphis, the Northerner noticed that he was being scrutinized by a sunburned individual in a broad-brimmed hat, a man with a squint of suspicion. Tim kept the stranger steadily in sight, but at the same time he carefully checked on the number of uniformed men who got on and off the train, the heavy guns at stopping points, the size of supply loads.

When Webster descended at Memphis, the wearer of the wide hat stepped down behind him. At the hotel where he registered (like Pryce Lewis, he nearly always used his own name), Tim saw an officer take down lists of newcomers, and then lead off a frightened youth. "Safety Committee's got that one," Tim heard a bystander murmur. So that was it. Fellow guests were excitedly talking about the incident: "He was from the North —enough to make him a suspect." "I'm for hanging every one of 'em that comes, without he gives full proof he's *not* spying!"

Despite the hostile atmosphere, Tim succeeded in sleeping well that night. The next day he had little trouble in discovering that a second Safety Committee man trailed him; the broad hat was nowhere in sight. Ah, well, Tim had his work to do. . . . In the hotel bar, standing beside three uniformed officers, he dropped a passing remark about Baltimore. Yes, he certainly expected Maryland would join the Confederacy, he said. From then on he needed only to listen.

The three officers said that there was a full regiment and four or five companies at their camp, and Pillow had more than thirty-eight hundred. Look, Mr. Webster must spend a day at camp! Mr. Webster replied that he welcomed such an invitation. The big man's camaraderie was infectious. An older major general, beaming kindly, began to treat Tim like a son. Infusions of Bourbon helped. By the time they left the hotel everyone was in a jovial mood and the three Confederates guided Tim into a store where they insisted on buying him, as a sign of good will, a corded, tasseled "secession hat." Webster donned it with delight.

For the temporary secessionist the day in camp was highly instructive, though even there the second Safety Committee man trailed him. Yet Tim was safe for at least a time; reports of his Baltimore connections spread through Memphis and men sought him out to shake his hand. Nevertheless, Tim suspected that if he moved a step back toward Union territory, he would be seized. He had learned a great deal, and it was time to start for home, but he would have to try to get there by a roundabout route. When he announced he must go to Chattanooga to meet a relative, his friends seemed genuinely sorry. Oh, yes, Webster assured them, he'd be back, and then he'd cast his lot with the Confederate Army he promised.

He left on the 5 A.M. train. Neither of his two shadows appeared, and he thought he was free of them. En route he changed from the Chattanooga-bound train to one heading toward Jackson, Tennessee—inside the Confederacy but in the right direction. Suddenly he glanced up and saw the wide-brimmed hat. Its owner and an ominous, Atlaslike figure, clearly a strong-arm helper, stood in the doorway looking at Tim.

Webster had a trick or two left in his bag, however. When he reached the Jackson station he asked the conductor at what time the train left for Humboldt, and inquired about the hotels there. "I'll be staying two or three days," he explained. As he boarded the train, so did the two men. By the time they jolted into Humboldt, it was raining hard. Tim left the coach quickly by the rear door, his shadowers more slowly by the front.

A pile of baggage stood on the platform, and he stepped behind it, his bag in his hand. A minute later Webster watched the pair of shadowers dart off through the rain for the hotel. The express for Louisville rolled in and the spy jumped calmly aboard. Just before he reached Union territory he slipped his "secession hat" into the bag and began to write up pages of notes.

Pinkerton had an even harder assignment for Tim back in Maryland. Baltimore revisited seemed a quiet city, under martial law. The Lincoln administration had arrested legislators, editors, and the chief of police, quelling outward hostility. Southern sympathizers were at work, however, and Webster was supposed to uncover their plans. For weeks the Union heard rumors of uprisings with tens of thousands of guns in the hands of organizations that were wary of outsiders. A number of Baltimoreans recognized Tim as a friend of Dixie; yet he had been away and he now had to re-establish his pro-Southern reputation under difficult circumstances.

So that the spy could move in the most elite circles, Pinkerton provided a lush expense account. Riding up in a gleaming carriage, an elegantly dressed Tim paraded into Miller's Hotel. To a few of his friends he explained that he had inherited money from a relative. To new acquaintances he groaned over "Yankee outrages," and predicted the inevitable Confederate triumph. And, when the doors were closed, to a very few he disclosed in great confidence the new role he had undertaken as a Southern agent against the North.

Tim declared that he was slipping in and out of Washington with messages for Southerners. He offered to take letters, maps, and other papers from Baltimore friends and see that they were delivered. He did, and the messages always arrived at their destinations in the capital—but the Baltimoreans did not know that Pinkerton's aides opened each one, copied it, and sometimes delayed it until they had used the information. From then on Webster was established in the most dangerous of occupations—that of the double spy.

His system worked well. At times the Northern agent took a warm Confederate sympathizer with him to Washington; the stories told on his return to Baltimore strengthened his standing. Tim introduced other Pinkerton men to his Southern connections. With another Northern agent, a wide-faced Irishman named John Scully, he went to a photographer's gallery. There the two spies posed virtuously and proudly with a big Confederate flag, and Webster put on his "secession hat" from Memphis. Meanwhile Tim was accumulating files of facts on various individuals, and when some of them suddenly fell into Union hands, the spy roared his indignation, and went on to trap his next victim.

Once he almost slipped into a hole of his own digging. As he stood in one of Baltimore's popular saloons, a dozen acquaintances around him, a sullen-faced character walked up. "Damn you, Webster, I'm going to wreck your dirty act!"

Caught off guard, Webster spluttered, and the man, Bill

Zigler, added: "You're a Yankee and a spy." To the others Zigler shouted: "I saw that fellow in Washington yesterday."

"Well, I *was* in Washington," Webster answered. "I've just been telling about it."

Zigler's voice rose again. "But you didn't say you had a long talk with the chief of the Yankee detectives!"

The spy gave a fine demonstration of righteous fury: "You're a no-good liar." When Zigler sprang at him, Tim's powerful fist hit him between the eyes and sent him sprawling. The other man scrambled up, a knife in his hand. He had no chance to use it, because Webster had drawn his gun: "Get out of here before I use this."

While his opponent backed away, the crowd voiced its approval. One man shouted that he'd just as soon call President Davis a spy as he would old Tim! As it turned out, the incident pushed Webster's Southern stock higher than ever. Yet he still had not succeeded in working himself into the inner Confederate organizations.

Then Tim conceived of another project to help the North and also build up his standing as a Confederate agent—a series of trips into lower Maryland and Virginia, carrying messages and scarce Southern goods. John Scully, his fellow counterspy, went with him. Tim received anxious warnings from his Southern friends in Baltimore: he must keep on guard constantly against Yankee soldiers; those men would do anything! The two agents, carrying secret Union passes, moved swiftly, contacting many people whose hostility to the Union had never been suspected and gathering dozens of letters with evidence of underground military organizations.

Tim's success filled Confederate Baltimoreans with admiration; why, this man could fool any Yankee on earth. The spy returned to find himself a hero, a man who had risked his life for the South. Moreover, he received the reward for which he had been hoping. A man sidled up and murmured that he and his friends wanted Tim to join the Knights of Liberty. They would meet that midnight.

Webster waited, long before the hour, at a deserted corner. Blindfolded, he was led to a gate opened only after a password was given, down an alley to a door where another password was required. Then in a dim room he took an oath, his blindfold was removed, and he proceeded to study the faces around him. That night and on the following nights Tim listened as men told how the Knights of Liberty worked directly with the Southern army, how they operated branches outside Baltimore, and kept their organization secret inside the city.

When he was called on for a speech, Webster summoned all his oratorical powers to attack Yankees and Yankeedom. He closed with a breathless denunciation, and saw the gathering explode in delight.

Hastily, Webster communicated with Pinkerton. It might have been possible for Tim to learn more by further attendance at the meetings, but the Administration did not want to take chances. The official order was to break up the Knights of Liberty before they made further headway. At the next gathering Tim rose and pointed a trembling finger towards the Northern abolitionists, calling for their final destruction——

By prearrangement, his last words were a signal; a squad of Union infantrymen swept in and trapped the panicky Knights. Only a handful escaped, and among them was Timothy Webster. That did not seem odd. Hadn't he always managed to get away from the Yankees? Besides, Tim had already whispered to a few Confederate partisans that his next destination was Richmond itself.

On October 14, 1861, the agent took off on a trip along the Eastern Shore. He had letters from Baltimoreans to Richmonders. At Eastville he made contact with a Confederate pilot who on dark evenings ran a sailing canoe, thirty feet long, across Chesapeake Bay. For several moonlit nights Webster and twelve others waited impatiently. Then under an overcast sky they set out on a tense voyage.

The mailbags which they carried had been filled with rocks. If the Federals intercepted them, the mail would be dumped overboard. The evening was not quite dark enough, and the passengers shivered when the sails bellied out for the thirty-mile trip. As the wind freshened, spray drenched them.

Acting as lookout, Tim spotted a point of light to leeward—a Union gunboat. But the canoe cut swiftly and safely through the water. On the shore a sentinel called to them, the blockade runner gave the countersign, and Webster made out a Confederate camp. After a few hours' sleep he made a quick survey of breastworks, battery, and personnel. Later a visit to the commander and a ten-minute conversation netted him a pass for Richmond.

The Union spy rode boldly into the city, registered at the crowded Spottswood Hotel, and sauntered about as if Richmond were his oyster. Before long he must present himself to some official, but first he would establish his identity with a few carefully chosen civilians. Tim strolled from house to private office, delivering letters, enjoying pleasant chats. William Campbell, to whom he brought a note from his father, was especially grateful, and conducted the companionable Mr. Webster on a tour of the town.

The spy listened and looked and missed little—batteries along the turnpikes, defenses of railroads from Manassas, earthworks, the size of gun batteries. Bill Campbell had a good friend in ordnance, whom they visited. The officer in charge described proudly how a British vessel, eluding the blockade, had just come in with thousands of Enfield rifles and rifled cannon. The latter proved to be of phenomenal accuracy, and the officer described why.

Next Tim called at the Richmond *Examiner*, and established an excellent relationship by saying that he would be happy to carry letters and information for the paper. After a few days he and Bill Campbell went to the office of the Secretary of War, and the Union spy sat down for a long talk with Mr. Benjamin. This was running a real risk, of course, but Webster's good angel must have hovered close, for he got away with it beautifully. When he told how he carried letters from Baltimore Confederates and hoped to deliver some of them in Manassas, the War Secretary gave him a pass to that important military point. With a cheerful good-by, Webster set off on the trip, made his observations, and returned to Richmond.

Fortune favored him again. He met a well-known blockade runner, about to go back to Baltimore, who took him to the provost marshal's office. With this introduction, Tim shook hands with a crowd of Confederates and left with a new pass. On the trip back to Maryland he accompanied the blockade runner, who escorted him to the headquarters of the Southern general in the Fredericksburg area. Webster's circle of Confederate acquaintances was growing. In Baltimore he conferred daily with Confederate sympathizers and agents, delivering letters he had brought from Richmond, gathering new ones to be taken South.

Webster masqueraded so well as a Southerner that once he fooled some of the "wrong people" in a ridiculous though dangerous mix-up. One day a man clapped him on the shoulder and thrust him into the arms of two Federal soldiers. The man was one of the new and eager members of Pinkerton's secret service, and since the staff had never been briefed on Tim's special operations, the tyro was certain he had met a truly dangerous Confederate!

Locked up incommunicado for hours, Webster finally managed to get a message to proper officials. News of the incident had traveled over Baltimore, however, and how could he be eased out of this muddle? Webster devised a method. While a crowd watched, soldiers led him that night from the jail to be taken to Fort McHenry pier. In the dark Webster "leaped suddenly" from the wagon and disappeared. Making his way stealthily to a Confederate friend, he stayed hidden for days. As usual, old Tim had turned bad luck into good.

A new trip to Richmond was due. Though he generally worked alone, Webster occasionally took along an assistant, and this time he chose one of the few Negroes who became full-fledged spies during the war. Pinkerton had discovered husky John Scobell among a file of "contrabands" taken to his office for questioning about Southern conditions. Much impressed by the man's intelligence, the detective added him to the staff.

John had been a Mississippi slave, property of a Scotsman who educated and freed him. Among his other qualifications, he could sing Highland ballads, Scottish dialect and all. He played a wide range of roles as a secret agent: a dull servant accompanying a "female agent," a steamboat roustabout, a blank-faced fisherman on a river bank. John's dark skin allowed him to move about without attracting much attention; his wits got him out of most tight situations.

On Webster's second journey to Virginia the two men went together to Leonardstown, Maryland, and then they separated for different assignments. At no time did they give any indication that they knew each other. At their transfer point Webster revealed his professional skill in converting a chance incident into a windfall. The hotel proprietor pointed to a nervous man who paced up and down the hall and identified him as a Dr. Gurley. Apparently the doctor had been with the Union Army on the Pacific Coast and had now decided to cast his lot with Dixie.

The manager spoke confidentially, as one good Southerner to the other: Dr. Gurley had vital dispatches from Confederate sympathizers in the North—messages intended for Secretary of War Benjamin. Because of their importance, the doctor had become terribly concerned about their safety. Perhaps Mr. Webster would help him on to Richmond?

Mr. Webster said he was more than willing to help. First, though, he must do one errand. Walking to the Negro quarter of the town, the spy caught Scobell's eye and managed a whispered conference. Then back at the hotel Tim met Dr. Gurley and showed a hearty good will. He'd make certain that the doctor found his way promptly into Virginia. Gurley gratefully treated Tim to several drinks and left him at dark to pack for tomorrow's journey. Webster was talking with the hotel manager when Dr. Gurley staggered back into the lobby, face ashen, clothes muddied.

Tim shook his head sadly at the tale of attack and robbery in the dark. What had the doctor lost? Those papers for the Confederate War Secretary, Gurley confided with a shudder of horror. The spy tried to soothe him: "Still, you can tell him what the dispatches said." The doctor groaned; he had no idea whatever of their content. . . . Alas, they had to start for Richmond regardless, and during the trip Dr. Gurley had the consolation of Mr. Webster's pity. The documents were by then in Washington.

For a while things were not so easy for Tim in Richmond. J. B. Jones, the War Department clerk to whom Webster applied for a passport, complained that all too often men of vague origin received permits from Secretary Benjamin or Provost Marshal Winder.

Letter carriers charged $1.50 a message, earning thousands, said the clerk, who himself was poorly paid. True, they brought in Union papers, but always seemed "particularly ignorant" about Northern military plans. Benjamin and the marshal, Clerk Jones thought, were simply "passing Federal spies out of the country." In his diary for December of 1861 Jones commented coldly:

Several of General Winder's detectives came to me with a man named Webster, who, it appears, has been going between Richmond and Baltimore, conveying letters, money, etc. I refused him a passport. He said he could get it from the Secretary himself, but that it was sometimes difficult in gaining access to him. I told him to get it, then; I would give him none.

Webster did apply to Benjamin and did get the passport. Yet the situation was definitely uncomfortable, and it was not politic to remind the War Secretary too often of his presence. After a calm Christmas in Baltimore, however, the spy made a third trip to Richmond, the most successful of all. There was only a preliminary mishap in crossing the water on a night of screaming wind and rain. The vessel went aground and Webster carried fellow passengers through the water to safety. Lacking a bed, he threw a blanket around his wet garments and tried to sleep.

The next morning Webster twisted in an agony of "inflammatory rheumatism." For the rest of his days he was to suffer from arthritis. When his pain lessened, he pressed on to Richmond, where he sent word to officials that he had brought information about Northern activity. Tim's charm worked its magic again. Judah Benjamin welcomed him warmly, and said he was much pleased with the intelligence. (It was, of course, a small selection of facts that could not hurt the Union.)

In return Webster received a boon—a passport allowing him to go much farther into Southern lines, to Knoxville, Chattanooga, and Nashville. On his return Webster "reported" to Benjamin, and this time he accepted letters and commissions from the War Secretary himself and from the provost marshal! Guardedly the Richmond press later admitted: "He was in the employment of one of the Departments here as a letter carrier between this city and Maryland." Southerners would whisper as he passed, "See that fellow? He's Davis' and Benjamin's man, carrying their messages."

In Baltimore again, while the Confederates read Judah Benjamin's secret messages with intense interest, Tim rested briefly, and his arthritic pains went away. His reports of Southern intentions and attitudes had already impressed General McClellan, who regarded Webster as a major asset. Like so many others, Little Mac liked the man and admired his calm precision. The general urged Pinkerton to make still further use of his star.

When Tim's Southern mail piled high again, he arranged for his fourth and last jaunt into Dixie. This time he had as companion Mrs. Hattie Lawton, of Pinkerton's regular staff, who had made several brief trips into Richmond with her husband or with Scobell, the Negro spy, as her "servant." Pretty, competent, Mrs. Lawton apparently lacked initiative, as her employer was soon to discover to his regret. Whatever espionage services Hattie was to have performed in Webster's support, asking her to accompany him was the first of a series of bad mistakes.

At Leonardstown, where Tim had deprived the nervous Dr. Gurley of his messages to Judah Benjamin, Mrs. Lawton waited for Webster to join her. They then traveled as sister and brother or, as some Confederate accounts claimed, as husband and wife. When they approached Virginia, the weather was bad; missing a connection, they wandered through winter rain. By the time they reached Richmond, Webster's pains had returned, worse than before. Days stretched into weeks, and for the first time no messages arrived in Washington or Baltimore from the resourceful spy.

McClellan was increasingly pressed by Lincoln and by Congress. He had delayed his long-planned major drive on the Confederates, but he must move soon. He wanted badly to know whatever new information Webster had. Both the general and Pinkerton were afraid of what might have happened to Tim and Mrs. Lawton. At last the secret service director decided to dispatch two trusted agents to Richmond—Pryce Lewis, who once played the English lord, and John Scully, the Irishman who had worked closely with Tim on his dangerous Maryland trips.

At the last minute Pinkerton realized a special danger. In Washington Lewis and Scully had investigated Confederate suspects, quizzing them, searching their homes. With two families, that of former Governor Morton of Florida and the Phillipses of South Carolina, they had had long conversations. Both families would remember their faces. Where were the Mortons and Phillipses now? Pinkerton consulted his files, conferred with refugees and escapees from the Southern capital. His informants were certain that the Mortons and Phillipses had left Richmond. Oh, no, they couldn't be wrong. . . . After long consideration the detective told Lewis and Scully to start. Not for some time would he learn that he had committed one of the biggest blunders of his life.

In Richmond the innocent-looking Pryce Lewis and his aide registered confidently at their quarters and walked over to the *Examiner*, the paper for which Webster carried letters. The editors answered their question at once: Mr. Webster was in the city now, in bed at his hotel. Hadn't they heard of his sickness? He hadn't left his room since his arrival. . . . Why Hattie Lawton had not communicated with Pinkerton is an unanswered question. Perhaps she was too frightened, or perhaps she feared sending a message through uncertain emissaries. Though the new arrivals had yet to learn of it, the very air of Richmond was thick with suspicion. . . . Somewhat relieved, Lewis and Scully proceeded to the hotel and there made their own errors.

Without preliminary inquiry they knocked at Webster's door. In the room they found their friend, as they expected, with Mrs. Lawton in a chair beside him and a Confederate guest, Mr. Pierce. Tim looked ill indeed, and distressed by their arrival. His uneasiness communicated itself, and the visit became very tense. After leaving, Scully and Lewis waited a while and then knocked again, only to discover another Southerner with their friends—Captain McCubbin of the provost-marshal's office. Once more they had no chance to talk privately with their fellow agent. Captain McCubbin asked: "Have you reported yet to our office?"

When they answered vaguely, the captain shrugged. "Well, do it in the next day or two." Conversation lagged, and the new arrivals could only leave. The next morning they called at the marshal's office and told a well-rehearsed story: They had arrived separately from the British Isles a few years earlier, and recently concocted a scheme for slipping goods into the South; they had come to make arrangements. On the way a Virginia friend gave them a letter for Mr. Webster. The note, prepared by Pinkerton, "warned" Webster that the Union had taken over his former route to the South.

The marshal nodded, and Lewis and Scully hastened to Webster's chamber. They had no more than entered when one of the marshal's detectives trailed them there. Regretting the intrusion, he said General Winder wanted to know where Mr. Lewis and Mr. Scully had lived in England and Ireland. After the messenger went off with their answer, Webster cried, "Leave right away, right away. Something's wrong, or they wouldn't have sent him!"

They had no chance to leave. Two men appeared at the door, a detective and a man whom both visitors recognized in a second—the son of Governor Morton of Florida, whose house the Pinkerton agents had searched in Washington! Scully lost his head and rushed out. Better controlled, Pryce Lewis stayed to acknowledge the introduction, gave no sign that he recognized the young man, and hastily excused himself.

They thought perhaps they could escape the hotel, but this was impossible. The detective dashed out of the room after them, telling them coldly that they were wanted in the provost marshal's headquarters. Downstairs other men were waiting, and at the office a second son of Governor Morton stepped forward. He immediately identified Scully and Pryce. The spies were taken to prison and separated, each wondering what the other was saying and how much of the whole story the Confederates knew.

Up to this point, it seemed, the Southern government did not comprehend Webster's role, and Tim, like the magnificent actor that he was, prepared to fight for the other two agents as well as for himself. A court-martial was ordered without delay for Scully, on charges of spying. When Webster received a call to testify and could not make the trip because of his condition, court was transferred to his bedside. With the frozen-faced Scully looking on, Webster spoke in his friend's behalf. No, he had no reason to consider Mr. Scully a Union agent; he regarded him as a good fellow Confederate. . . . When the court filed out, the sick man collapsed, and Hattie Lawton ran to his side.

The verdict was quickly pronounced against Scully—guilty. For Pryce Lewis a desperate hope had meanwhile presented itself. He joined a group of prisoners in a jail break one night. Huddled together in the dark, Lewis and the rest exchanged whispered plans. McClellan had advanced on the Confederacy and his camp lay at Yorktown; they tried to get to him. . . . For thirty-six hours Lewis crept across country in cold March winds and icy rains. Straining his eyes, he made out dim figures. They were his last chance. He could scarcely stand up, but he signaled, and they responded. When they moved closer he made out their uniforms—not Union, but Confederate.

They marched him back for his trial, and the verdict was what he had anticipated—guilty. He and Scully were to hang in a week.

The two men, on the basis that they were British subjects,

made frantic efforts to save themselves. They appealed to the acting consul at Richmond, F. J. Cridland, and in London the well-worn papers of the Public Records Office recount their attempt to get help from England. When they claimed the protection of Her Majesty's Government, Cridland went to officials of the court-martial.

In Scully's case, on which he first worked, Cridland soon became "convinced that the evidence . . . left no doubt of his guilt and that he had been a military spy." From the day of their arrival, the consul revealed, the Confederates had been wary of the two men. "Their movements were very extraordinary and suspicious, being watched by detectives."

Cridland doubted that he should intervene in cases of persons who "evidently violated Her Majesty's proclamation" of neutrality. Nevertheless, here were two fellow men and two Englishmen in distress, and the consul felt it was his duty to see them. The Confederates resisted his efforts, and a less conscientious man might have given up. Cridland plodded on, and finally succeeded—one day before April 5, the date set for their execution.

Though both Lewis and Scully admitted to Cridland that they had been paid as Federal agents, they pleaded with the consul to act in their behalf. Not only were they British subjects, but they had not been guilty of any offense in Virginia. Nor could they be convicted in Richmond for acts which, according to the testimony of the Morton family, they had committed in Washington. As a matter of fact, there was no proof that the two men actually spied within the Confederacy.

Cridland spoke frankly; he had to refer the matter to Lord Lyons, his superior in Washington. With the two capitals separated by the war, and with the thought that less than twenty-four hours of life was left to them, the prisoners despaired.

Yet Lewis and Scully, and perhaps others, had underestimated this quiet, conservative agent of Queen Victoria. Regardless of Cridland's own conviction, he saved the men. Calling on the Confederate Secretaries of War and State, the Consul said simply that he wished to place the matter before Lord Lyons. After all, he noted, the prisoners had received hasty trials, with scant time to prepare their cases. British understatement worked; within a few hours the Confederacy responded to his reasonable appeal and granted a reprieve.

Timothy Webster waited fatalistically for the next development. When his health improved, the young man whom he had first visited in Richmond, Bill Campbell, proved a good friend; Campbell asked Tim and Mrs. Lawton to stay with him, and they gratefully accepted. But Webster's position had become a delicate one. Most of his other Confederate connections were turning against him. "The style of his evidence" in defense of Lewis and Scully had aroused suspicion.

Gradually, the Southerners realized that Webster, the double spy, must have been the principal in the case, the others mere auxiliaries. Convinced it did not have the full story, the Davis administration sent agents to the two prisoners. According to one account, Scully, a Catholic, received a priest, to whom he confessed; the priest, it is said, was a layman in disguise.

Another explanation appears more likely. After days of brooding self-examination, Scully saw only one chance for liberty, and a return to his family; the alternative was death and the disgrace of hanging. Already the Southerners knew a great deal, and without doubt they would never free Webster. Scully broke down and told about the work of the friend with whom he had posed under the Confederate flag, with whom he had survived so many earlier risks. The officials then went to Lewis. The truth had come out, and to deny it now would benefit nobody.

Twenty years later Pinkerton spoke of Lewis and Scully with tolerance. They had often been brave, but they failed under terrible pressure. He said he would not attempt to pass judgment on them. . . . For the two men a further ordeal awaited: though they had saved their own lives, they had now to appear in court against their onetime colleague. Webster had testified to save them; they would now make his execution certain.

Tim remained composed as his former friends wove the rope for him, strand by strand. In contrast to their swift trials, his went on for three weeks. This time the Confederates had determined to build the strongest possible case. The verdict was hanging within ten days. Sitting beside the haggard condemned man, Mrs. Lawton cried quietly.

Serving in the field with General McClellan, Allan Pinkerton learned of Webster's conviction. He conferred with the general and sped to Washington to see Abraham Lincoln. The disturbed President convened a Cabinet session, which authorized the War Secretary to communicate with Jefferson Davis, and the Union did everything it could to save Timothy Webster.

The administration advised the Confederates that it had thus far been lenient in dealing with Southern agents. Many had gone free; none had been executed. The message hinted that if Webster were put to death, the Union might retaliate. . . . In Richmond Mrs. Lawton, too, tried desperately to have the sentence changed. She was permitted to leave prison, where she was still held, for an interview with President Davis. His staff reported him in conferences with General Lee. The trembling woman had a faint hope—an appeal to Varina Davis. But the President's wife said that, although she felt sympathetic, she could not intervene.

Many people in Richmond were certain that the Union spy would not hang. Stories circulated about mysterious Southern influences that would spare the man by whom Judah Benjamin himself sent letters through the lines. It was hinted that the double spy had bribed lesser officials of the provost marshal's office. A Richmond paper quoted Tim himself as saying that, before he went to the gallows, he would make several people at Confederate headquarters "shake in their boots."

None of the sensational rumors proved accurate. On the morning of April 29, 1862, a crowd gathered for the show at Camp Lee, once Richmond's Fair Grounds. Timothy Webster had spent an anguished evening, with Hattie Lawton praying beside him. His arthritic pains had returned and he was in physical as well as mental torment. At 5:15 in the morning guards led him from prison to spend the last few hours at a house near the gallows. Those who watched noted the difficulty with which he walked and his furrowed face. The actor who had played so many roles was now only himself, a man broken by mischance.

The day brightened, and the sun glittered on the soldiers' muskets and upon the edge of the coffin that waited to receive the spy. As the last moment neared Webster was led forth past the casket; he shuddered and the minister comforted him. An officer gave the signal, and Tim made his way, with an effort, up the stairs. He showed his suffering again while his arms were being tied behind him, his feet bound, and the black cap placed over his face.

The drums rolled, the executioner released the trigger that held the drop, and it hit the uprights with a cracking sound. There followed a thump as the heavy-bodied Webster dropped all the way from the scaffold to the ground. The hangman had done a poor job, the knot had slipped, and the victim had fallen to the earth with a thud. Several helpers drew him half dazed to his feet and led him up the stairs again. From behind the cap Webster's muffled voice cried: "I suffer a double death."

To make sure that the spy would not get off a second time, the executioner tied the rope too tightly. "You'll choke me to death this time," Webster mumbled. At almost the same moment the attendant sprang the trap, and the burly figure plunged down, to sway back and forth, back and forth. The second try had worked.

Webster's former assistants remained for a long time in Confederate hands. Despite Union protests Hattie Lawton spent a full year in custody; twenty-three months passed before Lewis and Scully were sent back North. When Rose Greenhow arrived in Richmond, the two men appealed to her to help them gain their freedom. Mrs. Greenhow had her revenge; she let them stay behind bars. . . . Meanwhile, with the swinging of Tim Webster's body in the springtime sunlight, the first phase of wartime espionage had reached its end.

Part Two

Chapter 5

Anything Went with Mr. Baker

In one of his lighter moments Abraham Lincoln smiled at an infuriated Washingtonian who called on the President with a complaint: a hand-organ player was interfering with the citizen's repose, and he wanted Mr. Lincoln to stop him. The President had a solution: let the taxpayer talk to the Secretary of War, and the Secretary would assign Lafayette C. Baker, the youthful new head of secret service, to the task. "Baker will steal the organ and throw its owner into the Old Capitol, and you'll never be troubled with the noise again," Lincoln chuckled.

Others made similar statements about Mr. Baker, without humor. Here was a man who would burn down a barn, not to rid it of rats, but of a few roaches. "Lafe" Baker might have had two or three friends in the capital, but the rest of the population strongly detested him. No more enigmatic figure ever operated in Washington although ultimately he acquired a degree of power held by almost no other official of his day.

Mr. Baker's career demonstrates the effectiveness of a single-minded purpose in life. The pleasant-looking Lafe knew precisely what he wanted—advancement for himself; whoever stood in his way found the position painful in the extreme. For him any means was justified, provided it worked for Lafayette Baker's ends.

He began as a vague figure in the war's shadows. Most Washingtonians had never heard of him, and those who had considered him an engaging rascal with more than a touch of gall. That quality was, perhaps, the true secret of his success, for Lafe accomplished what others only dreamed of doing. In time, however, the gall grew bigger than the man.

Before he reached his early thirties Baker had had several violent experiences. Born in 1826 in western New York, he was the grandson of the celebrated Remember Baker of the tumultuous Green Mountain Boys of Vermont. Lafayette grew up on tales of Colonial attacks and brutal retaliations. When he was about twenty he began to move restlessly from place to place, and finally went as far as California engaging in "mechanical pursuits." On his trip across the Isthmus of Panama he killed a native boatman and shot down another in a dispute caused, he said, by the mistreatment of an emigrant family.

In San Francisco, Baker leaped into the activities of the famous Vigilance Committee which scoured the city clean of election thieves, vice, and gambling rings. Vigilantes employed ruthless and rather questionable methods of their own, and Lafe evidently did not find them uncongenial. He also gave, according to an admirer, "unmistakable evidences of that peculiar adaptation to the detective service" which few could deny.

In January of 1861, just before the war started, Lafayette left the West Coast for New York. Of medium height, muscular, nattily dressed, he looked impressive with his straight, well-shaped nose, head of reddish hair, and full beard. He was remarkably strong and he could go for days with little or no sleep. But it was the Baker eyes that offered the real clue to the man's character: light gray, shrewd, and penetrating, they were hard as ice.

Lafe had become a magnificent shot; a friend regarded him as "probably the best in the country." He was agile, too, and he once jumped a man who had trained a gun on him and knocked it to the ground before it could be fired. And yet Baker showed an oddly contradictory side, also. He hated liquor. He joined the Sons of Temperance and, we are assured, never used even a mildly profane word. Such was the ambitious young man who now turned up in the East.

Sumter fell and, like thousands of others, Lafe went to Washington to get into the war. In the midst of milling soldiers, grasping contractors, and smooth politicians, he saw confusion, uncertainty—and opportunity. In the lobby of the Willard Hotel, he met two Union acquaintances who grumbled about the need for better information on the Southern Army. Not altogether modestly, Baker agreed with them that he was "the man of all others to go into this secret service."

His friends knew old Commanding General Scott, and took Baker to Scott's rooms. The tired chieftain beamed with satisfaction when he heard that Lafe's father had been one of his Mexican War veterans. Though other meetings followed, there is some evidence that Scott wondered what to make of the self-confident man. Baker, however, had his foot in the door, and he proceeded to push it open. The general mentioned the Union's lack of data on secession forces, especially the much-talked-about Black Horse Cavalry of Virginia. What followed was in the pattern of traditional American enterprise.

Like a good salesman, Lafe offered to demonstrate what he could do, and afterwards talk salary and conditions of employment. He would go to Richmond by any road he found possible, and do it in his own daredevil style. So he started his wartime spying the hard way, with a personal exploit that had its comic moments, but required unquestioned courage. Calamity always waited around the corner.

Winfield Scott handed Baker ten twenty-dollar pieces to finance him. He must not carry a gun, for the quiet civilian whom he was to impersonate would not be armed. Nor could he carry a Federal pass which might betray him. Walking into a "daguerrean establishment," the spy-to-be bought a big camera with tripod. He knew nothing about photography, and his outmoded camera no longer had a lens. In the early 1860s, however, the "box" was regarded as a toy, amusing and unreliable, yet every soldier hoped for a picture of himself to send to the folks back home.

Lafayette Baker had trouble even in getting through the Federal lines. During the next few days he mainly proved his relentless energy. With the camera slung over his shoulder, the itinerant photographer walked toward Alexandria. Reaching the 2nd Maine Regiment, he asked for the colonel's headquarters. The officer not only received him kindly, he also requested a panorama of the camp, with himself and staff in the foreground.

Lafe, who was hungry by then, had a good meal, and wondered how to get away. He surveyed the landscape and pointed to a hill—just the place to take a panorama of the camp. At its top he squinted into the camera, backed off a bit, backed again, until he was in the woods. Then he jogged toward Dixie, avoiding the soldiers on sentry duty. After an hour or two had passed and he felt sure he was well within Southern territory, he heard the cry: "Who goes there?" On a knoll, gun lifted, a soldier in Union blue stared at him as if he were a scorpion.

He soon faced the outraged colonel who had requested the photograph. The officer was now sure beyond doubt that Baker was a rebel agent. A squad took Lafe to General Heintzelman, the provost marshal, who swore at him: "I've a good notion to cut your head off, I'll fix you, though—send you to General Scott." Heintzelman probably hoped to impress his superior with his vigilance, and at the same time avoid the necessity of making a difficult decision. At Scott's headquarters the commanding general dismissed the escort and chuckled at Lafe, "Try again!"

A man of stratagems, Baker set out the second time on that day in mid-July, 1861. Union soldiers were marching steadily across the Long Bridge in a preliminary movement toward Manassas. Lafe lounged at the end of the bridge until night fell and a careless regiment straggled up; then he slipped into the ranks. A lieutenant noticed the interloper, unfortunately, and collared him. Put under guard, Lafe had a hard time persuading his captors to release him. After that he got rid of the camera; it presented too many problems.

Baker made his third attempt by another route, through lower Maryland. For miles he walked through a lightly populated region until he arrived at Port Tobacco, too worn to do anything except sink into a sodden slumber. On waking, he saw a Negro in a field, beckoned him over, and talked to him for a long time. They made a bargain: for one of the gold pieces, a tenth of Baker's retainer free from Scott, the farmer agreed to row him across the river below Dumfries.

At last he stood on Confederate soil. He went on foot through the countryside in the direction of Richmond, suffering in the summer heat, eating irregularly, drinking from shallow brooks. He had warily reached a point a few miles from the Potomac when a pair of gray-clad soldiers appeared, so close at hand that he dared not run. Lafe had a story ready and letters to back it up. They were not impressed and ordered him to tell it to the commander. They started with him toward camp, eight long miles away.

Dripping with perspiration, the Southerners paused before a saloon. Why not cool off? When they ordered, they offered their prisoner a glass, and for once the teetotaler accepted. Today he would drink for a purpose. As he wiped his lips, Baker suggested a round on him. His captors agreed, and the spy urged them to have another. They enjoyed this sort of pressure, and an hour afterward Lafe walked off and left them dozing near the stoop of the tavern.

Thus the pattern was set for a peculiar adventure in espionage. During his entire mission Lafe continued under suspicion, for much of the time under actual arrest. Nevertheless, he performed his spying errands with convincing ability. . . .

He maintained a lively pace as he traveled toward Manassas, until much the same thing happened as before. Out from a clump of bushes stepped four cavalrymen. To their questioning, he complained: "Look, I'm a peaceful citizen with business to do in Richmond. I can prove it!"

The searchers examined his several notes of introduction to Richmonders, concocted by himself in Washington. Baker had assumed the name of San Munson, because he had known a Californian who was the son of a Judge Munson of Tennessee. He also had a letter that he considered his trump card; originally written by a West Coast minister, it authorized Baker to settle his Southern land claims. Lafe expected to put this doctored message and his new name to good use.

The cavalrymen considered his story, and took him to their quarters at Brentsville. He gathered to his dismay that they regarded him as an important fish in their net. Late that night Baker stood before General Bonham, the same Confederate for whom Rose Greenhow's representative, Betty Duvall, unwrapped her black locks. This general was spy-conscious.

"How dare you come inside my lines?" Bonham thundered.

Baker was astonished. "I have legitimate business. All I want is to get to Richmond."

The general's mouth tightened. "That's just where you *may* go, eventually. I think you're nothing but a Yankee spy." Later that same day near Brentsville a disheveled, muddy Lafe Baker faced the dark-eyed General Beauregard, and the Creole frowned ominously: "If I could be sure you were here for the Yankees, I'd hang you to that tree out there!"

Still he could not be quite sure, and that gave Baker a chance. He was taken to a guardhouse inside the stockade, where he puzzled over his situation and then, daring as ever, proceeded to spy even while under arrest for suspicion of that offense! As a result of carelessness in Beauregard's headquarters, the stockade personnel had not heard why the newcomer was there. On being asked, Lafe said only that he did not know.

Casually he took out another gold piece, to buy a large breakfast and some good will. When wine arrived with the meal, the nonalcoholic Mr. Baker presented it to the guard. He asked, when he finished his meal, if he could stretch his legs around the town, accompanied by a guard, of course? Another gold piece ended any debate in the mind of the officer in charge.

With a confident air, the prisoner led his escort about the settlement and into a hotel, where a drink or two further mellowed that gentleman's mood. At the Confederate's side, Lafe proceeded to survey the troops in the area, getting names of brigades, numbers, commanders. He recalled General Scott's particular interest in the Black Horse Cavalry. Sure, he'd take Mr. Baker right there, said the guard. Finally the Southerner met an equally tipsy friend and wandered away from his prisoner.

Baker wondered if he dared try to escape? Under the circumstances he decided against it; even his audacity would not take him far. Unaccompanied, the spy walked back to the guardhouse and quietly sat down. It became evident that a message had arrived regarding him, and from the corner of those hard gray eyes he saw that several men were discussing his case.

Two fellow prisoners approached and complained to him about their treatment. Between protests they asked Baker a great many questions. One whispered a request: wouldn't the newcomer take a letter to his wife in Washington? Here . . . he thrust it into Lafe's hands. Baker answered him by going to the chief officer: "You've got a spy over there." The decoys had been too obvious to fool even a new hand like Lafe. . . .

Presently a striking young woman carrying religious tracts into the stockade, talked with Lafe in general terms, then bent closer to his ear. He had given his name as Munson, hadn't he? Well, he'd been right to hold off from those others. But he could trust her; she expected a pass from Beauregard, and would soon see her sister in Union territory. Couldn't she take a note for him? Politely Baker rejected this emissary as he had the others. Months later he met her again, and their roles were reversed; she was Belle Boyd, the Southern spy.

Long after dark a lieutenant summoned Baker; the orders were: "On to Richmond," and under guard. The Confederates were passing him on from one headquarters to another. He traveled some of the route in a badly ventilated freight car, the rest by slow passenger train which gave him a chance to peer out and inspect soldiers and equipment at crucial spots. The farther he went, however, the more sensational became the stories of his importance, though nobody knew just who he might be.

He stayed several days in a Richmond cell high up in an engine house, and he wondered if he would be imprisoned for the rest of the war, or if he would hang. The guards assumed an air of mystery. Warily Lafe questioned them and was given a smiling answer: President Davis wished to see him. In the early phases of the war Jefferson Davis concerned himself in many espionage problems, and Baker needed no one to tell him that this was a crucial hour.

Mr. Davis sat at a desk in his Spottswood Hotel quarters, wearing a light linen suit, minus collar and tie. His eyes moved slowly over the captive: "You've been sent here as a spy!" he stated. "What do you have to say?" Baker had a great deal to say, in angry complaint about the treatment of a law-abiding citizen with work to do in Richmond. He made no headway at all, for Jefferson Davis was thoroughly skeptical. Back in the engine loft, Lafe was kept in isolation and became increasingly nervous.

He received another summons, and this time Mr. Davis had another purpose in his questions: How many troops were there in Washington? Were the Northern forces fortifying Alexandria? How far were cars running on the Alexandria and Orange Railroad? Just where was General Scott at the moment? Baker offered scraps of information, trying not to tell obvious lies. . . . He felt better; he was making a little progress, he thought.

Then some instinct warned him of danger. The Confederate President looked thoughtful. So he said his name was Munson and he came from Knoxville, Tennessee; could he mention any people he knew there? With an effort Lafe recalled a few names he had heard. Perspiring hard, the prisoner understood only too well what was about to happen, as Mr. Davis rang a bell and handed a note to a clerk. They had located someone from Knoxville!

Baker sat near the door, trying to be as inconspicuous as possible, shifting in his chair slightly so that he could see into the outer office. He missed very little and noticed that people who came into the other room wrote their identities on cards which an orderly took to Davis. After a few minutes the clerk to whom Mr. Davis had given the note returned with a man who also put his name on one of the cards.

While Mr. Davis was occupied, Baker managed to glance at the card and made out the name—Brock. He had his cue and he had to carry off his plan or all was lost. . . . As the stranger entered, Lafe jumped up. "Why, Brock! How do you do?"

Jefferson Davis faced the new arrival: "You know this man?"

Caught by surprise, Brock stammered, "Yes. . . . But I can't think of his name at the moment."

Baker was more than ready to help. Before Davis could speak, he did: "Munson. Don't you remember Judge Munson's son who went to California?"

Again Brock paused. "Sam Munson."

"Of course."

"Oh, yes. Now I place you."

Jefferson Davis inclined his head. "That will do." Lafe departed with his guards, hopeful that his troubles were over. They were not. A day later Brock entered the loft, and Baker sensed that the man had been told to make certain of his identification.

The next few minutes would be critical. This time Lafe realized it was his turn to be silent and let Brock take the lead. The caller talked at length, pausing only for an occasional question. Baker gave brief replies or vague ones. Lafe threw in a few Knoxville names and places of which he had heard. When Brock mentioned a funny episode, Baker slapped his knee in amusement, though he had no notion of the story's background. . . . The interview ended rather cheerfully.

For several more days the spy waited tensely, until an officer walked in with a parole, which Lafe signed without a qualm. He had the freedom of the city, but he might not leave without approval of the provost marshal. Once more, while theoretically in Confederate hands, he proceeded to spy on the South. Still he suspected from time to time that he was watched and he was cautious.

One day as he was studying a board fence covered with military notices bearing useful information, someone pounded his back: "Baker! What are you doing here?"

Lafe felt a sudden chill. Nobody in Richmond should have known that name. He spun around and recognized the speaker immediately as his close companion during the trip across the Isthmus when he had killed the native years before. To admit their friendship would be fatal. "You're mistaken; my name's Munson," he said firmly.

The puzzled man persisted: hadn't Lafe gone West with him, and hadn't there been a fight, and . . . ? Baker admitted nothing and carried off the denial. But it was time to get out of Richmond. Lafe had most of the information he needed, and through a friend he got a temporary pass to Fredericksburg.

Once there, the spy again employed the device that had first brought him into Dixie territory. He found a Negro, who rowed him across the Rappahannock. He would work his way overland to the Potomac and across that river to Union ground. Skirting the farms, he went as fast as he could. Somewhere behind him the Southerners would soon be sending out an alarm; he must move faster than seemed possible.

He was crossing a road in a deeply wooded tract when two horsemen came around the bend and challenged him. One proved to be a Confederate officer. Making a show of unconcern, Lafe handed over the pass which gave him the right to travel, but only from Richmond to Fredericksburg. The Confederate shook his head: "I don't think this will do." Mr. Munson would have to go with him to have the matter checked. That would never do—and promptly Lafe acquired a pronounced limp.

Ah, the distance would be agony for a lame man, Lafe sighed. Well, the officer hesitated . . . he'd see about the pass, and leave the prisoner in the hands of his aide. Alone with the private, Baker suggested they move under the shade of the trees. As they sat and rested, the Union spy succeeded in making friends with his guard, who confided that he had missed his sleep the previous night. It was not long before the guard had stretched full length, his hat over his eyes. After all, could a cripple go far?

When the Confederate snored, the "lame man" used light fingers to slip the soldier's revolver out of its holster, untied his horse, and then rode off. In the rough woods the animal moved with annoying slowness; Lafe had covered only a few miles when it grew dark. Catching sight of a fair-sized house with several cabins, he talked to one of the Negroes on the place, who sold him bread and milk. Baker discovered after another hour's travel that he had circled back in the dark to the same spot. He had no choice but to rest until morning, but he crawled feet first into a haystack. He let the horse go; it had only slowed his progress.

It was not yet light when he heard pounding hoofbeats, and Confederate cavalrymen swept upon the farm. Lafe peered through the straw and saw several officers as they rode around the cabins, swords bared. The spy "prepared for the worst." Revolver in hand, he hunched forward to shoot the man who found him, resolved to try running for the woods.

One of the Southerners thrust a blade into the hay a few inches from Lafe's side, and then again. The second time the sword slid along his coat, and Baker's fingers tightened on the revolver. After a long moment the man in gray turned away. "Nobody in there, boys," he called. As soon as the party left, Lafe crept away. From then on, no more farmhouses.

The pursuit was so hot Lafe dared speak to nobody, ask no directions. He went without food, and still forced himself on, although his hunger was painful and his fatigue made him stumble. He came to a creek which he thought must run into the Potomac, and he followed it for a long distance. At last he caught the glint of the river a short way off, but on top of its sloping bank was a Confederate tent. Now what?

By now Lafe was really hungry, for nearly twenty-four hours had passed since he had eaten. A soldier walked toward the tent with a dripping catch of fish, and the Union spy could not take his eyes off them. Another Confederate came into view, and the two soldiers sat smoking pipes along the bank, the aroma of the tobacco drifting to Baker. That settled it for the spy. He craved their food, and he needed their help to cross the river. No matter what the risk, he must run it. Ambling out of the bushes, he explained that he was a farmer who lived up the creek and wondered how the boys were faring.

The boys grunted a reply; they were far from enthusiastic. Lafe went on: did they have anything to eat? Oh, he'd pay. . . . So he wolfed down a poor dish of fried fish that he thought tasted better than anything he had eaten for years. As dusk approached he sat smoking with the soldiers, pondering ways to get past them.

Baker saw the outlines of a small boat in the bushes along the creek. "What will you take for it?"

They would take nothing. "The Yankees are breaking up all the boats on the Potomac, and we need it bad." But he had to cross; one more day and he would surely be trapped. Dark settled upon them and Lafe grumbled that it was too late to make his long trip home. Could he stay with them? Rather indifferently the Southerners agreed and went inside the tent.

Still smoking on the bank of the creek, the spy hoped to slip away and row off in the boat. As the moon silvered the hills, he sat, praying that the men would drop off to sleep. From time to time he decided they were sleeping—then he would hear desultory talk. At midnight one called to him: "You comin' to bed tonight?"

Lafe had no choice. He found they had left a place for him between them. As he lay there exhausted, he tried not to doze off. He mustn't! He *had* to keep alert. . . . Suddenly he wakened with a guilty start. His companions' snores sounded in his ears, and cautiously he eased himself up, crawling toward the tent flap. Behind him one of the soldiers moved and Baker crept back, his heart thumping.

Several times he started to get away, only to return. Once the more wakeful of the pair stretched out his hand to make certain the stranger had not gone, and Lafe knew the man suspected his intentions. But dawn was near, and he could wait no longer. He had to take the chance. Crawling out of the tent, Baker descended the bank to where the skiff lay in the creek. There were no oars! Frantically he searched the grass and found a short one, its end rotted. It would have to do.

As quietly as possible he shoved off into the low water and headed toward the open river. Pulling his coat off, he flailed away with the decaying oar, swinging the boat in awkward circles, until he mastered its use. But he had barely started when he heard a shout:

"Meyer, Meyer, the boat's gone!" Peering behind him, Lafe saw the soldier snatch his musket. "Come back, come back!" The Federal agent rowed with his left hand, and pulled out his pistol with his right; he would now have to show his famous skill as a dead shot. The Confederate raised his musket, and Baker fired first. A cry, and the soldier fell. The second man appeared with a double-barreled shotgun. As Lafe applied himself more desperately than ever to his rowing, he discovered that the second Confederate was sliding through the bushes in an effort to surprise him. Forty yards off, the soldier fired.

Baker dodged and took aim, missed, and rowed on. The gunfire brought out other Southerners, and more bullets sang past the huddled figure in the skiff. Shots fell around him; several dug into the side of the boat. Dropping his pistol, Lafe struggled on to reach the river ahead. There the current helped him, and the bullets dropped in his wake. But his shoulder and back muscles tightened in pain; his head throbbed. The river seemed endlessly wide. . . . Still using the single oar, he worked on and on. He could only pause a few minutes at a time before resuming his frenzied, gasping effort. Finally the bow scraped sand and he staggered out and threw himself into the grass, where he lay for a long time.

That rest was about the only one Lafayette C. Baker had during the remainder of the war. He had shown what he could do, and General Scott, highly pleased, recommended him to the Secretary of War as a confidential agent. For months the general took a patron's interest in the remarkable Mr. Baker. On detached service, unconnected with the Pinkerton office, Lafe accepted assignments in and around Alexandria, Baltimore, and lower Maryland. From spying he turned to counterspying.

Under his questioning a child betrayed her father, a wife her husband. "Ferreting out sympathizers with secession," Lafe trapped such people as the owner of a vessel loaded with hay and oats "for the Union Army" covering ammunition for the Confederacy, Maryland postmasters who secretly used their offices to send mail to Richmond, and a lady with a hat that cached twenty ounces of smuggled quinine. For Baker, no assignment was too large or too small.

One day the hard gray eyes spotted a sickly looking young man in uniform in a bar. No one else noticed the youth as he lifted his fingers occasionally to stroke his hair. Gruffly Baker called him aside; two questions, and the lad broke into tears. Yes, sir, he was a lady and a spy. Again Baker tracked down a doctor and his wife from Montgomery, Alabama. After eavesdropping, the detective trailed them to their room. There the "wife" had a cigar in her mouth. The lady was a man, and both were Confederate agents.

Old General Scott faded from the war picture; his muscular protégé stayed on. Baker's trail can be traced through the account of the provost marshal, William E. Doster. One day the disapproving Doster received a "medium-sized, lean man of about forty, with a suspicious expression about his eyes." It was Baker, asking a prison commitment for a man he had arrested for "blackmailing Army sutlers."

Provost Marshal Doster knew of no one with authority to arrest anyone in that fashion. When he demanded proof of authority, Baker rushed off "in a passion." The next day Doster discovered that the prisoner had been committed after all and by authority of the Secretary of War himself; the suspect's name and offense were unlisted.

The provost marshal proceeded to inquire about the mysterious Mr. Baker. Superintendent Wood of the Old Capitol Prison said that the detective had a "roving commission" for the War Department; and Wood's opinion of him was "not good." The Pinkerton force held the same view, and Washington police put Lafe down as a "doubtful character." Doster went to the Assistant Secretary of War, who explained that the department used the man on the general principle of "set a rogue to catch a rogue."

Then overnight the department named Lafayette Baker as its "special Provost Marshal." Now he could operate unchecked, and Doster commented that "such an extension of power I esteemed a dangerous thing." It started, in this official's words, "a reign of terror." All kinds of people, infamous, questionable, or only vaguely suspect, suddenly disappeared, sent secretly to prison by Lafe and a new friend—none other than Superintendent Wood, who had once said his opinion of the man was "not good"!

The new team of Baker and Wood, or Wood and Baker, set up an inquisition alarming to many who saw it in action. A victim would be placed in bleak confinement for weeks or months; he would be approached only when this grim isolation began to tell. Then Superintendent Wood called as "a friend." He wanted to help; he could get the prisoner out if only he signed a confession. If the prisoner remained obstinate, an accessory was introduced, their conversation noted. Or Baker and Wood sent in a detective who pretended to be guilty of the same offense and urged the victim to confide in him.

When the prisoner still did not give in, Doster claimed, counterfeit testimony by others was prepared and read to him. He might be advised to speak in his own defense. But spurious passages were inserted in his testimony and when it was read back to him the captive would sometimes become so hopelessly confused he would "throw himself on the mercy of his torturers." This unpretty picture reflected "a growing spirit of absolutism in the War Office." One major obstacle stood in Baker's path to power—the organization of Allan Pinkerton.

Without warning that organization broke apart. For nearly a year and a half "Little Napoleon" McClellan had been the Union's hope. The Northern public gave him fervent support, Lincoln backed him, and so did a powerful section of Congress. Pinkerton had always been McClellan's man, fiercely loyal to him. By November of 1862 the general's methods had produced only meager results; the Union was disappointed, disillusioned, and after long deliberation Lincoln replaced McClellan as commander of the Army of the Potomac.

Pinkerton and his staff could have remained in operation, but abruptly the detective ended all espionage activity. The Pinkerton force had achieved a number of outstanding successes, but their work in general revealed serious defects. They had no military training, no previous experience in handling Army intelligence. They had operated primarily as detectives, with McClellan as their client. Their work was hampered by their devotion to that highly individualistic commander and by his own weaknesses.

Serving an overcautious McClellan, Pinkerton followed the inclinations of his superior. The general consistently saw the enemy as better prepared, more formidable than it was. He asked always for more men, more material; until he received them he would wait. Lincoln could fret, Cabinet members storm, abolitionists charge him with sabotaging the Union effort—McClellan still was not quite ready. When he interpreted the data from his agents, Pinkerton also overestimated enemy strength. He and his chief leaned on one another in building up a picture of a vast opposing force that did not exist. The crisis came for McClellan, and the detective departed with him.

Pinkerton later served in other military matters, investigating claims and the like, but his role as spy chief had ended.

A confused situation followed. For months the former Pinkerton office gathered dust, until the shrewd Colonel George H. Sharpe of the 120th New York Regiment took over and formed a new Bureau of Military Information. Sharpe stayed in charge until the war's end, operating efficiently. He confined himself to actual army affairs and did not handle civilian espionage, as had the Pinkerton staff. Lafayette Baker had no difficulty in inserting himself into the vacuum. He became chief of the War Department's detective organization. In that capacity few people thought of him, as had earlier Washingtonians, as a rather amusing rascal.

Under the coldly efficient direction of Secretary of War Stanton, Baker distinguished himself for ruthlessness. With increased funds he delved into all kinds of irregularities. He did trap a good many spies, corruptionists, deserters, and the like. A White House staff member once commented that, although many of his colleagues might not know Baker, "if any man has been here long enough, with anything dubious about him, Baker knows him."

Historians have shared a generally unfavorable opinion of him: "one of the worst rapscallions of an age in which rascality paid high dividends" . . . "cruel and rapacious" . . . "that most notorious character" . . . "the American Fouché" . . . "a Baron Scarpia of the Potomac." In subsequent years several dubious figures in European secret service paid Baker the honor of seriously studying his techniques.

For all his authority and success, Lafe frequently appeared to lack judgment. He also showed a childlike blandness in admitting tricky errors. The Register of the Treasury said he once trapped Baker in forgery, or at least connivance in it, and without a blush the head of secret service smiled: "That game didn't work, did it?" So he went on to another! And in postwar years Baker himself was accused of corruption and questionable dealings.

Throughout the war, despite his natural suspicion of others, Lafe proved gullible and careless when Confederate women spies asked for passes. Washington gossip had it that any lady who played siren could get whatever she wanted from Baker. But there was one "Southern female" who asked no favor from him, one whom he could not quite faze. He and Belle Boyd had already met, but they were to become even more dramatically acquainted.

Chapter 6

"Cleopatra of the Secession"

Belle Boyd played the role of spy as if the war were a light-hearted game of charades. And she lived as if she were fashioning her days into the plot of a romantic story. During her lifetime she could have read about herself in at least two historical novels, although neither did justice to her dashing exploits.

The zestful Miss Boyd became an espionage agent when she was seventeen, and served the Confederacy throughout the war, in Dixie, the North, and England as well. She matched the boldness of any man, galloping headlong into the dark with cipher messages, or creeping into rooms to eavesdrop on Union Army conferences. On at least one occasion (when she could persuade none of the men to do it for her), she daringly entered battle lines to carry back important information.

But Belle Boyd was above all overwhelmingly feminine; she made good use of her womanly appeal, of which she had an enormous amount. Unlike others who impersonated the inconspicuous female and made themselves up as a drab housewife or dowdy traveler, this spy played her own personality to the hilt, with a dramatic air and sweeping gestures, wearing rich reds and greens and feathers in her hat. Belle had a "joyous recklessness," as one reluctant admirer phrased it. She looked at men through her long lashes, assuring them that she had no intentions hostile to the North, while she stole whatever secrets were at hand and filched others practically from their pockets.

Belle possessed at least one additional asset—perhaps the best pair of legs in the Confederacy. Even a lady must get in and out of a carriage or with a flurry of petticoats dismount from a horse; at such times Miss Boyd showed a pretty confusion, and very fine ankles.

Her actions were puzzling to her opponents, for at times she seemed cunning, at others naïve. Always an individualist, she spied "by ear," after her own special fashion. Belle obviously did not believe in the virtues of silence, for what she thought, she generally said. Despite her failings, she proved a remarkably good agent.

Belle Boyd loved the South passionately. After the war she said she had never "had a consciousness that I was a spy. I only wanted to help my people." Nevertheless, as Carl Sandburg has observed, she could have been "legally convicted and shot at sunrise" on the basis of the evidence against her. Yet Belle had critics among Southerners themselves. She traveled alone, to the horror of more conventional women. A "brilliant talker," she conversed easily with anyone she met, and her lack of self-consciousness in the company of men was unusual in a woman of her class.

She shocked her conservative friends by visiting camps, calling on generals and colonels in their tents, and accepting carriage rides in the warm afternoons. She even danced and flirted with Northerners as well as Southerners. When she bothered to defend herself, Belle said that it was necessary for her to be on good terms with both sides. Yet, there was no doubt that Miss Belle liked the boys in blue as well as those in gray. And she obviously liked spying; she performed her duty to the South and had a nice time, too.

She could always rely on a hidden weapon—male gallantry. When Federal commanders discovered that she had given information to the South that might wreck their plans, she would look sad, speak half gaily, half pathetically, and Northern chivalry would prove as strong as Southern; they would release her. Before she reached twenty-one this Virginian had been imprisoned twice, "reported" nearly thirty times, and arrested six or seven. In one romantic feat she persuaded her Northern captor to marry her and switch sides. Nearly everybody liked Belle or enjoyed hearing about her. In Piccadilly, English crowds hailed her as if she were a Sir Walter Scott heroine. French newspapers termed her "La Belle Rebelle." It can be surmised that she approved the title.

Her birthplace was the Shenandoah Valley, whose rolling hills, "broad, clear, rapid streams," silver maples, and rocky borders Belle pictured in affectionate memory. Her native town of Martinsburg, then in Virginia, now West Virginia, lay in a peaceful area which eventually exploded in action and shifted from Southern to Northern hands.

As Belle later told a Chicago interviewer, she came of a "well-known family of Virginia," having ties "among the best in the state." The Boyds traced themselves back to an ancient Scottish clan; they had highly placed kin in New Orleans and parts of Kentucky, and a family connection with George Randolph, later Confederate Secretary of War. Although Belle was reluctant to admit it, her branch of the Boyds had done less well than others. Her father ran a store and managed a tobacco farm.

To her English admirers Belle described an idyllic childhood in a "pretty two-storied house," its walls "hidden by roses and honeysuckle." Idyllic it may have been, for a relative recalled that Belle had been a reckless tomboy who climbed trees, raced through the woods on a nettlesome mount, and dominated brothers, sisters, and cousins. It is said that her mild-mannered mother never disciplined her; what little Miss Boyd wished to do, she did. There is a story that when she made a visit to

Tennessee relatives she encountered a stricter home regime and, to her surprise, liked it, "although it was the first time in her life she ever had to conform to family rules." She did not conform for long; in her own phrase, she preferred to be "on the go."

Despite their lack of money, the Boyds gave their daughter a good education. After some preliminary schooling, she was sent at the age of twelve to the Mount Washington Female College at Baltimore. A minister was head of the college, but despite his influence Belle remained "on the go." At sixteen her training was "supposed to be completed," and her family and friends arranged a debut in Washington. Cousins made certain that the tall, graceful girl met the proper hostesses and received invitations to the best affairs.

Secretary of War Floyd, soon to join the Confederacy, was one in whose drawing rooms Belle became a favorite. For the impulsive adolescent the waltzes and cotillions, the bright conversations with uniformed officers, judges, and senators were a heady experience. The season was that of late 1860, however, and more and more often she heard the echoes of clashes over slavery's extension. Then came secession.

With Sumter's fall Belle headed home for Martinsburg, "enthusiastic in my love for my country, the South." There she discovered that her forty-four-year-old father had volunteered for military service. Sedentary, highly unmilitary, Ben Boyd nevertheless insisted on taking his part in the war. Offered "that grade in the army to which his social position entitled him," he had instead enlisted as a private. Beside younger and more hardy men, Ben was to suffer greatly in the war; but Belle reacted with hearty approval, contributing to town funds for his regiment, the 2nd Virginia, and joining other Confederate causes as they sprang up.

To nobody's surprise, she soon found these employments "too tame and monotonous to satisfy my temperament." When her father went to the camp at Harper's Ferry, she helped organize a festive visiting party. Officers and men were "gay and joyous," she wrote, and "many true hearts" were pledged. To this Belle added: "A true woman always loves a real soldier." Not yet seventeen, Miss Boyd considered herself a "true woman."

So, perhaps, did others. Observers did not always agree about her looks, for while some considered her beautiful, or at least handsome, a few noted that she had a prominent nose, and ultimately Northern and Southern journalists would debate the momentous issue: did Belle have freckles, or didn't she? One man said that her face possessed "too much character in it to be called merely pretty." Still, Belle had shining blue eyes, a heavy head of light brownish hair, and, last but not least, a fine figure which many commented on, despite Victorian proprieties.

Early in July 1861, Ben Boyd's regiment prepared for battle, and sorrowfully the girl and her mother bade him good-by, and returned to Martinsburg. The 2nd Virginia met Union forces and fell back; still more sorrowfully Belle watched as her father and his comrades retreated through the home town. She had already met the commander, old "Stonewall," for whom she acquired an admiration that approached, then exceeded worship. To her, General Jackson, the bearded, reticent genius, was "that undaunted hero, that true apostle of Freedom."

Belle promptly went to the hospitals to help the wounded, and she was there when a triumphant Union officer entered. Waving a flag over the soldiers' beds, he referred to them as "damned rebels."

Belle snapped at him, commenting scornfully on the bravery of a man who insulted men when they were "as helpless as babies."

The Federal soldier was taken by surprise. "And pray, who may you be, Miss?"

Belle glared, and her maid spoke up for her: "A rebel lady."

"A damned independent one, at all events," remarked the Northerner as he left the hospital. The next day Belle had what she termed her "first adventure," when she killed herself a Yankee soldier, in a highly controversial incident.

Half the town of Martinsburg knew that the forthright Belle kept Confederate flags all over the walls of her room, and word of this reached the Union forces, who were planning a great July Fourth celebration. While the Boyds stayed at home, the men in blue drank heavily, smashed windows at random, and broke into houses to hunt for Southern souvenirs. One party staggered into the Boyd place, tore down pictures, and stamped toward Belle's room. "Where's the secesh flags?" they demanded.

As Belle and her mother stood tight-lipped, the maid slipped out and removed the flags. The thwarted Northerners then announced that they would make sure the damned family *looked* loyal, anyway, and one pulled out a big American flag and started to climb to the roof to hoist it.

For once Belle's mother lost her meekness and called out: "Men, every member of this household will die before that flag is raised over us." The soldier cursed and pushed Mrs. Boyd aside. According to Belle, "I could stand it no longer; my indignation was aroused beyond control. . . . I drew out my pistol and shot him." A near riot followed, with Union soldiers firing shots at the house and threatening to burn it down. Then guards arrived.

The Confederates considered Belle's act one of simple justice. The Union commanding officer hurried up to investigate, held a hearing—and exactly nothing more happened. Belle put aside her gun and employed tears and smiles. The result was that a guard was posted at the house to make sure no further incidents occurred, and "Federal officers called every day to inquire if we had any complaint"! Belle recalled that in this way she first became "acquainted with so many of them." Before long she had set a good many teeth on edge by fraternizing with the enemy, which astonished and horrified conservative Martinsburg.

Belle explains, however, that she had begun to experiment in espionage. Whatever she learned, she "regularly and carefully committed to paper" and sent to her beloved Stonewall Jackson or to Jeb Stuart. Soon her first mistake tripped her. A true novice, she had no cipher and made no effort to disguise her handwriting. One of her notes reached Union headquarters, and the colonel in command summoned her. Reading the articles of war, he asked sternly if Miss Belle knew she could be sentenced to death?

Belle declined to be frightened. She made a full curtsy, and her eyes swept over the officers in the room. "Thank you, gentlemen of the jury," she murmured in irony, and swirled out. But she had to be more careful, and for a time she used as helper an old Negro, who carried messages in a big watch from which the insides had been removed. A certain Sophie B. also assisted her. Lacking Belle's superlative horsemanship, Sophie once had to walk seven miles each way to Jackson's camp.

In her memoirs of these salad days of her spying, Belle gives only a few details, but reveals something of her inspiration. One day she heard of the exploit of Rose Greenhow's famous helper, Betty Duvall, with her market girl's disguise and the dispatch hidden in her black locks. Spy inspired spy, and Belle sought out Colonel Turner Ashby, Jackson's sharp-faced cavalry leader, head of military scouts in the Shenandoah Valley.

Ashby was no mean spy himself when he put on civilian clothes and rode around Union camps in the role of a dreary veterinarian. For days Ashby would treat ailing horses, then jog back to his own lines with all he needed to know about the enemy. From him Belle received several assignments as courier for the Confederate forces. She learned the use of a cipher, and in the shifting battle areas she frequently carried messages on brief runs, pounding through back country and over short cuts on her horse. Her tomboy days were paying off.

Restless as ever, she worked in one town after another, until she heard in late March of 1862 that fighting was on again at Martinsburg. Her place was there, she felt, but as she passed through nearby Winchester an enemy tipped off Union authorities. At the railroad station, officers begged Belle's pardon—and arrested her. She would have to go all the way to Baltimore with them. The experience might have been terrifying to the girl, but, while friends watched glumly, Belle adjusted a bright new beribboned hat and assured them that nothing was going to happen to *her!* They'd see.

They did. Her prison in Baltimore was a comfortable hotel, where she held court and chuckled at, then with her captors. A week passed pleasantly as officials puzzled over what to do about her. General Dix, who had presided at the Greenhow hearing, found no specific evidence, and let her leave with a fatherly warning. With another deep bow and a raised eyebrow, the junior spy swished out.

After this adventure she rejoined her family at Front Royal, forty miles south of Martinsburg, where Belle's aunt and uncle had a small hotel. To her surprise, Union forces had taken over the building and the remaining members of her family had moved to a cramped cottage. Such restriction made Belle's Confederate heart sink. She knew precisely where she wanted to be—in Richmond, the heart of everything that interested her. As Belle understood life, the way to get a thing was to ask for it, especially if the one to be asked were a man. So she sought out the commander, General James Shields.

The good-humored Irishman beamed at the bold, pretty girl.

Ah, he clicked his tongue, if he gave Miss Belle the pass she wished, she would have to go through General Jackson's lines. Shields shook his head in mock regret; those Confederates had been so demoralized that he dared not trust Miss Belle to their mercies. Then with a twinkle he added that in a few days Jackson's men would all be wiped out, and she could go through!

So assured was the Union officer, Belle said in her memoirs, that he forgot "a woman can sometimes listen and remember." Sensing a chance for a real exploit, she changed her plans in a second. She would stay right here. When she twinkled back at Shields, he grew expansive and introduced her to his staff. A younger, handsomer Irishman seemed definitely worthy of cultivation and quickly Belle let Captain Keily think *he* was cultivating *her*.

The spy rode out with the captain, and Keily talked freely. To him, as she said wryly, she was "indebted for some very remarkable effusions, some withered flowers, and last, not least, for a great deal of very important information. . . ." Belle gathered that a major Federal drive would soon be mounted, and her aunt's hotel was a rare observation point. One night in mid-May she learned that a war council was about to be held in the hotel parlor. Directly above was a bedroom with a closet, and, as Belle had once noticed, the closet floor had a small knothole. Perhaps the energetic spy enlarged it a bit for her purposes.

When the men gathered, she lay down in the closet and put her ear to the opening. For hours she stayed there, motionless, cramped, catching every murmur as the men, sitting over cigars and maps, argued strategy. Belle's mind filled with names, figures, placement of scattered armies. There was much she did not understand, so she memorized most of it. The meeting ended about one in the morning, and, after waiting for the halls to clear, Belle scurried to her cottage and wrote out a cipher message.

She had to leave with it at once. To wake a servant was too great a risk, so she saddled her horse and led him softly away. A few minutes later she was galloping toward the mountains. In her pocket she had a pass left her by a paroled Confederate. A sentry stopped her, and as she thrust it into his hands she talked nervously of sickness in the family, her need for haste. He let her by.

She had to rein in and chatter out her story to another guard, and he nodded. With that she sped across fields, along marshes, past cabins. Fifteen miles away was a house where she had been told she could send an emergency message to Colonel Ashby, Jackson's head spy. At last, breathless, she jumped from her horse and hammered at the door of the dark building. A suspicious voice demanded who she was. After she gave her name, the friend opened the door and gaped at her: "My dear, where'd *you* come from?"

Belle ignored his questions as male irrelevance, and asked her own. Where was Ashby? How soon could she reach him? Told that his party was quartered up the road, she started to turn, when another door opened, and Ashby himself frowned at her. "Good God! Miss Belle, is that you?"

The girl told all she knew and left hurriedly, for she had to get back home before dawn. She was nearly there when a drowsy sentry, waking just as she rode by fired after her. But she was lying exhausted in her own bed by the time General Shields's forces rolled out of Martinsburg. The next ten days or so would see vigorous action, she felt sure.

Rumors arrived soon of Federal movements at Winchester. Feeling the need to be "on the go" once more, Belle asked for a pass. The provost marshal was suspicious, and put her off with one excuse after another. He sometimes left on short absences, however, and she waited until he rode out of town. Then Belle applied prettily to a young cavalry lieutenant in the provost's office. She, a girl cousin, and her maid were anxious to make the trip, and surely he wouldn't object. The lieutenant hesitated, and Belle moved closer. . . . Well, he had to go thereabouts himself, Miss Belle, and he'd just ride along. Though she had not expected quite that arrangement, she took full advantage of it. For the young Union officer the trip was a gay adventure. He escorted the girls through the lines and they stayed briefly at Winchester.

There, unexpectedly or perhaps not so unexpectedly, a new opportunity opened to the alert Miss Boyd. A "gentleman of high social standing" found her and murmured an anxious message: He had several papers that should go to General Jackson or one of his subordinates. He shoved them into Belle's hands. They all dealt with the impending clash between Confederate and Northern forces and were of varying importance. The first packet she examined was vital, and Belle slipped it to her maid, reasoning that the Federals would probably not search a Negro. A paper of less import the girl dropped casually in a small basket; another of the same sort she gave the bemused lieutenant to hold. A final document, of great significance, she held in her own hand. The blithe party started back.

They did not get far, for they had just reached Winchester's outskirts when a pair of detectives flagged them down. They were all under arrest. At headquarters the colonel in charge asked a direct question: was Miss Boyd carrying any disloyal messages? The lieutenant was flustered. Belle knew that the less important packet in her basket would quickly be found, so she promptly passed it to the colonel. In her hand she still held the most vital of the papers. "What's that?" the colonel demanded.

Belle employed elementary psychology. "This scrap? Nothing. You can have it." She moved forward as if to give the note to him; had he reached out, she said later, she would have swallowed it. Instead, the colonel turned his attention to the lieutenant. From his pocket that luckless man fished Belle's paper, and caught the brunt of the older man's rage. What did *this* mean—carrying messages for the secesh! Didn't the unwitting fool know . . . ?

To the girl's regret, the lieutenant stayed under arrest. Belle herself, according to a newspaper of a few days later, "with her usual adroitness and assumed innocence, got clear of the charges of treachery." She had not only kept the essential note in her hand, but also the valuable one in her maid's possession!

In May of 1863 Jackson had launched perhaps the most astonishing action of his career, his first Valley campaign, which bewildered and terrified his Northern opponents. He started several times in one direction, and the Union shifted forces to meet him; a day or so later he reversed himself in a long, secret march in the opposite direction, and fell on other units of the unprepared enemy, smashed them, and moved on to repeat the performance. Each time the Federal military leaders declared that the maneuver was incredible, impossible—yet there it was. . . .

Jackson had fewer than twenty thousand men in the Valley; the Union had several times that number, at different points, under Generals Banks, Frémont, and McDowell. McDowell was preparing his army to join McClellan in a mighty drive to take Richmond. But now Stonewall had gone to work to wreck that plan. Furthermore, he was making such a powerful movement toward Washington that the Union would have to divert thousands of men from the push against Richmond.

In Front Royal, Belle Boyd was puzzled: what could she do with her accumulated information? Then, on May 23, 1862, she found a way to make proper use of it.

As she sat in her living room, her reliable maid announced excitedly: "Rebels comin'!" From the door Belle saw Northern soldiers running in every direction. When she called out to a friendly officer, he told her nervously what had happened: Southerners under Generals Jackson and Ewell had surprised the Union pickets. Stonewall was within a mile or so of town before the Federals had wind of an attack!

"Now," explained this talkative fellow, "we're trying to get the ordnance and quartermaster's stores out of reach."

"And the stores in the big depot?" Belle asked quickly.

"We'll burn 'em!"

"Suppose Jackson's men come too fast?"

"We'll fight as long as we can show a front. If we have to do it, we'll draw back on Winchester—fire the bridges as we cross, and join General Banks. . . ." As he disappeared, Belle snatched up opera glasses and ran to the balcony. The Confederate advance guard was about three quarters of a mile from town. She thought of her poor father, trying to hold his own with younger men, advancing with that army, and all at once her hopes overcame her fears.

She went over her assorted information: the messages handed to her in Winchester, the military conference overheard at the hotel, and data gathered on her visits to the camps. It added up to a great deal. In her own words, she knew "that General Banks was at Strasbourg with 4000 men; that the small force at Winchester could be readily reinforced by General White, who was at Harper's Ferry, and that Generals Shields and Geary were a short distance from Front Royal, while Frémont was beyond the Valley; further, and this was the vital point, that *it had been decided all these separate divisions should co-operate against General Jackson*." The Confederates *had* to be advised of these facts. . . . She hurried downstairs.

Out on the street Belle spoke to several men whom she knew were Southern sympathizers. Wouldn't one of them carry her information to General Jackson? "No, no. You go!" they urged her gallantly.

Snatching up a sunbonnet, she went. She edged her way through the Union soldiers, past heavy guns and equipment. Finally reaching the open fields, Belle was fired on by Union pickets. She felt the rifle balls "flying thick and fast" around her in a cross fire between Confederate and Northern skirmishers.

A Federal shell hit the earth twenty yards ahead of the girl and just before it burst Belle threw herself to the ground. A moment later she was dashing on again, in terror and determination: "I shall never run again as I ran . . . on that day." She scrambled over fences, crawled along the edges of hills and fields, and at last approached the oncoming Southern line.

Her Confederate spirit leaped within her, and she waved her bonnet to the soldiers as a sign to press on. Astonished at the sight of a woman at this exposed spot, Hay's Louisiana Brigade and the First Maryland Infantry cheered and quickened their pace. (Three years later Belle still heard in her dreams "their shouts of approbation and triumph.") Exhausted, tearful, she fell to her knees, then rose as the main body of men moved toward her. She recognized an old friend, Major Harry Douglas. In his own memoirs Douglas, taking up the story, explained that Stonewall Jackson had been trying to take in the situation facing him, when:

I observed, almost immediately, the figure of a woman in white glide swiftly out of town on our right, and, after making a little circuit, run rapidly up a ravine in our direction and then disappear from sight. She seemed, when I saw her, to heed neither weeds nor fences, but waved a bonnet as she came on, trying, it was evident, to keep the hill between herself and the village. I called General Jackson's attention to the singular movement just as a dip in the land hid her, and at General Ewell's suggestion, he sent me to meet her and ascertain what she wanted. That was just to my taste, and it took only a few minutes for my horse to carry me to meet the romantic maiden whose tall, supple and graceful figure struck me as soon as I came in sight of her.

(Even at such moments Belle's proportions were not to be overlooked!)

As I drew near, her speed slackened, and I was startled, momentarily, at hearing her call my name. But I was not much astonished when I saw that the visitor was the well-known Belle Boyd, whom I had known from her earliest girlhood. She was just the girl to dare to do this thing.

"Great God, Belle, why are you here?" He asked the same question that others often put to her. Trying to catch her breath, the girl spoke in gasps.

I knew it must be Stonewall, when I heard the first gun. Go back quick and tell him that the Yankee force is very small—one regiment of Maryland infantry, several pieces of artillery and several companies of cavalry. Tell him I know, for I went through the camps and got it out of an officer. Tell him to charge right down and he will catch them all. I must hurry back. Goodbye. My love to all the dear boys—and remember if you meet me in town you haven't seen me today.

Harry Douglas raised his cap, Belle kissed her hand to him and started back. While he stood talking over her message with Jackson, she waved the white bonnet and re-entered the village. Some of what she told Douglas the Confederates had already heard; but she confirmed the facts, and she gave them new data on which to act. Now they moved on with brilliant effect. While Maryland and Louisiana troops raced forward, Jackson "with a half smile" suggested that Douglas might see if he could "get any more information from that young lady."

More than willing to try, Douglas galloped off. A bit later he met Miss Boyd in conversation with Federal officer prisoners and a few Confederate Army friends. Forever Belle! "Her cheeks were rosy with excitement and recent exercise, and her eyes all aflame. When I rode up to speak to her she received me with much surprised cordiality, and as I stooped from my saddle she pinned a crimson rose to my uniform, bidding me remember that it was *blood-red* and that it was her 'colors.' "

Spurred by Belle's information, Jackson and his men pounded through the town. According to plan, the Union troops set fire to the bridge, which had begun to blaze when Jackson galloped up. The Confederates defied the smoke and flame, burned hands and feet as they pulled and kicked at the scorching timbers and tossed them into the water. They succeeded in saving the bridge and pushed on in another of Jackson's unorthodox performances.

To Banks's amazement two days later, on May 25, Jackson hit his column near Middletown, smashed it in half, and chased it in a rout back to the Potomac. In this campaign Jackson had taken three thousand prisoners, thousands of small arms, and hundreds of thousands of dollars' worth of stores that the Federal army lacked time to destroy. In years to come, men of both sides would study with admiration this military performance.

As Stonewall intended, Washington officials felt a flash of terror. The Union capital itself was endangered; Lincoln sent out peremptory orders, and hastily the Federal armies took action to save the situation. Tens of thousands of men had to be pulled out of the drive on Richmond. On May 29 Stonewall could draw back satisfied. He snatched a moment to express his regard for Belle and her work:

> I thank you, for myself and for the Army, for the immense service that you have rendered your country today.
>
> Hastily, I am your friend,
>
> T.J. Jackson, C.S.A.

A week later, Southern forces abandoned Front Royal. A Union sympathizer (a woman, of course) stepped forward to denounce Belle as a dangerous enemy, and an officer arrested her in her house and surrounded it with sentries. Then General Shields, the Irishman who liked her so much, rode up, and, regardless of what his fellow Northerners thought, he released her.

Belle found herself famous. Northern newspapers, while admitting her cleverness, sneered at her as "notorious," "abandoned," "a camp follower." One account claimed she had helped Jackson by "playing Delilah to General Banks," dancing before him at a ball, draping "a large and elegant secesh flag" over her fatuous admirer, while Stonewall was supposedly fooling Samson Banks with a surprise attack. In another story "La Belle Rebelle" had caught up a sword and led the whole Confederate charge!

A Federal writer found her "the sensation of the village." "The intensely loyal Confederates idolized her and . . . she had a large following of Federal officers who were ready to do her homage." Apparently Belle had not been greatly stirred by any of the men she captivated, but a change was on its way. She was to betray herself in love and in war as well.

One day Belle saw a prepossessing young man in Southern uniform. He interested her strangely, and she learned he was a paroled Southern officer waiting for a pass to Dixie. She invited him to dinner with her and the family, and he later accompanied her to a party at which Belle played "The Bonnie Blue Flag." The handsome fellow stood beside her and they sang a duet; presumably that proved him worthy of full trust. Smiling at him, Belle made a whispered request: when he left to go South, could he take a dispatch to Stonewall for her? He promised gladly.

The girl's maid warned her. Miss Belle had better watch out; she'd seen that man among the Yankees, and mighty friendly with 'em, too. Ever direct, Belle asked him bluntly: *was* he a Northern agent? He said no, and for her that settled it. Actually he was C. W. D. Smitley, a scout for the 5th West Virginia Cavalry.

Belle became still more enamored. When the next party broke up after midnight the other officers envied Smitley, who walked her home in the moonlight and paused with her in the dark for a long good-by. The next morning, however, Belle suddenly began to sense danger. Hurrying to Smitley's boardinghouse, she frantically demanded the truth about the rumors that he was a Union agent. Again he denied the rumors flatly. Then he promptly reported to his superiors, who communicated with Secretary of War Stanton, and Stanton acted.

Union officers appeared to arrest Belle and take her to Washington, among them a squat, ugly man called Cridge. (Could Dickens have thought of a better name? Still, Federal records show that Belle did not make it up.) Belle and her relatives were lined up against a wall, but her better-than-fiction maid succeeded in running off with handfuls of records and burning them. The men broke open a desk and found other papers, however. Finally Belle, white with anxiety, was led away through a crowd of people, some of whom had come to sympathize, some to jeer.

The girl wept on the way to Washington. This was no situation to be escaped by flirtation or bravado. Moreover, in her first real love affair, she had been completely taken in. . . .

In the national capital, as the chill walls of the Old Capitol loomed before her, she shivered. The doors were swung open by Superintendent Wood, Lafayette Baker's partner in the handling of malefactors: "And so this is the celebrated rebel spy. . . . I am glad to have so distinguished a personage. . . ." Standing with hands clenched at the window of her cell, Belle had a view of Pennsylvania Avenue, and she made out the former home of Secretary Floyd, where she had danced at her happy debut. She felt more alone and frightened than ever before in her life.

Soon Belle was confronted by Superintendent Wood and Lafayette Baker himself. At the sight of the stony-faced director of the Federal detectives, her rage welled up. In his customary fashion Baker took the lead, and she later quoted him, a bit unkindly: "Ain't you pretty tired of your prison a'ready?

I've come to get you to make a free confession now of what you've did agin our cause."

After a long silence Belle made a contemptuous reply. "When you've informed me on what grounds I've been arrested, and given me a copy of the charges, I'll make a statement." Baker "harangued her" and offered an oath of allegiance. "Remember, Mr. Stanton will hear of all this."

Belle's reply was withering. "Tell Mr. Stanton for me, I hope when I commence that oath, my tongue may cleave to the roof of my mouth. If I ever sign one line to show allegiance, I hope my arm falls paralyzed to my side." Then she ordered Baker out of the room: "I'm so disgusted I can't endure your presence any longer!"

Cries of "Bravo" roared through the jail, for her fellow prisoners had been listening with delight. Superintendent Wood took Baker's arm. "We'd better go," he said. "The lady is tired." —a masterpiece of understatement. Belle had won the first encounter. Baker came again, but she answered none of his questions and told him nothing at all. . . . That first evening she heard a cough, and a small object rolled across the floor of her cell. It was a nutshell with a Confederate flag painted on it; from inside she drew a note of sympathy. Belle's eyes filled; even in Yankeedom her people were with her!

Young Major Doster, the provost marshal, became a grudging admirer. "The first time I called on her," said Doster, in his record of the Boyd affair, "she was reading *Harper's* and eating peaches. She remarked that she could afford to remain here if Stanton could afford to keep her. There was so much company and so little to do." Never did he find her in bad humor, he noted.

Editor Dennis Mahony of Dubuque, Iowa, who was in the Old Capitol for siding with the South, described how he heard her sing "Maryland, My Maryland" with "such peculiar expression as to touch even the sensibilities of those who did not sympathize with the cause." In a silence that spread over the prison, the girl threw her "whole soul" into the words of devotion to the South, defiance to the North.

Another inmate declared: "When Belle sang, it made you feel like jumping out of the window and swimming the Potomac." If she walked the narrow yard for exercise, fellow prisoners craned their necks to see her. Editor Mahony recalled her passage "with a grace and dignity which might be envied by a queen." On Sunday, if she gave inmates "a look or a smile, it did them more good than the preaching."

Belle made a different impression on her guards. In her favorite song she often emphasized the line, "*She spurns the Northern scum*"*!* At that point they stormed in one day to stop her, and as they went out, she took up a broom to sweep up after them. They could never fathom how she obtained the small Confederate flags which she wore in her bosom or waved on sticks from her window!

One story Belle omitted from her own recollections was her prison courtship by Lieutenant McVay, an appropriately good-looking young man with a properly romantic background. He had known Belle in his boyhood, but they had not met for some time, and now his war record intrigued her. The lieutenant told her, when they had a chance to talk, how he had been badly injured in the battles before Richmond and left for dead by his Confederate comrades. When the Union army moved in, attendants lifted him into a basket for corpses. Lieutenant McVay moved, and they brought him to Washington, where he slowly recovered.

His cell was across the hall from Belle's; the circumstances and setting combined to stir her affections. Whenever they were allowed, the pair sat together in the yard or whispered across the corridor; eventually Belle announced her engagement to McVay. They planned a wedding as soon as they won their freedom, and gaily Belle asked permission to buy her trousseau in Washington. The War Department coldly denied the request.

The girl's confinement in prison had begun to tell on her. Because she put up a picture of Jefferson Davis, smuggled into the prison by a friend, she had to spend stifling summer weeks without leaving her cell. She was listless and thin. Major Doster declared that "open air and horseback exercise were in her case constitutional necessities." In a pathetic talk with her doctor, she asked when she could get the medicine he prescribed—freedom.

In late August great news ran through the prison. Belle and some others would be sent South on exchange. Much stronger action might have been taken against her; but in the Civil War nobody shot eighteen-year-old girls, even though they were secret agents. There was only one drawback in the exchange order: Lieutenant McVay could not go with her. They had long talks, and promised to meet again at the first possible moment. Superintendent Wood in a burst of friendliness bought her trousseau and sent it after her, under a flag of truce!

Belle's departure was a triumph. She looked tearfully out of the carriage window as crowds pressed forward, calling her name. In the Confederate capital the celebrated Richmond Light Infantry Blues drew up to present arms in her honor. Generals visited her, women stopped her on the streets to praise her. She appeared in a gray riding costume, that of an "honorary captain" of the Confederacy, and sat happily on horseback at troop reviews. When her trousseau arrived, Belle excited the ladies with glimpses of her finery.

For Belle and her lieutenant, however, there was misery ahead. Months passed and he stayed on in prison, whereas Belle moved all over the South. Their letters became infrequent. Slowly their interest cooled, and the engagement ended. If they met again, it is not known.

The Union caught up with Belle a second time when she returned to Martinsburg. A Belle Boyd within Federal lines was a serious hazard. Soon after Northern units swung into the town, Secretary Stanton ordered her arrested. In July of 1863 she was at Carroll Prison, involved in a mysteriously romantic experience. One twilight she felt an object brush past her foot; startled, she discovered an arrow on the floor, with note attached. "C.H." wanted her to realize she had many sympathizers. Thereafter he would be in the square opposite on Thursdays and Saturdays, to communicate with her!

Miss Belle must not worry, C.H. added. "I am a good shot." She was to obtain India rubber balls, insert her messages, and toss them out as energetically as she could. Somehow she did get the balls and carried on a lively correspondence, receiving clippings, confidential word about the Federals, and admiring messages. She also assisted the Confederacy when a fellow inmate, a Southern mail runner, planned an escape. At the crucial moment she asked the superintendent to come to her cell. Several prisoners cried, "Murder, murder!" And in the excitement the mail runner crawled to the roof, slid down, and got away.

Once more summer heat and close confinement told; after three months of being caged, the volatile Belle became ill. As before, she was sent to Richmond, but with a sharp warning: let her show herself again inside Federal lines, and she would be in the worst trouble of her life. There followed a sad time for the girl; after several sieges of sickness brought on by the war, her father died, and as she grieved her own illness dragged on.

Doctors told her she needed a long trip, and Belle had an inspiration; she would improve of necessity if she carried Southern dispatches to England. Starting on one of her most flamboyant exploits, she went to Wilmington, the North Carolina port where Rose Greenhow met death—but for Belle the trip produced the great love affair of her war days.

On the night of May 8, 1864, the three-masted schooner *Greyhound*, her decks piled with cotton bales, moved out to sea, lights covered, crew and passengers tense. For Belle, who had assumed the name "Mrs. Lewis," the risk was heavy; the Federal Government looked with particular disfavor on bearers of Southern messages to European powers. With lookouts stationed at vantage points, the *Greyhound* hoped to avoid the Federal fleet which lay somewhere nearby. Hours later, when the darkness lifted, there was a shout: "Sail ho!"

The *Greyhound's* frantic captain increased her steam pressure, set more sails, but the pursuing Federal vessel drew closer and closer. As Belle and the other passengers rushed aft, the Northern gunboat began firing on the *Greyhound*. One source says that Miss Boyd sat calmly on the highest cotton bale, the better to see the show. The first shells landed in the sea with a smothered roar, but the Union aim became steadily more accurate.

The crew threw valuable cotton overboard, and when the captain hurried past Belle, he called: "If it weren't for you, I'd burn her to the water's edge before they could take a single bale!" La Belle Rebelle shrugged. "Don't think of me. I don't care what happens, if only the Yankees don't get the ship." As the *U.S.S. Connecticut* moved in, the crew tossed over a keg of money containing twenty-five thousand dollars, and Belle burned her dispatches.

As the girl watched with growing concern, Northern officers removed the Confederate captain for questioning, and a prize master, young Ensign Samuel Hardinge of Brooklyn, took over the *Greyhound*. Belle made no secret of her first impression of Mr. Hardinge:

> I saw at a glance he was made of other stuff than his comrades. . . . His dark brown hair hung down on his shoulders; his eyes were large and bright. Those who judge of beauty by regularity of feature only, could not have pronounced him strictly handsome . . . but the fascination of his manner was such, his every movement was so much that of a refined gentle-

man, that my "Southern proclivities," strong as they were, yielded for a moment to the impulses of my heart, and I said to myself, "Oh, what a good fellow that must be."

When Ensign Hardinge asked permission to enter her cabin, Belle replied pertly: "Certainly. I know I am a prisoner." He was now in command, he said, but, "I beg you will consider yourself a passenger, not a prisoner." Belle took Sam precisely at his word, and apparently he was as romantically bemused as she.

The *Greyhound*, astern of the *Connecticut*, started north for Fortress Monroe. A more cozy atmosphere spread over the *Greyhound;* Belle, the ensign, and the Confederate captain got along increasingly well. One night the three sat together as the moon lighted the ocean, "just agitated by a slight breeze." Waves lapped the vessel, and the young Hardinge raised his voice in a gentle song. Later Belle wrote in relaxed mood of the "soft stillness" and "sweet harmony."

When the Confederate captain made a tactful withdrawal, the ensign quoted Byron and Shakespeare; "and from poetry he passed on to plead an oft-told tale. . . ." Soon Sam was asking her to marry him; but Belle indicates that she hesitated. Twice before she had been hurt by love, and the fact that Ensign Hardinge was a Yankee had to be considered.

A "very practical thought" also suggested itself; if Sam really loved her, "he might in future be useful to us." Us, of course, was the Confederacy. She replied that the matter involved serious consequences, and he must wait until the trip ended. She admits that at the same time she and the Southern captain were studying ways to arrange the latter's escape!

Her alias of "Mrs. Lewis" gave her no protection; the truth slipped out, and at New York and Boston newspapermen panted for interviews with Belle. She had become more lustrous than ever, and newspapers described her every move, quoted every word of hers that could be caught. As some Yankees fretted over this female's prominence, or merely gaped at her silks, one excited correspondent proclaimed her the Confederacy's Cleopatra.

By then Belle had seen enough of Ensign Hardinge to make up her mind—this time she had found the man she really wanted, and she would marry him. True, their politics differed, yet "women can sometimes work wonders," she remarked. She promptly managed a neat bit of wonder-working, when she sent Sam on an errand and helped the Confederate captain to get away. She had helped the South again, but her fiancé was in trouble. There was an official inquiry into the escape. Very much under her spell, Sam appeared more interested in Belle's plight than his own. While officials pondered his case, he made a trip to Washington in an effort to secure her release.

Belle told the Northern authorities that she wanted to go to Canada, and Sam Hardinge applied for a month's leave, to join her there. Instead, he was arrested, tried, and dismissed from the Navy for neglect of duty. Deeply humiliated, Sam had just one consolation. Belle had been sent north, and if he ever got out of the United States, he could go to Canada and claim the bride for whom he had risked so much.

American agents in Canada watched Belle closely, to guard against any fresh mischief, until she sailed for England. There she could at least work for the Confederacy. Sam went to London after her and learned she was not there, raced on to Paris, only to discover she was in Liverpool. At last they met and their marriage was a great event for Southern representatives in London, the newspapers, and a delighted part of the public—American, British, and French.

At St. James's church in Piccadilly the ceremony took place on August 25, 1864, "in the presence of a fashionable assemblage of affectionate and admiring friends." As one Englishman declared: "Her great beauty, elegant manners and personal attractions generally, in conjunction with her romantic history . . .

concur to invest her with attributes which render her such a heroine as the world has seldom if ever seen." An American account claimed, erroneously, that the Prince of Wales himself attended the wedding.

One excited correspondent revealed that Belle had "succeeded in withdrawing her lover from his allegiance to the United States flag, and enlisting his sympathies and support for the South." Sam intended to leave England with his bride, run the blockade, and join the Confederacy! Belle had demonstrated indeed that "women can sometimes work wonders."

If the new Mrs. Hardinge went back home, however, the Union might make good its many threats against her. Belle had to stay in London, and Sam, therefore, returned alone. It was said that he carried Confederate dispatches. He was a brave man, or at least a foolhardy one. He slipped into Unionist Boston, visited his family in Brooklyn, and went on to Virginia to "meet Belle's family" or to perform a Confederate errand, or both.

Promptly the Union trapped its former ensign, arresting him as a Southern spy, and again the country had a Belle Boyd sensation. A wild, baseless story spread about the country to the effect that Belle herself had sneaked back. As poor Sam went from one prison to another, over in London a saddened Mrs. Hardinge received funds from friends and sympathizers, but in the last days of the Confederacy Belle had unending trouble over money.

In prison Sam Hardinge fell sick, and Belle had to sell first her jewelry, then her wedding presents. British papers carried one or two accounts of her "very great distress of mind and body," and many of her London admirers rallied around. She wrote her memoirs, which appeared at the war's end and had a large audience for a time. Sam returned to her, but only for a few months. The young man who had given up so much for her died of ailments growing out of his imprisonment, and Belle was a widow at twenty-one.

Before long her *joie de vivre* returned, and she went on to a theatrical career in England and America. She lived out a full life, surviving until the year 1900. Death came on a speaking tour in Wisconsin, and she was buried far from home. A Southerner put up a tombstone, "erected by a comrade," which proclaimed her officially "Confederate Spy." In many ways she was the most appealing one of the war.

Chapter 7

Scholar in Blackface

Prince Georges County, Maryland, was a strategic spot in the Confederacy's secret affairs. It bordered Washington, D.C., Baltimore lay only a short way off, and Federal troops frequently marched through it. Though the Union maintained its hold on the state of Maryland, an important line of Southern communication ran through the county's sleepy town of Upper Marlboro.

At obscure points along the river, hidden under trees or along scantly populated stretches of the shore, Marylanders waited with boats to take Southern agents across the Potomac. In a high dormer window a dress or shirt which hung casually, as if for an airing, told these agents by its color whether the North's watch was close or inattentive.

A hundred or more times in early war days a tall, calm-faced young man with bent shoulders passed over this route, until Federal officials spotted him and placed him high on their list of wanted spies. He was Walter Bowie, as gentle-looking an individual as ever made Lafayette Baker sigh and fume.

Oldest of nine children, most of them girls, Walter was the son of a lawyer who had made a name for himself in the Prince Georges area and then retired to planting. At twenty-four Walter was, as he had always been, "the serious type," a youth with many responsibilities and a willingness to carry them. His worst enemy, Lafe Baker, referred to him as "a young man with considerable culture." A good student, Bowie prepared himself for law and settled down to a stable, undramatic practice.

Nobody in Upper Marlboro would have expected the young lawyer to live out his life in anything except the most conservative fashion. "Wat," his close friends called him; to others he was Mr. Bowie or Mr. Walter. Maryland neighbors, seeing the dreamy look in his blue-gray eyes, the wide forehead, the long, full mustache, considered him a "type." As far as available records go, bachelor Bowie had never shown any romantic interest in the girls of the neighborhood.

The year 1861 was one of change for Walter Bowie. Though it was many months before he joined the Southern Army, few Marylanders ever criticized him. According to Lafayette Baker, the Southern Secretary of War sent a message that he had a number of chores for the attorney. Wat put up his legal books and documents, attached a lock to his small office near the courthouse, and abruptly became another man.

It was almost, his friends declared, as if a second Wat had been waiting inside the familiar shell. He was a one-man agency working against the North, a source of schemes and plans, and a spy of courage.

Repeatedly during the war's first ten months he had himself ferried across the river to Washington, where he conferred with Southern friends, gathered messages for Richmond, medical supplies, and Union war information. In his travels back and forth he was almost always a night operator. At dawn he would knock discreetly on a farmhouse window, or crawl through the foliage in a town-house garden, and sleep all day in safety.

Lafayette Baker recalled that Wat "raised squads for the rebel service," and arranged their transfer to Confederate camps through Union territory. In time Wat grew especially adept at finding holes in Federal patrolling systems and slipping through the one unprotected spot.

Bowie succeeded so well that Union officials decided that something decisive had to be done about him. Northern sympathizers told as much as they could about Bowie's habits, and a net was spread. One girl had now captured Wat's interest, and he often visited her and her family. Baker knew where to watch for him. In early October of 1862 a local informer whispered to one of the Federal detectives that the spy had arrived again at the girl's house.

A dozen Union detectives crept in darkness around the gray, two-storied building. Wat, alert as always, sensed their presence and called to the family to put out the lights, all of them! The Federal agents were puzzled, but one man with especially good ears heard a slight sound and made out a lean form climbing out of a second-story window. It was Wat, preparing to lower himself. Despite the long drop, he might have made it and sped away, gun in hand, to the grove of trees that grew close to the house. Luck, however, favored the Baker forces; as Bowie thudded down, three pairs of hands seized him and he was taken at once to Washington. The Federals wanted no rescues or demonstrations by sympathizers.

In the Old Capitol, Lafe Baker delightedly took over. For weeks the old hand at ruthless questioning worked harder than usual. His victim sweated but admitted nothing whatever. Very well, let him hang! A hearing followed, with a verdict of guilty, and an order for execution.

The Bowies had dozens of Washington and Maryland friends, a number of them close to the administration, and many sent appeals to Stanton and Lincoln. The Secretary of War ignored the petitions; the President, who reprieved or spared scores of men in similar situations, is said to have considered the matter and declined to intervene. The time for the execution approached. By some method the prisoner's friends sent word that Wat was not to lose hope; they would manage something.

The prison guard was increased. Two days before the scheduled hanging, Wat's aunt arrived to beg that Superintendent Wood allow her and her nephew a farewell meeting. Faced with a weeping woman, Wood hesitated, and finally agreed. He reminded her that a guard must stay with them all during the visit.

The guard heard and saw nothing untoward. As his aunt kissed Bowie a sad good-by, however, she passed a piece of paper from her lips to his. He gave no sign of surprise and when he was alone again he spread out the note, which outlined the escape plan and warned him to be careful to follow directions in detail.

As he suspected, the Bowies or their friends had spread money heavily in the proper places, and a Washingtonian with influence had organized the affair. In a few hours a Negro would bring his food as usual. Tonight, however, the servant would not lock the cell door. A moment or two after seven—Wat should be especially watchful—the light in the hall would go out. A few feet down the passage he would discover a ladder to the roof. After he had jumped to the sidewalk and walked a few blocks, someone would meet him with a horse. A few minutes later he would be on his way out of the city, in disguise. . . .

Bowie waited tensely. He started at a sound outside his cell, and the Negro entered carrying his meal. While the prisoner pretended not to look, the servant fumbled at the lock. Suppose he lost heart and turned the key? Instead, the attendant went quietly away. Eating little, Wat stared at his watch. Five minutes to seven—seven o'clock—one minute after—the light went out. Prisoners in adjoining cells fell silent; Wat had already whispered the escape plan to them.

He felt his way down the hall; yes, the ladder was there.

With nervous agility Wat reached the roof, thrust himself over the ridge pole, and then slid slowly downward to the top of a woodshed. It had begun to rain steadily and that would help. But a sentry was patrolling the dark street, much too close for Bowie's comfort. At last the soldier turned at the corner. It had to be now. Wat lowered himself and let go.

His fall almost betrayed him. Landing on his ankle in the wet, mushy earth, he sprained it badly. When he got to his feet he realized he would have trouble walking and the guard had heard the clatter of his fall. The man came toward him, and for a moment disaster seemed certain.

The once pedantic lawyer thought fast. Slapping his hands together, he called on the soldier to help him. Damn these streets; even an old Washingtonian got tired of slipping and falling. "Why don't they have lights and clean up the muck? Here, take my hand."

The guard hesitated.

Bowie grew still more irate. His confidence carried him through, and, apologizing, the soldier escorted him until he was within reach of his friends. Federal records gave the escape time as 7 P.M., November 17, 1862.

Back in Maryland, Wat sat out the man hunt, remaining hidden for weeks. There were many places in which he was safe. The Union detectives finally gave up the search, and Bowie moved on to a new assignment.

One morning he threaded his way through a wood, and walked right into a huddle of Northern soldiers around a fire. One already had his hand on his holster; Wat could not withdraw.

Taking the initiative again, he went up to the enemy. They had a hell of a nerve, burning his fence rails to warm themselves! He played the angry landowner with considerable cleverness, and as the Unionists argued, he allowed his temper to cool. Well, yes, he'd have some coffee. During the next few minutes he listened quietly while they talked of their present activities. Had he heard, they asked, that they were after that scoundrel Bowie? No, he hadn't.

Then the "landowner" remembered: He'd talked to Wat just a week ago; he'd known him for a long time. He had seen the man go over in that direction. . . . Then Wat rose, stretched his arms, and realizing that one or two of his listeners might recall the description of Bowie—lean, light eyes, long mustache, shoulders slightly stooped—the "landowner" chuckled: "It's a good thing you fellows are on my property. Might've had trouble; they say I look like Wat."

Not long afterward, when they met the real owner of the land, Wat was a long way off. The year 1863 passed, and several times Baker's men almost trapped Bowie again. They would trace him for miles, only to lose the trail. Lafayette Baker, however, had discovered something of which he could make good use. Bowie had cousins, the Warings, who lived on the banks of the Patuxent River; sooner or later he would go there.

The Union detectives felt certain that planter John H. Waring had made his house a headquarters for blockade runners and mail carriers. They had been told that Waring helped two of his sons swim their horses across the river in order to join the Southern armies. But the planter took care not to express himself publicly, and had yet to be caught in any dubious action. The Warings had no way of learning that Baker had a secret ally in John, their coachman. John met a Union agent at discreet intervals, and in July of 1863 gave his contact big news: young Bill Waring of the Confederate Army had just come home, with Mr. Wat Bowie himself!

About dusk a few hours later the Union agents surrounded the Waring home. The father had spent the day supervising the work on a plantation at some distance from his house. As he returned home, the detectives seized him. He tried to warn the family, and Baker wrote that "the proximity of the men somehow became known to the inmates of the house."

Wat Bowie held a hurried conference with the younger soldier and Bill's sister, Elizabeth Waring Duckett. Elizabeth showed herself a woman of nimble mind and strong will. She reminded them that she had a heavy bag of Confederate mail, due to be sent South; she shoved it into a hiding place. She asked Wat if he had anything that she could put into a safe place, and he held out a fine map of the newest Washington fortifications. He could burn it, of course; still, he would rather try to save it. He and his friends had gone to so much trouble to get it. . . . Elizabeth thrust the map into her bodice.

The big problem was what to do about Wat. The house was large, and they might be able to delay the searchers for a while, so Elizabeth suggested that he hide in a corner behind the kitchen fireplace. Perhaps in the dark they would be able to slip him out of the back door.

Hours passed. Baker's men waited all night, and each side prepared for the test that would come with daylight. In the early morning the Union agents finally acted, pounding on the front door and crying: "Open in the name of the government, or we'll burn the house over your heads!" Wat and Elizabeth made a swift inspection, finding all five entrances guarded. The pounding grew louder; young Bill Waring went to the front door, and was arrested on the spot.

Elizabeth motioned Wat to get behind the fireplace. The coachman John had disappeared, but the rest of the servants remained faithful to the family. As the detectives searched room after room, their annoyance increased and, calling for the keys, they began to lock the doors of each chamber as they left it.

In the kitchen Elizabeth was improvising again. Wat was going to become a Negro girl. Over his objections she told

Peggy, their gaunt old slave, to get one of her dresses. She slipped the gingham costume over Wat's head and tied it at the waist. "Kick off your boots," she ordered. "I know you've gone barefoot before. And give me your gun."

Again Wat protested, but she won out. Stolidly he allowed her to rub "black cosmetic" over his face, neck, hands, and feet.

Now she had to find an excuse that would allow Wat to leave the house with Peggy. She ordered a manservant to break the kitchen pump. He complied, and a minute or two later they heard the steps of the Federal men coming toward the kitchen. Wat took a chair in the corner, and sat there quietly while the intruders searched the room. As Elizabeth had anticipated, the detectives asked for something to drink. "I'll have to send to the spring below the hill," she explained, and summoned Peggy.

The old servant balanced a tub on her head and Bowie, her "helper," slid another under his arm. No one in the kitchen paid any attention as the pair walked out into the yard. In front of the house were two detectives, who looked up casually. "That's a mighty tall colored girl," one snickered.

A moment later the Union agent spotted a younger servant standing a short way off, holding a horse. The boy had followed Elizabeth's instructions but had come too close to the house. "Whose horse is that?" he was asked.

The confused boy stuttered truthfully: "Marse—Marse Wat Bowie's!"

Peggy and her "helper" had by then reached the edge of the ravine that led to the spring. Throwing away the bucket, Wat scrambled down a steep decline. The detectives ran forward, fired several times, and shouted for help. Bowie crawled behind a bush and suddenly disappeared. He was on home ground now.

Before the Federal men returned, Elizabeth burned most of the Southern correspondence and Wat's precious Washington drawings. The furious Northerners had lost their main prize;

they retaliated by arresting the whole Waring family, charging the brother with being a spy, and accusing the father of hiding a spy, "harboring rebels," and possessing illegal Southern mail.

Months later, Elizabeth heard that her brother William might be hanged as a Southern agent. He had never been a spy and for help she appealed to a man who was unquestionably one, Walter Bowie himself. Receiving her message by Confederate underground, Wat went to Robert Ould, the Confederate Exchange Commissioner. Ould dispatched a white-hot note to the Federal Secretary of War: let William Waring suffer any injury, and the South would not lose a day in executing one of its outstanding prisoners, General Cochran—a close friend of Stanton's. Bill Waring did not hang.

Walter Bowie had come a long way from his scholarly lawyer's life. Famous as he had become, civilian spying was now almost impossible for him. He therefore took a not illogical step and joined the celebrated Mosby Rangers. Mosby's men were known to the Union as cutthroats, lawless pillagers, "entitled to nothing except powder and ball." To the South they were hard-riding, glorious adventurers who struck hard at the Yankees however, wherever, whenever they could. Wat Bowie found the organization very appealing.

He was under Colonel John S. Mosby, the little rooster of a man whose background paralleled Wat's at several points. They had both known a quiet early life; they belonged to well-established families; they had practiced law before the war. Those who saw Raider Mosby seldom forgot his wiry figure, tight lips, penetrating eyes, and clean-shaven face, a rarity in that period. Like Stonewall Jackson, Mosby hated advance talk about his plans. Usually even his own leaders did not know their destination on a raid.

Early in the war Mosby had seemed to many observers a poor soldier, careless and unmilitary in appearance. Then he gathered his small band and they won a reputation for terrorizing that might have been won by a hundred times their number. Behind Federal lines the Mosby partisans so dominated the rolling terrain of Fairfax, Loudoun, and Fauquier counties that the region was dubbed "Mosby's Confederacy." Like the Commandos of World War II, they burst out of nowhere, struck in the night (or morning or afternoon), and disappeared victorious.

Walter Bowie became first lieutenant of Mosby's Company F, and one of the three or four most proficient of the organization's scouts. Mosby depended heavily on Wat's advice in his Maryland activities, but, daring as he himself was, the chief sometimes found his subordinate too much of a gambler. . . . Mosby liked to stay alive for the next fight.

In the fall of 1864, Bowie received some information that stirred him: the Federal governor's mansion at Annapolis was almost unguarded. Wat conceived the most bizarre scheme of his career: to raid the place, kidnap the governor so hated by the Confederates, and drag him to Richmond. It would be a magnificent piece of propaganda, and they might store away His Excellency as hostage for Southerners held by Lafayette Baker in Washington!

At first Mosby would not hear of it. His lieutenant argued, almost begged, "with so much earnestness" that he won the Ranger's approval. The leader provided a band of twenty-five, and the party swept out from Upperville, Virginia, to Mathias Point on the Potomac. At dusk of the second day, a bad evening in late September, they stood before the wide, sullen river.

Wat decided to proceed with only seven aides; they could do better as a smaller group. Reluctantly they agreed that they had to leave their horses behind. The blockade runner who was to take them across grumbled at the weather, and at several points the fragile yawl almost capsized. Federal boats hovered in the distance and the terrified runner insisted he couldn't make it; they *had* to go back! A gun at his temple kept him moving ahead.

On the Maryland shore Wat and his men rested, wet and discouraged. He led them into the woods, and most of them tried to sleep on the chilly earth while he reconnoitered his home territory. Wat returned with excitement in his eyes; at nearby Port Tobacco he had come upon a fine lot of horses. All they had to do, the eight of them, was take the animals from twenty-odd Unionists.

Part of the 8th Illinois Cavalry was quartered in the courthouse; the eight men walked quietly into the shadow of a cedar tree in front of the building, waited until the guard passed on his beat, and "put him out of action." One of the Rangers stood at the entrance, with orders to shoot down any Yankee who tried to get out. By the light of matches, Wat and one or two others crept into a big room, the court chamber itself, in which soldiers lay asleep, and worked their way to a vantage point, the judge's bench.

A big German soldier awakened, sprang up, and rammed his pistol against Bowie: "By dams, me shoot!" Quickly one of Wat's aides shoved *his* gun into the German's ribs and the German backed away.

According to arrangement, four more Bowie men broke in, shouting, pounding, "making more noise than the whole of Mosby's Battalion would have done." It sounded like the vanguard of a great force, and when Wat called out, "Surrender, surrender, or you'll be shot down where you are," the whole group gave up.

Facing Confederate pistols, the Union soldiers signed an agreement to stay in the courthouse until daybreak. Mosby's men took the horses and rode off with the cry: "Big Walnut by dawn!" They went in the opposite direction, of course, thirty-five miles to Upper Marlboro. There they rested through the day in Wat's home, and there Bowie had an affectionate reunion with his mother and father, his sisters, and his younger brother Brune, another Confederate soldier on furlough, recovering from war wounds.

In the morning brother Brune asked to be allowed to join the group in capturing the Yankee governor. He didn't want to miss that fun! Wat agreed, and as they galloped off they waved a cheerful good-by to the other Bowies.

As they approached Annapolis, the party took to the woods while Wat quietly scouted the territory. He discovered to his profound disappointment that the information on which the whole enterprise was planned had been wrong. By one account, Bowie found the governor's mansion all too well guarded; according to another, the executive had simply gone away on a long trip. The town was filled with newly arrived Union soldiers; even for a Wat Bowie, the place was too warm. . . . Glumly the party mounted their Yankee horses for the long return trip.

They might have made it safely but for a short halt at a country store at Sandy Spring settlement. They were hungry, and the stop may have been a raid, in which they seized whatever they wanted—cans of meats, smoked foods, and bread. One of the Mosby band said only that they "opened negotiation" for supplies. Even then there might have been no trouble if one man who lacked shoes could have found his size on the shelves. The clerk wore a pair that would fit, and Bowie's helper "insisted upon making the exchange."

Finally they leaped into their saddles for a forced ride to the Potomac. As it grew light, they went into the woods to eat and rest. They had scarcely settled themselves when they heard hoofbeats and a shout: "They've gone in there." It was not Federal cavalry, but a posse of village men, already upon them. The furious clerk had organized it; the party had shotguns, and for once someone had really surprised Wat and his men.

"Boys, we'll charge 'em on foot!" Bowie yelled the order and the eight Rangers advanced in an uneven line, shouting as they plowed into the enemy. Gunfire blazed; the villagers fell back. Several of the Mosby men, with Wat in the lead, jumped onto horses abandoned in the rout and dashed after the fleeing enemy. The sound of Wat's laughter trailed him in the sunny morning. At a curve in the road a blacksmith hidden behind a cedar tree took aim, fired twice, and Bowie took a full load of buckshot in the side of his head.

His brother and his other companions came upon him, bleeding and gasping in the road. Weakly Wat warned them: "They'll be back—the whole country with them. Leave me. . . ." Despite the hazard, his aides remained and hunted until they located a wagon. Lifting him gently, they took him to a farmer's house. At his desperate urging the Rangers went on, but Wat's brother Brune stayed at his side with the women of the house until Wat's eyes glazed and his dark head dropped back. Then Brune followed after his friends.

Federal soldiers intercepted him, and the younger Bowie sat out the balance of the war in the Old Capitol Prison. For a long time Mosby and his men talked admiringly of Wat, and retold the story of his final hour, when he laughed as he had never laughed in his dull days as a plodding lawyer.

Lafayette Baker could scratch one name from his list, but he would never check off that astringent little enemy, John Mosby. The Federal detective did the next best thing by capturing a girl he felt certain spied for the Rangers. She was Antonia Ford of Fairfax Court House, Virginia, a twenty-four-year-old who played Belle Boyd in a more placid, yet quite lethal way.

Dreamy Antonia had her own technique. She seemed to do nothing, talked of everything except actual military affairs, and allowed the other fellow (generally it *was* a fellow) to presume she sided with him. Her soft, dark hair was parted in the center and drawn loosely back on her small head. Heavy lashes and brows, a slightly tilted nose, and full lips with a suggestion of a pout gave Miss Ford a smiling prettiness. She also had "a way with her." Like Belle, she had gone to nearby Washington to parties and was known as "a wit and conversationalist." When war came, Antonia continued to live at Fairfax, where neighbors knew her as a Confederate, though a discreet one.

Her brother joined the Southern forces, and died in battle; her merchant father gave information and aid to Southern messengers. But soon the big Ford house had a new use: the family entertained Union officers and also took some of them as paying guests. More and more military men crowded into this strategic area. One observer said the gentle-voiced girl received all sorts of information "in an apparently very careless and no-interest-to-me-I-assure-you manner, which quite deceived the men." Lafayette Baker commented acidly on her "pleasant, insinuating manners . . . impressing her admiring guests with her loyalty and intelligence."

Antonia made good use of that intelligence. Early in the war, the first invading Yankee officers ordered a thorough search of houses in the section. Warned in advance, Miss Ford carefully gathered up heirlooms and important documents and hid them. When the soldiers arrived Antonia sat reading in her parlor, her crinoline skirts spread wide around her chair. Calmly she told them to hunt as they wished; during all of their visit she bent her head over a book.

At the end the officer in charge stood before her; would she get up? Miss Antonia's dark eyes were points of fury. "I thought not even a Yankee would expect a Southern woman to rise for him." The abashed officer went out, and the papers were safe under the skirts.

Antonia did her first spying for Jeb Stuart, sending him

intelligence by any means available. Shortly before Second Manassas, in August of 1862, with the vicinity in tumult, the girl chanced on information that she knew had to go to the Confederates. Nobody else could take it, so she and a frightened but still strongly pro-Southern aunt hitched up a pair of horses and plodded twenty miles through a rainy night along broken roads, "dodging prowling troops," until they reached Stuart's camp.

The general rewarded Antonia with a document—later a famous one—commissioning her his honorary aide-de-camp. Because of "special confidence in the patriotism, fidelity and ability of Antonia J. Ford," Stuart ordered her to be "obeyed, respected and admired" by all of Southern heart.

By March of 1863 the Union concentrated more and more troops in Fairfax as protection for Washington. And John S. Mosby acted as a burr in the enemy's rear, tantalizing the Federal forces by sudden assaults, sneak raids, and withdrawals. Resentment spread in the North. They'd get him yet, and once they did. . . . Mosby answered: First let 'em try to get me!

Some people, including Lafe Baker, said Mosby had already come boldly within Union reach, staying for days in Antonia's home. Federal officers who saw her sitting on the gallery with the lean, unimpressive civilian took him for a "simple, green, raw" countryman. At that moment any Union man who had snagged this supposed yokel would have made himself a hero. Baker reported that the astonishing Antonia once went riding with a member of a Northern general's staff and met Mosby in disguise. She introduced the Confederate under a false name and sweetly went on at the Northerner's side, "with loyal words upon her traitorous lips"!

General Edwin H. Stoughton, a prepossessing young New Englander, who found living pleasant in Fairfax, thought Antonia as attractive a rebel as he hoped to encounter. When Stoughton's mother, sister, and friends visited him, they stayed with the Fords, and the general and staff became very regular callers. While Edwin Stoughton enjoyed himself, others in Fairfax wondered about his common sense. In early March of 1863 a Union soldier wrote to a fellow Vermonter:

> General Stoughton, who commands the Second Vermont Brigade, has his headquarters in the village, although his Brigade is five or six miles away. What he could or would do in case of an attack, I don't know, but it seems to me that a General should be with his men. If he is so fancy that he can't put up with them, the Government had better put him out. . . .
>
> There is a woman in the town by the name of Ford, not married, who has been of great service to General Stuart. . . . Why our people do not send her beyond the lines is another question. . . . *If he gets picked up some night he may thank her for it.* . . . So things go, and it is all right. No wonder we don't get along faster.

Unfortunately for the Union, this letter did not reach official eyes until much later. On March 8 Stoughton planned a gala evening at Fairfax, a military party complete with champagne. Though it rained, nothing dampened the general's enthusiasm. Something of a dandy, and as proud of his social grace as of his military reputation, General Stoughton supervised preparations for a night he would never forget.

About twenty miles away, John Mosby mulled over a fat dossier of facts, and made up his mind to steal himself a Union general and most of his staff. Mosby had recently interviewed a deserter from the 5th New York Cavalry, who gave him vital information. Mosby's suspicious associates grumbled that the fellow looked just like a spy. The shrewd partisan shook his head; he trusted the man. As ever, Mosby told his followers nothing of his purpose. On this wet, windy afternoon—the night would be ideal for advancing in the dark—he and about thirty Rangers rode out on horseback from the town of Aldie.

Fairfax lay well inside Federal lines. To all appearances the road was well blocked, but Mosby had learned of one unguarded point. Through the rain, up a slope, down a dim lane the band plodded in their Confederate uniforms, bundled to the throat against the weather.

Once half the party lost the others, and for more than an hour the troops tried to locate one another; then, behind schedule, they pressed on. They skirted Federal infantry camps, and once a sentinel called to them, and they answered that they were the 5th New York Cavalry. He let them come nearer, and they made him a captive. Others saw them from a distance and allowed them to pass. They were assumed to be Union scouts, of course; who else would be inside the lines like that?

They reached their goal without a single loss or a single warning. Near the courthouse, Mosby broke his company into squads, each with its mission—one to go to the stables and take all the best mounts; one to regimental headquarters, or to the houses of different army officers. Obviously Mosby had been well briefed as to the town's layout. Telegraph wires were cut, sentries taken off duty one way or another. Federal sources verify the story of the astonishingly efficient descent.

At the red brick residence of General Stoughton, Mosby approached with picked men. He wanted this prize for himself! A member of the party beat with his sword hilt on the door, and a drowsy sentry answered. "Fifth New York Cavalry; bearing dispatches for the general," the Confederate replied. When the door opened, a hand clapped over the guard's mouth, and other hands pinned him down. The Mosby men subdued several of the general's aides, and the chief Ranger tiptoed into Stoughton's bedroom.

The proud Union officer was deep asleep after his big party. Beside the bed lay several empty champagne bottles. Hunched on one side, the general snored happily. Mosby drew back the quilt, gently raised the general's nightshirt, and slapped him hard on the rump. The general snorted and sat up.

"Did you ever hear of Mosby?" the Ranger asked.

"Yes!" Stoughton, who thought he was looking at one of his own men, answered thickly. "You've caught him?"

"He's caught *you.*"

Mosby and his men hustled the general and his staff into their clothes and marched them out at gun point. The dismayed Yankees made little attempt at resistance; they were certain the Confederacy had captured the village with an overwhelming force. Mosby, however, faced even greater danger now. Federal pickets had to be eluded and much territory covered before dawn. Somehow it was done with everything intact, including the general. At Southern headquarters Stoughton, sick with dismay, greeted his old West Point classmate, Fitz Lee, and was given a stiff drink to console him.

The North was electric with excitement. How, in God's name, had Mosby managed it? The Washington *Star* spoke for millions when it remarked: "There is a screw loose somewhere." Though Stoughton's reputation was ruined, Abraham Lincoln realistically shed no tears for him. Told that the Union had lost nearly sixty magnificent steeds, the President sighed: "I'm sorry for that. I can make generals, but I can't make horses."

Lafayette Baker probed and analyzed. He read the unfriendly soldier's letter about Antonia and General Stoughton (somebody sent it to the *Star*, which ran it complete), and he heard endless rumors and speculations. He dispatched an able "female detective" to Fairfax. The lady agent posed as a Confederate from New Orleans, who hoped to reach Warrenton and take refuge behind the Southern lines. Several people believed her and Antonia, who of all the villagers should have been suspicious, was glad to provide a room for such an ardent Southerner.

The woman stayed for two nights in the Ford home, and she lost no time in working on Miss Ford. Before retiring on the second night they exchanged feminine confidences. The newcomer spoke proudly of her work for the Confederacy; Antonia lifted her chin and said she could match it. The girl told how she had given Mosby particulars about the Union strength, the location of officers' quarters, the picket points, the officers' habits, and so on. She even showed the stranger her prized commission from Jeb Stuart.

In the morning the "Confederate from New Orleans" said good-by, and soon after Federal agents arrived at the Fords's house. Unprepared, Antonia could only stand aside as they searched her room. They uncovered a large supply of Southern mail, including notes to prove she had been in touch with Richmond authorities. Between an upper and lower mattress, as the woman spy had indicated, the searchers located Antonia's commission. Baker confiscated it, and Washington newspapers reproduced it as a horrendous document.

A Union officer went to escort Miss Ford from Fairfax Court House to the Old Capitol; he turned out to be Major Joseph C. Willard, a Northerner who had met her before and taken her to several parties. Eight or ten others in Fairfax were arrested, among them Antonia's father, but attention centered on Antonia and her connection with Mosby's brilliant raid.

Years later Mosby denied that Antonia had helped him. He admitted he had known her, and several Confederate observers have thought that the Ranger was more careful than factual in his disclaimer. In any case, Mosby himself pointed out wryly that the girl "got her revenge"; she married Major Willard, the Union officer who had come to arrest her! On March 10, 1864, while the war still raged, the ingenious Miss Ford, like Belle Boyd, took her Yankee for a husband. For the Fords and the Willards the brothers' war ended long before it did for the rest of the country.

Chapter 8

Espionne, Creole Style

Behind the garish footlights of Wood's Theatre in wartime Louisville, a well-curved brunette in a tight-fitting man's costume stepped forward and paused for a long minute. Though Pauline Cushman had a painted mustache that curled across her olive cheeks, no one in the overcrowded hall had any doubt of her gender. For once, however, even the males in the front rows concentrated less on Pauline's figure than on the thing she was about to do. All day long Louisville had been stirred by rumors of impending excitement at the theater.

Most Kentuckians did not think of La Cushman as "political" at all. She usually sang a romantic song or two, pranced around the stage, and took off a few of her clothes. Not many clothes, of course, in the 1860s, but enough to make Pauline a girl that few men forgot. Now, dressed as a gay young blade, she lifted a champagne glass, and her voice rang out over the audience:

"Here's to Jefferson Davis and the Southern Confederacy. May the South always maintain her honor and her rights!"

Union sympathizers sat stunned, Confederate hearts missed a beat, and then there were shouts of approval and wild applause, mingled with curses and threats. Hats flew in the air, frenzied men punched at their neighbors, and women ran out screaming. The manager, aghast, ordered the curtain down, and caught Miss Cushman's arm: what the devil did she think she was doing?

The rest of the company looked scornfully at the actress and edged away from her. Pauline gave a belligerent laugh: "I'd do it again. I'm not afraid of the whole Yankee crew!"

And thus Pauline Cushman made her entry into the secret service on the Northern side.

Mademoiselle Cushman is in the grand tradition of the European actress spy, who talked for one side and acted for the other, while she exchanged favors for information. Nature cast her to type. She had the rich dark coloring of her French mother and Spanish father, the heavy-lidded look of the professional temptress.

For months Pauline operated in a highly dangerous area, the Southwest. She slid in and out of officers' quarters and her own hotel rooms on her spying errands, and saw dozens of enemy soldiers melt under her charms.

Like many another "man's woman," Pauline was her own worst enemy. Some of the wartime operators were self-controlled and strong-willed, but unfortunately Miss Cushman allowed emotion to rule her. As a result, she came closer to being hanged than any woman in the war.

She was born in an appropriately flamboyant setting, the Creole town of New Orleans. It is ironic that the Queen City of the Mississippi, stoutly Confederate in most respects, should provide as its most famous spy a woman who used her arts for the North. Pauline gave her birth date as June 10, 1833, the time of the river town's booming cotton prosperity. Her mother was the child of a winegrower of Bordeaux, her father a Madrid merchant; the parents had eloped to Louisiana. Both the girl's names, Pauline and Cushman, were chosen for the stage. Her original name was Harriet Wood.

Pauline claimed that her childhood was troubled. Her father had a harsh temper, her mother a placid sadness. Mr. Wood, who had Anglicized his name, succeeded for a decade or so in

New Orleans as a merchant in the thriving French section. There were other children, all boys, and they lived in a house on a crowded thoroughfare, with Creole markets and theaters at their elbow, and the teeming Mississippi wharves a few squares off.

Then the girl's father lost his money in speculation, and the family rode upriver toward a far less glamorous spot, Grand Rapids, Michigan. The settlement was then known less for furniture than for Indian trade, and Mr. Wood started again in that field. Pauline had young Indians as friends, and learned to ride, paddle a canoe, and make her way like an Indian scout through wood and swamp.

Though she would eventually be presented to her public as a thoroughgoing siren, Pauline grew up as a tomboy. She enjoyed hunting and shooting. One gushing biographer declared: "She could converse upon all manly sports and habits with the ease and polish of a high-born gentleman," and she had "the dash and daring of a headlong, headstrong boy." When she reached her teens, however, Pauline suddenly blossomed into a *femme fatale*.

The girl had long hair with a blue-black sheen, which she let hang straight, regardless of the current fashion. Her lips were wide and full, her nose firmly carved, with a piquant tip. Before long the Indian youths were yearning after her. She said they gave her a special name, "Laughing Breeze." One in particular wooed her, but Laughing Breeze had her bright black eyes on other things, among them a career in New York.

There was trouble between her parents, and Pauline, who had "a volatile and susceptible nature," did not stay out of the family quarrel. She differed violently with one of her brothers, and they were never reconciled. In any case, Pauline wanted change and adventure, which she loved "with an intensity that bore down every other feeling." Having heard of the cafés and theaters of the East, she took the road that led to them.

When she arrived in New York, with only a few dollars, she went directly to the stage managers.

This novice could not claim any theater background nor any training, but she had something more important, her personality and her high spirits. Manager Thomas Placide of the famed New Orleans Varieties suggested a season in her old home town, and Pauline followed him there. Others besides Mr. Placide promptly noticed her special qualifications.

According to one newspaper description: "Her form is perfect—so perfect that the sculptor's imagination would fail to add a single point, or banish a single blemish. Her arm is equally beautiful, resembling in mold the marble efforts seen in the great art galleries of Europe." Before long the Creole town was doing its own excited cataloguing of Pauline's attractions. She worked for Placide when she was nineteen or twenty, and photographs confirm some of the descriptions. Posing in a loose shawl, Miss Cushman displayed dimpled shoulders over which, it is said, the city went wild. It is reported that one man, beholding her, "seemed to lose all restraint over himself."

From New Orleans, Pauline went to other towns where she was almost equally successful. Her biographer expressed the conviction that she would have made a fine "pirate's bride," a woman of fire for a man of fire. Pauline thought otherwise; she became the wife of an actor.

The official account omits entirely her marriage to Charles Dickinson, a fellow player who doubled in the orchestra. As they played the circuit, the actress lost the last of any strong Southern identification that she might have had. She kept her New Orleans look, her soft Creole voice, and that was all. Neither Dickinson nor his wife were stars, but Pauline always possessed what might be more important than technique, "a direct communication between her fair self and the audience." She went on communicating for years.

The Dickinsons had two children; both died early, within a

day of each other. At the beginning of the war, Pauline's husband became a musician with the Union Army. Not many months later he succumbed to "camp fever" and died after a short illness. His widow carried on, and in March of 1863 she appeared in popular John E. McDonogh's production of *The Seven Sisters* at Wood's in Louisville. Kentucky continued in the Union ranks, but the city had a large, intense, and resourceful Confederate population.

One day Pauline received a call from two paroled Southern officers, "whom she had, apart from all political considerations, admitted to a certain degree of friendship." They reminded her of a skit in which she played a man about town; tonight they wanted her to surprise everybody at that point with a rousing Southern toast. In effect, they dared her to do it.

"I'd be locked up," Pauline protested. But she was curious to hear what purpose they had in mind.

"They'd never lock up so charming a lady," they insisted. "Do it, and we'll give you three thousand dollars–Union money."

"Let me think it over." Pauline's Union sympathy was aroused, and quietly she went to Colonel Moore, the Federal provost marshal. After he heard the story he looked seriously at her. "I advise you to drink the toast. I'll be there when you do." The marshal immediately made plans to attend the performance with several aides and let Pauline flush out coveys of Confederacy-lovers.

That night Pauline provoked her riot. An hour later, as the marshal had forewarned her, the manager fired her. For good effect, Federal guards arrived at the theater to arrest her and a crowd gathered. Defiantly she offered a repeat performance, her chin lifted in scorn. Back at the marshal's headquarters, however, she was cautioned. Her reputation as a "Southern sympathizer" had been well established, and she must not overdo the act. She should talk "only moderately secesh," as if she had been reprimanded.

Pauline agreed; she was in the service now. Again the marshal proved a good prophet. Southern friends materialized from everywhere, sending messages to her boardinghouse, stopping her on the street. She began by doing what was, in effect, counterespionage. She drew up lists of secret enemies of the North and gathered information about shipments of supplies and operations of guerrilla bands in the vicinity. She learned a good deal about the best Southern spies and the way they worked.

Occasionally, she said, she rode out into the country for especially secret meetings and on spy errands in neighboring areas. She discovered how Confederate sympathizers sent letters across the lines by folding them lengthwise and stuffing them into the craw of a chicken carried by an innocent-looking farm wife. She also reported that some Southern dispatches were pushed inside the handles of farmers' butter knives.

Miss Cushman made use of her acting skill. Though she was as emphatically feminine as anyone on either side of Mason's and Dixon's line, we are assured that she masqueraded as a man —a clumsy country boy, a dandy, a gruff farmer.

After her introduction to spying in Louisville, a wider field opened. The manager of a Nashville theater sought her out. Although her last employer said that Pauline was "a good-looking woman and an accomplished actress, but she *will* talk secesh," the Nashville man offered her a job, and the Union provost marshal approved of her accepting it. Nashville was also in Federal hands, but it lay "pretty close to rebeldom," and was the heart of Southwestern army operations.

Pauline's arrival at Nashville City Hotel was something of a civic event. Opening in *The Married Rake*, La Cushman was the town's delight. She spied again, as much as ever, but the Confederates considered her their own and Federal soldiers "could not help admiring so magnificent a specimen of a woman—rebel or not."

One day she received a summons from Colonel William Truesdail, head of the police system of the Army of the Cumberland. One of the Union's canniest field detectives, Truesdail managed a large network of scouts and couriers. For months, however, the South had been infiltrating positions along rivers and at railroad terminals. The Confederates kept a sharp watch on all known Northern agents. Truesdail told Pauline he had a difficult assignment for her—to visit the camps of General Bragg's forces.

She was rather alarmed, for Bragg was one of the most spy-conscious generals of the war. Nevertheless, Truesdail had made careful plans. Pauline's beauty and her now pro-Confederate reputation gave her opportunities open to none of the others on his staff. She would go to each settlement or camp, request an interview with the general, and in leaving, ask for a "kind letter" to the next commander. Pauline remembered her estranged brother, now somewhere in the Southern Army, and Truesdail was delighted. That gave her a fine peg on which to hang a story.

The actress was given full stage directions. She would have "many attentions" from military men; whenever possible she should ride about the fortifications with them. First, however, let her hesitate, with "*seeming caution* as to the propriety of such excursions," then let herself be talked into it. She was never to make direct inquiry about military details, but look well at everything. She must also ask with great sympathy to visit the sick and the wounded. At the hospitals she could inquire innocently whether they had medicines and where these supplies came from. She must remember everything without making a single memorandum or tracing! She was especially warned against anything of this sort.

Thus coached, Pauline prepared for "public expulsion" to

the South. Late in May of 1863 the Union removed many women who were Confederate sympathizers, and she received star billing among them. Three miles out of Nashville, an attendant waited for her with a fine bay and also a "friend in need," a six-shooter. She was on her own, and she would have all the adventure she could use. Riding steadily through "neutral-ground" territory, the actress threaded dangerous bogs and skirted swollen creeks until she halted before a rickety gray cabin on the bank of the Big Harpeth River.

Pauline gazed into the shifty eyes of an unshaven individual who chewed tobacco and listened without comment to her graphic story of Yankee mistreatment. If only she could get through to Dixie, she said in a yearning voice. . . . The man relaxed. In Nashville he had the reputation of a Unionist, and had taken the loyalty oath; now he told her of his extensive smuggling operations. Yes, he operated in the Southern trade, running the lines with muslins, sugar, muskets, and people as well.

He had a partner, ma'am, and if she paid proper, they'd get her through in a buggy. "Paying proper," she also gave up her bay for a hundred Confederate dollars. The trip was a wretched and risky one, yet she survived; her Indian friends had taught her something after all. The smuggler's partner took her to Columbia, Tennessee, and introduced her to a friend, a major, who in turn introduced her to a captain. Establishing herself at a hotel, Pauline used a bit of her old method of "direct communication."

Surveying the field, Pauline picked the candidate most likely to help her in her work, a certain Captain Blackman. This natty individual was a quartermaster, just back from the vital Confederate bastion at Vicksburg, and he had dozens of friends in Columbia. The actress' charming naïveté about cannons and such mysteries intrigued Blackman, and he lectured her in some detail.

Pauline concluded this pleasant instruction by announcing she must go on to the next military point, Shelbyville, in search of her lost brother. The sympathetic captain offered a "letter of safeguard," recommending her to the protection of all good Southerners. On leaving, she gave Blackman her solemn promise that she would surely return to see him. So far, so good!

In Shelbyville's best hotel the spy played the game primly at first, while she sized up the situation. Pauline saw scores of Confederates. Obviously they saw her, too, but she contented herself with sitting quietly at the dinner table listening to the conversation. She noticed a tight-lipped young engineer captain who was also a guest, and found out that he was working day and night to finish important new fortifications in the area.

Her interest in the captain increased rapidly. Here was a man dedicated to his labors. He paid no attention to the arresting female only a few feet away from him, never suspecting that he had become her target. First Pauline presented her "letter of safeguard," and the captain grew slightly less indifferent. Soon he smiled and, even as had the New Orleans admirers, seemed to begin a mental inventory of her charms. He would be happy, ma'am, to give her his own letter, to General Bragg himself.

This engineer captain certainly had the right friends! As they talked he was called to his office upstairs and he regretfully gave up La Cushman for blueprints. . . . Very soon he heard a tap at the door. Pauline stood there, all blushes and apologies. She had to leave earlier than she had intended; could he let her have the letter to General Bragg?

"So you're leaving us so soon?" he asked, and we are told that his once indifferent eyes "rested admiringly on her beautiful figure." Pauline nodded, but then, demurely, as in the case of her quartermaster friend pledged herself to come back. The engineer said he would have to go to his desk downstairs to write the note, and when he had left Pauline tiptoed to a table covered with drawings. The chance was altogether too good to pass up; picking up what looked most interesting, she slipped the papers into her dress.

In the morning Pauline went off serenely. For the first time she had ignored her superior's clear instructions: no papers, no notes. . . . At her next stops, although she missed General Bragg, she met many other officers who helped in their own fashion, taking her over the fortifications, explaining about depots, medical supplies, and gun emplacements. One step in the direction of note taking led to another. Pauline was learning so much she felt she had to be certain of her information by putting it on paper. Nobody would catch *her;* she had thought of a perfect hiding place. She chose a spot that would have occurred to any tyro, the lining between the inner and outer cork soles of her extra shoes.

Back at Columbia, Pauline reworked the field there. Blackman, the receptive quartermaster from Vicksburg, beamed at the sight of her. So she *had* returned. . . . "Venus, alone, conquered Mars," her biographer puts it, cryptically. Captain Blackman had a "whim" to take her on long country rides about the fast-filling camps in the vicinity; La Cushman was willing.

Our heroine, we are informed, withstood "with casings of steel, the temptations of the camp." Blackman came up with an unusual suggestion: Why didn't Pauline put on men's clothes and join the army as his aide-de-camp? Smiling, she agreed, in her words, to "don the unmentionables" in the near future. In delighted anticipation, the quartermaster had a complete gray uniform tailored for her. For Blackman, it is apparent, the war took on a sudden new interest; who else would have a lieutenant to compare with his?

The time had now arrived for Pauline to go back to Nashville. She located the smuggler who had brought her over from "neutral ground." Stuffing the Confederate uniform in her satchel, she set out again in the buggy, only to collide sharply with a few facts of life in espionage.

The two smugglers had been willing to escort her into Southern territory, but to set her back in the Union area, that was a far different matter. This gallivanting lady now knew a great deal about their tricky operations; if she told any of it, they might be lucky if they merely fetched up in jail.

Although they did take her back, at the cabin on the Big Harpeth Pauline sensed their hostility. If only she could get a horse and gallop away . . . Suddenly in walked a Confederate scout, who demanded her pass. Didn't she know General Bragg insisted that nobody could leave his lines without one? The smugglers had sold her out. As she was led off, Pauline could not even reach for her satchel, which contained the shoes with her precious papers in the soles. She grimly determined to get it back, somehow.

On a borrowed horse the Confederate led her through the woods, riding carelessly ahead of her. Like a number of other men, the scout underestimated Miss Cushman's potentialities. Her hand touched the gun in her pocket, the "friend in need" presented to her by her Union employer. One shot and she could race to safety. . . . She could not pull the trigger.

At scout quarters at Anderson's Mills Pauline spent a number of nervous hours. Higher authorities had to be asked what to do with her, and while she waited she made note of one Southern agent after another, bearded men in hunting dress, smooth-shaven youths in overalls, deserters, bushwhackers, men of a dozen types.

Then she found herself in the charge of a light-haired, smiling man—the celebrated John Hunt Morgan, Southern partisan fighter. Morgan liked what he saw; so, evidently, did Pauline. He introduced himself with a low bow. Could he be her new guide?

"Not guide, jailer," Pauline corrected him, flashing him a

bright smile. "I have no objection to my new jailer." Taking her hand, Morgan drew her to the crude dinner table, and from that time on she found him "the tenderest of captors . . . gallant and even elegant . . . though dealing once in a while in a little sentiment, as charming a companion as one could wish." He called her Pauline, Pauline called him Johnny, and together they rode on to the next camp.

At Hillsboro the idyll ended, for the war's more prosaic demands made the chivalrous Johnny turn her over to another scout. Again Miss Cushman swore that she would meet her admirer before too long. Taken to a farmer's house, she found luck temporarily with her again. A report arrived that Yankees were racing toward the spot, and Pauline's captors ran away. This time she was able to snatch the reins of a waiting horse and start toward the Union lines.

She had to pass six pickets. The spy had learned the password and she used it successfully, for each picket was young and impressionable. Pauline of the New Orleans Varieties had no trouble with any of them—until she drew up before the last. He proved to be old and, worse than that, conscientious. Pauline cried, touched his arm, pressed his hand; he remained adamant. Ma'am, you *got* to have a signed pass.

The Confederates caught her. Pauline learned that they regarded her as a war prize, definitely as an enemy agent, and with apprehension she heard one officer exclaim: "Damn her, she could be as beautiful as Venus, but I'd hang her on the highest tree." She felt even more concerned when the scouts brought her before fierce-tempered General Nathan Bedford Forrest, who gave her a hostile smile: "Miss Cushman, I'm glad to see you. You're pretty sharp at turning a card, but I think we've got you on this last shuffle."

Pauline would now have a chance to meet the Confederate officer whom she had tried vainly to find, General Bragg. Forrest ordered her taken to Bragg himself, now quartered at Shelbyville. It was the town in which she had recently romanced with the overobliging quartermaster. She could hardly triumph this time. The actress sat tensely before the small, bronzed general, a man with iron-gray hair and iron-gray enmity in his eye. Pauline had no hope of "direct communication" with him.

Bragg and his provost marshal put dozens of questions to her. If she were really pro-Confederate, why hadn't she brought in quinine and other supplies from Nashville? Yes, she "let on secesh," yet could she offer a single proof of Southernism? Pauline assumed the role of injured sincerity, of the woman who had suffered and still suffered for her side.

Her pulse jumped when a guard carried in her satchel. She was asked why she had carried a Confederate uniform. Wouldn't that make an excellent disguise for a Union spy? Pauline had not used it, of course, if only because she lacked the time. She did not need to play innocent in this instance, so she told the simple truth about the quartermaster and his plan to use her as his aide-de-camp. Look–she reached into her pocket–she had a letter from him to prove it. At this point the Southern officers acted in a way she had not quite expected. They arrested her admirer!

Bragg's provost marshal produced several papers–removed from the hiding place in Pauline's shoes. As she realized that they were the only tangible evidence against her, she wished heartily that she had followed instructions.

For days Pauline had gone with little or no sleep. In the woods she had suffered from exposure and tension. All at once she became so ill that she could not leave her bed. On top of that, she received the news that she would have a military trial. The June heat was savage in the town of Shelbyville; she was weak and her moods ran the gamut from hope to despair.

The Southerners had her taken to a private home, and, as on so many other occasions, Pauline enlisted a sympathizer, an army captain named Pedden. He was twenty-seven, blond, and "good-looking, which is no small consideration with a lady." The captain knew that his predecessor, the quartermaster, sweated in jail for his love of the actress. Still, Pedden called daily, then twice a day, paying her "a thousand delicate little attentions."

The trial took place and Pauline awaited the verdict in desperate fear. She was found guilty and the news was brought to her sick room. She buried her head in the pillow.

By now she had only one comforter, the captain, who found Pauline his kind of woman, enemy agent or no. From him she heard the first faint rumors that Union General Rosecrans had launched a drive on Shelbyville. History tells of many spies, due to be killed, who were rescued by the advance of their own military forces. Would she have such luck?

As Pauline tried to reassure herself, her captain came in to report that the alarmed Confederates were quitting the town and would leave her behind. He promised that he would look for her after the war. The actress made still another of her future dates, they kissed, and she fell back on her pillow. . . . A day or so later the Federal troops marched in and Pauline, wrapped in a blanket, stood happily on the balcony to greet them.

The incoming Union soldiers, learning of her role as a spy, made a great fuss over her, with flowers, candies, toasts. But Pauline had been too close to death to recover quickly; she said she "dreamed of gibbets," with rebel guards lined up at her side. After turning over all the information she had, Pauline whispered that she wanted only one thing—to get deep inside the Federal lines. On a rainy day in June of 1863 an ambulance arrived to take her to Nashville. Two generals carried her down from her room in a chair, while a major held an umbrella over her head!

In Nashville she still suffered spells of tears and depression, and Washington records confirm the fact that grateful Union officials paid for her convalescent care. General Rosecrans and other Union officers came to see her and as a "testimonial of appreciation" she was declared a major of cavalry. Union women presented her with a shining blue riding habit, "with dainty shoulder straps." From then on, Pauline wished to be called "the major," and sometimes she was saluted as "Miss Major Cushman."

Her spying days were over. Everybody, including Mathew Brady, took her picture; there could be no secret activities for a woman stopped on the street by autograph seekers. La Cushman went back to the stage as a monologist. She was wildly applauded in Boston and other cities before the war ended, and afterward in New York, San Francisco, and Western towns, which appreciated a woman of Pauline's explosive quality. In her military garb the "major" told all about her exploits and, perhaps, about a few of her military romances.

Yet Pauline married none of the captains, generals, or privates whom she had pledged herself to meet again. It might have been better had she done so. Pauline fell in love again and again, often unwisely, always with zest. She toured America as a lady who gave a dramatic if uneven performance off stage as well as on, swirling through hotel lobbies in trailing velvet, riding in an open carriage with armfuls of roses, slapping an occasional manager's face, doing everything in the grand style.

For years her slumberous Creole look, the suggestion of the South and of France that remained in her voice continued to stir male pulses. Eventually her beauty faded and people got tired of her story, but in the end the Grand Army of the Republic did not desert her. It gave Pauline Cushman a military funeral with a big white coffin and thousands of white flowers around it. She went to her grave with flags, an honor guard, and rifle fire splitting the December air.

Chapter 9

Tightrope Walker

Six generals paid Philip Henson of Mississippi to act as their spy, and he provided information for each of them. This fact might indicate only that Phil was a most energetic fellow—except that four of the generals were Confederates and two Federals, and he served them all.

Like Timothy Webster, though on a far bolder scale, "Colonel" Henson was that rarity in America, the spy who played both sides. He followed a twisting course that doubled back on itself and then doubled again; many mystified observers never decided which side he favored, North or South. A Confederate officer would help him over the lines as his man; a Yankee commander would send him back as *his!*

Phil Henson was "a Southern man, born in the South, reared in the South, married in the South," with his ties and interests there. But always, he said, in his conscience he favored the Union, hated secession and whatever went with it. In his secret service work he insisted that he really favored the North. He admitted that he gave data to some of the Confederates, which might possibly have assisted them on occasion. Yet his employers in the North knew that Phil withheld the truly important material and poured into Union ears everything he could learn about the rebels.

His unquestionably was a tightrope performance; one slight

error, and Philip Henson would be destroyed. Ranking officers of both sides swore to kill him if they set hands on him, and one exasperated Confederate called him "the most dangerous man in the Confederacy." In spite of everything, a few friends regarded the colonel as a true Southerner at heart, a maligned man; and after the war he continued to live among his former neighbors.

Sympathizers have pictured Phil as "a talented eccentric," "one in ten thousand"; the descriptions are understatement. He went so calmly about his spying that his exact role was unknown to most of his relatives, his brother-in-law, even his wife. Mrs. Henson realized he had something to do with the war, but in which way she could not be sure. . . . He assures us she did not discover the truth until close to the end of hostilities. That might be considered Mr. Henson's greatest accomplishment.

Devious though he was at times, Philip Henson has contributed what seems to be the most candid of war narratives, in which he tells with easy matter-of-factness about all, or nearly all, the tricks of his trade, and concedes acts of bribery and deception of which men seldom boast.

His earlier life had taught him how to protect himself. Born in 1827 in what was then Indian territory, later northeast Alabama, Phil had grown up among the red men. His father, well liked by the Indians, became one of the commissioners in their removal to the West. The boy's only education was had at the Indian mission school. Like Pauline Cushman, Phil recalled long rides through the woods and vigorous training in hunting.

At that time the boy mastered an art that would mean a great deal to him, as it did to other spies—that of swift, silent movement. He acquired a remarkable hardihood. Never bookish, he had a memory that friends thought phenomenal; he seldom forgot names, facts, or figures. When Phil was twelve his father died, leaving seven children, and from then on young Henson made his own way. He cut pine knots for a quarter a day, carried mail through potentially hostile Indian country, led herds of cattle over difficult trails.

At twenty-five, in 1852, Phil had a taste of future strife when he went to Kansas, the territory so tragically divided on the slavery question, and met John Brown himself. Later he ranged about the uncharted West and Southwest, learning primarily how to remain alive and intact. From Kansas and New Mexico he returned to roam Alabama, Georgia, and other parts of the South, and finally settled down in northern Mississippi to a dull job in a country store in the town of Rienzi.

At maturity Phil stood six feet two inches tall, a wiry, muscular man of great endurance. He was taciturn, with a deceptive slowness of speech and action. Nobody who looked like that could be a dangerous fellow, some people said, but anyone who took advantage of Henson quickly learned otherwise. With thick, slightly wavy hair growing long and close about his cheeks and forehead, he had the appearance of almost any rural Southerner. That "average" air would, of course, be a tremendous asset in espionage.

In early 1861, as war approached, thirty-four-year-old Phil picked a bride, and he recounts with an engaging frankness how he eluded conscription. When one of his brothers joined the Confederacy, Phil decided he could not follow him. Southern regulations allowed a slave overseer to be exempt from war service, so Henson asked a friendly plantation owner to hire him. For a time he stayed put and watched the war from a distance; then the Confederates fell back, and General Grant pushed into Mississippi.

Many of his neighbors took the Union oath for simple protection, but Phil Henson took it "because I believed in it." Before long he met Union General Rosecrans and a man we have already encountered, detective chief Truesdail. Phil agreed to help them buy cotton supplies, as part of the Northern war effort on Southern soil. After Truesdail saw how shrewdly and silently Henson performed, he asked him to try a stint of spying.

Phil agreed. When Truesdail said he wished to "discover the plans" of Confederate General Price, the Mississippian knew just what to do. He simply rode over to the Southern lines, chatted with the sentries, and went on through; then he walked up to Price's headquarters and hung about until the army marched. A bit later he rode back the same way, waved good-by to the sentries, and soon was telling the Union officer all he wanted to know. Truesdail, as pleased as he was surprised, urged him to continue.

Henson informs us in a curious passage in his memoirs how he "laid down a principle." For his own safety and usefulness, he decided he must "always tell the truth; in this respect he treated rebels and Union men alike"! He would reveal as little as possible to the Southerners, but he would never twist a fact. By this means he gained the confidence of his real employers as well as of "his rebel friends," whom he fooled in the Union's behalf. "It was the secret of his prolonged success."

Phil had several other secret assets. With his phenomenal memory he "never made a note," avoiding the trouble that Pauline Cushman and others made for themselves. He concentrated on speed, using up two or three horses on a single trip. He carried a hidden weapon, a bottle of "good old rye," and many Confederates felt that no one so honorably equipped could be a Yankee.

Perhaps his greatest advantage, however, was his friendliness. The way to get along best in the world, Henson thought, was to do favors for people, weaving a network of grateful recipients. He was no mere dispenser of smiles and vague kindliness. With sharp practicality he arranged a loan for one person; for another he provided a load of bricks; for a third he spoke a good word to the sheriff. It was the Henson Friendship Plan, a system of services that returned services.

In October of 1862 Confederate General Bragg was moving toward Murfreesboro, Tennessee, and the Northern forces wanted to learn about his plans. Henson thought he had friends right about there, and the route lay directly through his native section of Alabama. He was off. For three days he rode steadily, along river valleys, over hills, and down narrow roadways overhung by vines and trees.

At Sheffield, Alabama, he collided with the outposts of Southern General P. D. Roddy, a cavalryman who squinted his eyes at Henson and clearly disapproved of him at first look. Put under guard, Phil fumed, and then asked a few questions about the camp: who was there now, whose names did the guard know? At once the Friendship Plan proved its worth: he located no less than six men, one a colonel, another a captain, who spoke to the general in his behalf, respectfully yet firmly. Old Phil was a fine Confederate; they'd swear it, sir! They'd as soon believe treachery of their own fathers.

General Roddy's face indicated that he still had a doubt or two about this angular character, but Old Phil rode away again. Near his former Alabama home he renewed acquaintances, talked like a firm Confederate, and received some valuable information. Soon afterward he met advance guards of Bragg's army in Tennessee. Phil had heard that his own Confederate brother served somewhere under Bragg. Like Miss Cushman, he had a good family reason for his presence in the neighborhood.

Between inquiries about the brother, Phil learned all he needed to fulfill his mission and start home. At that point he again fell into the hands of his nemesis, General Roddy. The scowling officer was again displeased by the sight of him and asked why the devil Henson wasn't in the Confederate Army? Phil was glad the general had brought that up. You see, he said, his home at little Rienzi lay inside Yankee territory, and he first had to get his family out, because the Yanks were "the meanest, worst people on earth." That was the very reason he had just been in north Alabama, to arrange to take them back there, among real Southerners!

General Roddy pursed his lips. Well, Henson could go along, on condition that he soon joined the Confederate Army. With this proposition, Phil earnestly agreed; why, he'd come right into Roddy's own cavalry, he promised. The relieved spy spurred his horse homeward, but five or six hours later he was snagged a third time, by pickets for his own side, the Union.

Once again Henson had to argue his way out of a spot. Demanding that he be taken to the nearest headquarters, he succeeded in identifying himself, and passed on his information. For the first time Phil met the man with whom he was to be deeply involved in the future, Union General Grenville Dodge. Though the world would remember Dodge mainly as the builder of the Union Pacific Railroad, he served the North as a resourceful secret service chief. Dodge knew a good agent when he saw one; he took on Phil for greatly extended spying activities.

Two armies faced each other in Mississippi late in 1862, maneuvering for position—the North at Corinth, the South at Columbus. When a rumor came to Dodge that the Confederates were mounting a powerful attack, he asked Henson to get to Columbus at the first possible moment. The agent made good time, and reached the Southern command in a far more direct way than he or Dodge had anticipated. At a turn in the road six cavalrymen in gray surrounded him.

"Just come along. . . ." They waved aside his explanations and took him into headquarters. Nor did Confederate General Ruggles have much to say when Henson stood before him; he simply glared, silent, unfriendly. Phil went to work. He mentioned as friends a dozen Southern names and he let the general understand how he regarded the dastardly Yankees. He threw in several interesting (and also accurate) facts that he had observed about the Northern forces.

General Ruggles listened with growing attentiveness, then motioned Phil to a seat. He asked his own questions and nodded at the answers. After a time he not only released the spy, but arranged for Phil to be *his* scout, at once and for pay! Ruggles had a task for Henson—to get inside the Federal lines and gather information for the South.

That was precisely where Phil hoped to go, to report what he had learned about the Confederate position. Within a few days he sat with his Union boss, Dodge; a week after that he made his way once again to the Confederate Ruggles. . . . Such was his pattern of operation during the next eighteen months. Somewhere along the line he assumed the title of colonel, and kept it for the rest of his life.

Phil's method was suddenly put to severe test. The Confederates held the almost impregnable town of Vicksburg on the Mississippi. Dodge's secret service needed definite information about the defenses, and the general turned to Colonel Henson. "It may be a delicate piece of work," was the spy's opinion, but again, when he consulted his mental file of friends, he thought he had a solution.

Nobody could be more ardently Confederate than Jesse Johnsey, a man with seven sons in Southern armies, including several around Vicksburg. Phil asked Jesse if he wouldn't like to see his boys? He could ride Phil's extra horse, and they could go over to Vicksburg together. Gladly the neighbor accepted the invitation. The two men met dozens of pickets and guards on the way. "Goin' to see our boys in Vicksburg," they explained, and the words opened all roads.

Phil had managed to extend his friendship program in a highly unorthodox fashion. Most spies automatically tried to get the best of an enemy agent when they met. But if Phil bumped into a Confederate scout, he generally did a favor for him—not a large one, perhaps, yet a favor. Why draw the line against the enemy, especially if the enemy thought you were with *him?* And so, on the way to Vicksburg, Henson and his friend stayed several times at the homes of Southern scouts whose families had heard of Phil's kindnesses to their boys. In time it appeared that half the South felt under obligation to the colonel!

Reaching Vicksburg, the men asked to meet General Pemberton. That officer seemed merely polite, but a Captain Murphy stepped forward with a warm smile, a firm recommendation, and Pemberton unbent for a long chat. When Phil tapped his usual stock in conversational trade, the harsh treatment of Southerners in Yankee-held territory, Pemberton had an inspiration: why didn't Colonel Henson go right out and tell his soldiers all about it? It would spur their resolution and help them to realize what they were fighting for.

The colonel was pleased to oblige. He walked unhampered over every part of the Vicksburg fortifications, talking and looking. Whenever Henson needed some explanation of the defenses, his fine friend Murphy was there to give it. Phil went home more than satisfied. His Union superior demonstrated his own satisfaction with a gift, a superb horse named Black Hawk. Henson continued to lope about the Southern camps and before long established firm "understandings" with two more generals, Gholson and Ferguson. Like Ruggles, they unknowingly provided him with information which he took to the Union side at the same time that they paid him for supposedly spying on the North.

Nevertheless, Phil admits that he did one quite definite service for a Confederate general, whose wife yearned for hats, gloves, and other luxuries obtainable only in the North. Colonel Henson's Yankee employers provided an expense account for the purpose, and the Southern lady's costume proved to be a good Union investment.

Phil traveled with convincing credentials, a variety of passes that identified him as an agent for both sides. If a Southerner saw the pass signed by General Dodge, it could be his death warrant; Phil hid it by unscrewing the brass section of his revolver handle, cutting out a tiny rectangle of wood to hold the wadded paper and screwing back the brass plate.

On another trip to the Southern territory Phil took with him a bright-eyed Confederate blockade runner who considered it fine fun to ride beside "a real spy for the South." At or near Okolona, Mississippi, Henson expected to meet his trusting friend, General Ruggles. At that time, however, the Confederates of Mississippi had become alarmed at the prospect of an immediate Federal drive, and their forces were shifted. Arriving at Okolona, Phil collided with a newcomer, a red-haired provost marshal who "thought he owned the Southern Confederacy." Strutting like a "turkey-gobbler," said Henson, the fellow swept aside the fine-looking passes and arrested him.

Phil's companion, the young blockade runner, heard the marshal's murmur that Henson was a Yankee spy; he knew it! Obviously the Southerner had found some damaging information, and Phil told himself he must act quickly. A break for liberty? The guard looked entirely too alert. One way remained —cash, and the ever practical Henson was ready to use it.

Fortunately the Confederate guard proved corruptible. For a hundred dollars in Southern currency he went quietly to sleep, and Phil stepped over his prone figure and escaped on Black Hawk. . . . It was simple, but he marked Okolona as a danger spot to be by-passed in the future.

By the end of 1863 the Southern military situation had deteriorated badly. Union General Dodge moved into Alabama, and Henson felt it wise to "report" for a time to one of his Confederate employers, the friendly Mississippian, General

Gholson. Dog-tired after a long jaunt, the agent received permission to spend the night on a cot at the back of the general's tent. Under any circumstances it would have been a vantage point; tonight it became the place of all places for a spy.

Worn out as he was, Phil quickly realized that something vital was afoot. One man after another arrived for long talks with General Gholson; they were his military scouts, and they had a great deal to say. Making a show of steady snoring, Henson missed few of the important details—the shifting of troops, the placement of emergency bridges, the movement of ammunition and supplies. A few hours later even the taciturn Phil had trouble in remaining calm when a dispatch arrived from General Nathan Bedford Forrest: General Gholson was to send all his men to West Point, Mississippi, for a major action.

This was truly news for the North, and in the dark Phil puzzled how to get it quickly to the other side. He didn't get much sleep that night. In the morning Gholson had his own instructions for Colonel Henson—to make a trip behind Northern lines. The colonel accepted the new assignment bravely, and they parted as friendly as ever.

It was a harder task, however, than either man realized. For two days the Confederate passes helped Henson make his way to the Tennessee River opposite Florence, Alabama, where he discovered that every boat along the bank had been destroyed. To get across he had to follow the stream far up its course. With each mile Phil felt more desperately anxious. A ten-strike such as he had just made, and now this frustration!

He was gloomy when he reached Guntersville. Suddenly he thought of somebody who could help—his own brother-in-law, Yancey Nobles, who believed Henson to be a Southern agent. Racing to the Nobles home, Phil dispensed with family greetings and described his problem, though not quite accurately: it would help the South if Yancey could get him across the river.

Yancey was sympathetic but nervous. He mentioned some lawless guerrillas who dominated the area. If any of that crew saw Phil trying to cross the river, they'd shoot him first and then ask who he was later. Still, there might be one safe stretch. Dropping his work, Yancey guided Phil over the mountains on a rainy, thirty-mile trip to an overgrown spot on the river. On the opposite bank stood a Federal camp.

They located the owner of a canoe who had a young Negro helper. The boy said he would row Henson over for a hundred dollars, but the canoe owner was pessimistic: "Man, even if you do make it, those Yanks'll grab you, and you'll be gone." Soberly Phil said he'd take the chance. Then the man pointed toward the river: look, the rain was coming down harder and the water was already mighty high; the strong current, carrying trees and logs, could capsize them in a minute. "I'll take that chance, too," Phil shrugged. "I've just got to do it."

The trip was decidedly nerve-racking. Several times big logs hit them, swinging the canoe in a circle, half filling it with water, and the current swept them three miles downstream. Bedraggled, muddy, they finally touched the other bank, and Phil scrambled up and accosted Union pickets. Just as the owner of the canoe had predicted, the Yankees arrested him at once.

Henson informed his captors that he had to see the nearest commander. They took him to General Logan at Huntsville, to whom he hurriedly told everything he knew, and he knew a great deal that was important to the North. Among other things, he said he had learned that General Sherman was at that moment falling back to Vicksburg.

To his astonishment the Union general jumped up, shouting: "Now you're lying, and you're nothing but a rebel spy! Trying to tell me a thing like that. . . ." He tossed over the latest Union papers, which announced that Sherman had gone in the opposite direction. The general would hear no more, nothing at all;

summoning a guard, he ordered Henson put into close confinement. Dirty and hungry, Phil spent a miserable night, reflecting on the sad and uncertain lot of men in espionage.

The following morning he was brought again before the general, who greeted him with a sheepish smile. He was sorry, very sorry. A batch of newspapers had just arrived, and he realized that Colonel Henson had told the full truth.

Phil now had one urgent request: to go to see his old Union employer, General Dodge, who was stationed nearby. Under cavalry escort, he was taken to Athens, Alabama, where the general greeted Phil warmly and took down all the facts that Henson unloaded. Then at last Phil could have the bath he needed so badly.

Even for the adroit spy, a baffling problem remained: what to do about General Gholson, who had sent him toward Federal territory to make a report for the Confederacy? Henson decided to cross that bridge when he came to it.

Meanwhile, he had a reward, for his next assignment was the hardest that he had ever been given. Dodge proposed a long survey of the whole Southern army in the region. Most spying jaunts lasted a few days; this was to take thirty-one. For the first time, General Dodge showed the extent of his confidence in Phil. "Henson," he said, "go to my desk and take whatever you think will help you most with the rebs."

The agent selected several timetables of military projects. They looked impressive, but their value was apparently less than it seemed, and Dodge approved their removal. The general promised that if this feat succeeded, Phil would get a good, long rest.

On March 9, 1864, Henson headed toward an objective that might present enormous difficulties—the headquarters of that tough old warhorse, General Forrest. No suspicious person would ever get past Forrest, people said; the general could scent a Yankee a mile off. Phil would now test Forrest's sense of smell.

On the way he made perilous crossings of swollen rivers, and once his mount threw him and he nearly drowned. The colonel got past pickets by using his several passes, his Southern talk, and, not least, his bottles of rye. But he admitted that the prospect of facing Forrest left him uneasy.

At the Southern camp near Tupelo in North Mississippi, Phil lost his nervousness. He "met a friend," a good-natured captain who would, of course, be glad to vouch for him. Yet the recommendation failed to impress the dark, hard-eyed Confederate general. Forrest asked pointedly: "Just *where* did you come here from?"

Phil had to gamble, say something drastic and dramatic, and so he told the truth. "From Union headquarters—General Dodge's."

"And what were you *doing* there?"

Henson recalled that the gullible Confederate, General Gholson, was quartered somewhere nearby, and, after all, only two weeks or so had passed since Gholson ordered him to go to Union headquarters. . . . "I was sent there by General Gholson, sir. And I'm here to pass on what I found about the Yanks."

Forrest immediately summoned Gholson, who was nearer than Phil realized, and when he arrived Phil had a bad moment. Forrest spoke quickly and to the point, but Gholson merely smiled. "Yes, general, that's true. I sent him for our side. Sure, he's a good Southerner."

Forrest relaxed, but only a bit. Now Phil had to make his "report" to the Confederates, under most difficult conditions. He presented convincing facts, some of which, as he expected, they knew to be accurate. When he handed them the timetables from Dodge's desk, they were more impressed. Then Henson pulled out his full bag of tricks. Leaning forward, he spoke in an especially confidential tone: he had learned that General Dodge had ordered a band of new spies into Confederate Georgia.

"You're certain of that?" Forrest's eyes widened.

"Oh, yes. I can describe every last one."

Now, it was true that Dodge had sent the men to Georgia; Phil neglected to add that all of them had failed in their objective and had already returned to Union lines. Forrest spoke intently: he wished Henson to get right over there and help track down every last Yankee of them! Here, he'd give him a letter to General Polk and sign a sixty-day pass. And one of Forrest's own scouts, the best he had, would accompany Henson.

Calmly the colonel took the papers—treasures of which he could make full use. In Confederate territory anything signed by the mighty Forrest had great value. Still, there would be Forrest's scout, a shrewd observer, at Phil's side. He discovered later that the general had also set a detective to shadow him. Here was a curious situation: a double spy, serving with the North but pretending to be a Southern agent, going about with a real Confederate spy, and trailed by a second. Ultimately the second Confederate told Henson of his assignment, letting Phil understand that he had seen "not one suspicious action" and concluding that he was "all right"!

In mid-March the group set out for General Polk's headquarters in Georgia. On arrival, Phil sat for nearly a whole night with Polk and two of his staff. The Southerners went over papers, took down Henson's information, and set traps for those Union spies. Colonel Phil "had the game in his hands."

Giving him five hundred dollars, General Polk directed him to Atlanta, with a Confederate captain as an assistant. They crept through alleys, inspected hotel registers, visited prisons. They met nobody who looked like a Federal spy, but Henson's diligence impressed his collaborator. When he announced that he wanted to hunt those fellows in other towns, the Southern captain let him go alone. The captain had now been added to the friends of Phil Henson.

With a freer hand, Colonel Henson visited a series of towns on behalf of his real employers, the Northerners. He returned finally to General Polk, who thanked him for his trouble, and now, like other Southern generals, instructed Phil to spy for *him* against the Yankees! He wished the colonel to cross the Federal lines at the first possible moment.

As always, the colonel was glad to oblige. His heart light, he used one of Polk's passes to re-enter Union territory. Dodge made no secret of his delight; Phil had done even better than they had hoped, and he could finally take the long rest he merited. But after only a few days the Union chief asked Henson to make one more trip, positively the last. This time the Union hoped to learn more about General Forrest's plans, and as blithely as ever Phil rode forth—to disaster.

Like an avalanche, Phil Henson's past thundered down upon him. He fell into the hands of the last person he should have met, General Roddy, the bitter Confederate who had mistrusted him from the start. Long ago Phil had promised Roddy he would enter the Southern Army without delay. Where, Roddy shouted, had he been all this time? The general gave him no time to answer; he had had enough of excuses. Throwing Henson into a stockade, Roddy studied the case. Then, because he lacked authority or perhaps evidence, he sent the alarmed Henson to General S. D. Lee at Tuscaloosa, Alabama. In an accompanying letter Roddy called the captive "the worst man in the Confederacy."

At Lee's quarters Henson looked into a circle of faces, every one unfriendly. The staff, West Pointers all, examined him and spoke without hesitation: the general should take no chances; try this man and hang him. Lee hesitated, fearing injustice. He ordered an alert young lawyer, with a reputation in such cases, to interview Phil.

Without a quiver Henson answered each query, clearly, impressively. Even if he were executed, he said with earnest sincerity, he did not mind dying for his beloved South. . . . The lawyer was much moved. Henson, he said, was clearly innocent!

General S. D. Lee announced that he would question Phil himself. On such and such a night, had the prisoner been in a certain Union-held town? Here, once more, was a crisis. Lee knew something, and Phil answered instinctively, "Of course I was, and I can explain why." The story he told sounded very believable.

The general went on: where did the prisoner think Federal forces would strike next? Henson gave him a direct reply, and a truthful one. (It was too late for the Southerners to act on such information, in any case.) A few minutes later a telegram brought news that the Union had struck precisely where Phil had predicted, and Lee was impressed.

Phil sighed in relief; he would not hang, at least for the time being. General Lee would pass him on to General Polk for his superior's decision. At Polk's quarters at Demopolis, Alabama, Phil Henson saw something that made him thoughtful. Polk had just hanged another Union agent, and several soldiers grinned at Phil: "The rope will fit your neck real nice."

Though the prisoner forced a smile, he wondered if his friend Polk would now support him. Polk, it developed, was happy to see his good friend Phil. The whole thing had been a mistake; the general was ready to send him right through the Union lines to take up his spying again for the Confederacy! Polk made out the pass.

Phil still feared the hatred of General Roddy and felt he needed protection from that man. Polk agreed to grant it, forwarding Henson through Roddy's lines with an escort. Yet Phil had been right to fear Roddy's fury. Just as Henson and his escort reached Tupelo, General Forrest also arrived in that town, and one of the first messages he received was a burning wire from Roddy. All of Forrest's own latent hostility came out. As Phil was preparing to leave, one of the general's men arrested him.

Forrest now made good his reputation for firmness. Henson tried to see him, for he must have believed he could talk his way out of this spot as he had all the others. The general absolutely would not receive Philip Henson. For many days, beginning May 20, 1864, Phil stayed under heavy guard. He made an enforced tour of Southern prisons as the Confederates shifted him from place to place. On a trip to Mobile, he learned how deeply some Southerners suspected and hated him.

Manacled by the wrists and ankles, Phil was recognized by a mob, and some of the men tried to drag him off to lynch him. Only the intervention of military authorities saved him. Henson remained in custody while the infuriated crowd shoved him, kicked him, and spat tobacco juice into his face. In other towns men yelled: "Burn him! We know what to do with him!" In Mobile officials observed the Fourth of July by parading the spy through the streets.

Phil spent months in a narrow cell, an unventilated chamber known as "the sweat box," suffering severely in the humid heat of the Gulf area. With some difficulty he obtained a lawyer, who told him that the Confederates doubted the strength of the evidence against him. Though they considered him guilty of spying, he had written no notes, signed no papers. No court-martial was held; his captors continued simply to hold him.

In confinement Henson grew thinner, paler, and his years of exposure had their effect. He developed throbbing pains in his arms and legs, and he asked himself if he could hold out for the rest of the war. In time he was transferred to another prison, in Meridian, Mississippi. In mid-February of 1865 the Confederates came to a decision. In these desperate days, Southern generals cried out for men—men from anywhere, anything that had hands and feet. . . . Forrest remembered Henson and dispatched a message: draft him into the Southern Army; at least they'd get some use out of the fellow!

Phil, his hopes somewhat restored, asked if he could join "the old bloody 26th Mississippi," and his captors granted the request. Neither the blood nor the regiment itself appealed to Phil; he knew only that it had gone to Virginia, and that on the way there he might escape. General Dodge implies in his record that his own Union operatives used bribery to get Henson free. Phil wrote simply that a "kindhearted Colonel" winked when he jumped off the train.

The spy used care in picking the place to jump—a stop on his old friendship route. A former employer lived in Selma, Alabama. The taste of freedom helped the weakened Henson to make his way on foot for nearly twenty miles. The friend welcomed him, and introduced him to his nephew, a wounded Confederate. The nephew had something that Phil needed as much as anything on earth—Southern identification papers. With them he might yet get through the three hundred miles between Selma and the Federal lines. For a thousand dollars in depreciated Confederate money, the nephew gave up the papers.

For days Henson dragged himself on, his pace alarmingly slow. Not only must he fight increasing pain, but he could travel only after dark and by back roads. The exertion weakened him so that he wondered if he could somehow reach the last safe harbor that seemed at hand—his sister's place in Blount, Alabama. Phil's determination won; he staggered into the house and collapsed.

Timothy Webster's old complaint, arthritis, had trapped Henson. For weeks he could not rise from his bed, and he was constantly fearful of the Confederates who were after him. In this emergency he had to give up any claim that he was a Southern agent. Phil told his relatives everything that had happened; they were startled, but they were loyal to him and took extra precautions. . . . Then late one afternoon his sister came to Phil, terrified. Somebody had been talking about his presence in her house. For his own safety Phil had to go, at once!

He could hardly put his feet to the ground, but his relatives found a solution They bundled him up and took him after dark to the nearest river bank. Federal gunboats were expected to pass soon; to avoid suspicion, they had to leave him to reach the gunboat by himself.

All the next day and the next night, with food and water beside him, Henson lay hidden among the rushes. Suppose the Union vessel never arrived? In the middle of the second day he made out a dark shape in the distance. The gunboat drew up, slowly, too slowly. Phil forced himself to the water's edge, waved, shouted, sweated as he struggled to attract the crew's attention, to indicate his plight. If they passed him up, everything would be over . . .

The captain spotted him and sent a boat to pick him up. At long last the spy felt safe again. He wanted most to rejoin General Dodge, and Union officials helped him to get to Chattanooga and then to Dodge's St. Louis headquarters. The general's mouth dropped open in amazement. "Phil," he declared, "the rope hasn't been made yet to hang you!" Weakly, Phil agreed.

At home in Mississippi, Mrs. Henson had been taken into Confederate custody for a time. Receiving no word of Phil, she thought him dead. But now he sent word to her secretly, and without telling anyone of her plans, she met him inside the Union lines. When the war ended they returned to Mississippi and Henson, his health recovered, went briefly into newspaper publishing, with a pro-Republican journal.

In his later years things went less well for the colonel, and he tried to get a pension through Congress. To his chagrin, he discovered that many Northerners mistrusted him. But General Dodge came out emphatically for Phil and testified that he was "probably the ablest man in our secret service . . . one of the most important men we ever had within the Confederate lines."

Chapter 10

One Man Remembered

There are always some people who seem born to bad luck, who, through no fault of their own, go from one difficulty to another. . . . Almost everyone who met Spencer Kellogg Brown, of Kansas and Missouri, liked him. Again and again people did things for him because they admired his looks, the candor in his light eyes, his obvious generosity of spirit. Yet, during most of Spencer Brown's short life, misfortune dogged him. Finally he was trapped by a casual accident in which a stranger passed a street corner and remembered that he had seen the boy once before.

For Spencer Brown the struggles over slavery lasted, not four years, but eleven of his twenty-one, beginning with peacetime conflicts between the North and the South. But through it all, he moved quietly, submissively, accepting his fate.

Originally of Massachusetts, the Browns had transferred in the late 1700s to New York, where Spencer's father eventually operated a store in the village of Belleville. They were a devout, strict family. The boy's earliest recollections were centered about Bible lecturers who stopped overnight on their circuit, and dark-skinned slaves who stayed briefly in the Browns' house on a well-traveled route of escape to freedom in Canada.

The Browns viewed slavery as a poisonous evil, to be removed by men of conscience and conviction. O. C. Brown, the father, was an individual hated bitterly by some, admired passionately by others—a man ready to sacrifice his world in the struggle with wrong as he saw it. The family went to New York City, where the older Brown became increasingly involved in the abolitionist crusade. In 1855, when the boy was twelve, the family rode out to the new territory of Kansas and became part of the violent opposition to the proslavery settlers who had migrated from the South.

Spencer was a studious, dreamy boy, who showed an occasional flash of quick wit and imagination. For years he had one great ambition—somehow to get a fuller education. Existence on the prairie farm gave little chance of leisure; the Browns and their several children struggled long hours to set out the 160 acres that surrounded their log cabin. Spencer would sit in the evening before the fire, writing poems and stories and whispering to his older sister Kitty, always his confidant, of his hopes for another kind of life.

But violence quickly became part of their daily existence; "Bleeding Kansas" was a byword for savage partisanship, house burnings, attacks with hatchet and ax. In 1856 almost anyone living in Kansas was subject to insult, harassment, perhaps murder. Fear of these brutalities persuaded O. C. Brown to send his wife and the girls back East.

One day when he was alone in the farmhouse, Spencer heard shots and ran outside to find a proslavery mob attacking the small settlement on the edge of his father's farm. Before his startled eyes, neighbors were wounded, and part of the embryo town put to flame. (The famous John Brown had settled near Spencer's father, and the two families were friends. Because they shared the same name and the same locality, many slavery hotheads mistakenly thought they were related.)

Suddenly furious men surrounded the white-faced boy, taking him captive. He watched his home burned to the ground by the angry mob. "That's John Brown's son," one of the

Missourians shouted, and for a time he feared that, young as he was, he might be shot. Then he was removed with other prisoners, to be held for many weeks in Missouri.

Spencer's stormy father appealed to the territorial government and secured his son's release. Meanwhile the boy's reserved, courageous behavior had made him popular with his captors. Several of them retained their interest in him.

After the Browns were reunited, economic conditions became very bad. In his diary Spencer made solemn entries: "Christmas passed with very little notice. Hard times press. . . ." He tried to get work, but no one needed him. The year 1860 brought a disastrous drought; "we have not had six hours of good rain in ten months." Once more the Browns had to separate, this time to keep alive. The mother and girls returned East again, and it became clear that the burnt-out farm must be abandoned.

At seventeen, Spencer canvassed everyone he knew in his hunt for work, including his former captors in Missouri. "You will perhaps remember . . . the little prisoner you had. . . . I am young and willing to try any honest labor." He took a temporary summer farming job, and in November heard of a small teaching post in Missouri which required scant training. To the family's delight the ambitious boy was given the job, and his hopes were high. For the first time in years Spencer felt happy; things had taken a turn for the better, at last.

Two days after he started teaching, dissension over slavery caught up with him, and he received a frightening anonymous note: He had come from Kansas, and he was one of that cursed clan of John Brown, wasn't he? If he didn't get out of town right now, he'd never live to regret it!

Spencer had to escape in the night, leaving behind his clothes and small possessions. Supporting himself by day labor, he worked his way toward St. Louis, and wrote the family of his whereabouts. He made an urgent request that from now on they address him as "Spencer Kellogg." Also, since his mail was likely to be opened, they should never mention Kansas. It was a depressing time for the boy, and an even worse one for the nation. After Lincoln's election, the Southern states withdrew from the Union one by one, and Missouri was in violent tumult.

The Browns, scattered and living in several different places, soon lost track of Spencer. They wrote to him repeatedly, but received no answers. In January of 1861 a letter arrived from Newport Barracks, Kentucky, telling the family that he had enlisted as a private in the Union Army. To his worried mother Spencer admitted that he had been ill and had nearly died, but now he felt almost well again. His affectionate sister Kitty wrote to their father. "It seems dreadful . . . you could claim him, as he is under age." He was not yet eighteen.

But Spencer, so long lonely and friendless, found the army and its companionships a pleasant change, and the family decided not to intervene. He was transferred to St. Louis, as a company clerk, and he felt more cheerful and secure. Even now, however, as a precaution, he continued to call himself Spencer Kellogg. The boy's alertness attracted official attention and he was made a military scout.

For several months he moved about the Missouri area; by one report he rode nine hundred miles on scouting service. In a mysterious note he asked his older brother to report on Confederate military operations in his vicinity. "Be very careful to send as correct news as possible, something that can be relied upon, as it will be of great importance to me if correct. . . . Do not express wonder at what I ask."

After several months, Spencer's fortunes improved still further. In September of 1861, General Frémont gave him an honorable discharge and named him first lieutenant to recruit for the "Lyon Legion," scouts of the 12th Regiment, Missouri Volunteers. He wrote Sister Kitty an elated note:

"Ah, your little, unpractical, theoretical brother has had many of the sharp, uncompromising corners rubbed from him, and is getting, more than ever he thought, a man of the world. I am sorry! almost ashamed! When I look back it seems that if I had married happily, with the old notions and greenness, and retired to some out of the way town, life would have been full of much keener enjoyment than can ever come to me, as worldly as I have got to be."

In a manner much less worldly than he thought, Spencer went on to describe his hopes and his delight in his changed role. He wished to send a large part of his pay to the family. "Let me do for you what I can, not reluctantly but with joy and love. . . . Remember how much you have done for me—as I remember. . . ." Only a few weeks later, the pendulum swung heavily in the other direction. The Administration replaced General Frémont as commander of the Western Department, and Spencer received curt notice that his commission had lapsed.

For months the family was again in the dark about what had happened to him. Then they learned that he had turned to another branch of the service. He enlisted as a sailor on the *Essex,* one of the astonishing new ironclads that were beginning to churn along the Mississippi below St. Louis.

The Western flotilla had been created almost overnight, in haste and partial secrecy. Speedy, heavily plated, armed with big guns, the monster boats now awaited the signal to steam downstream to fight Southern vessels for mastery of the great river. . . . The Browns waited for word, until one day in late January of 1862 a cousin picked up a St. Louis paper and read the startling news that Spencer Kellogg of the *Essex* had deserted with a companion, to join the Southern Army.

The family would not believe the statement. When they petitioned Navy officials for details, they learned only that the youth had disappeared one night. The authorities insisted there could be no mistake in the identification. . . . The family was horrified and worried. Could Spencer's personal difficulties, his alternate high hopes and disappointments, have led him to do this terrible thing?

In April Spencer's grandfather in St. Louis sent an exciting message. He had just seen the boy, and learned everything that had happened. Spencer had *not* shifted sides; he had gone as a spy on a "secret expedition to Dixie." The false account had been inserted in the paper to make the rebels believe the story, but now the truth could be told. Spencer himself wrote warmly to Kitty. During his first days aboard the gunboat, he had talked with a new friend, one Trussel, about his experiences in scouting enemy territory for the army. Afterward he went to the executive officer and received permission to approach the somewhat forbidding Captain W. D. Porter.

"Come in, young man. Speak quick!"

This invitation made the sailor stammer, and he had trouble in speaking at all. Nevertheless, Spencer explained that he and his friend wanted to sail downriver to explore the Southern batteries and fortifications. They could pretend to be dissatisfied Union recruits; Spencer had already learned how to handle such an assignment. . . . Captain Porter thought over the proposal and agreed. He added a sharp warning, however, to the effect that they must be careful not to be mustered into Confederate service, or they would be in real peril.

About twenty-four hours later, on January 31, the adventure began. Captain Porter ordered a skiff attached to the *Essex's* stern. At 3 A.M. the two boys dropped into it and drifted down the black stream. A cold winter wind was blowing and water froze on the sacking with which they tried to muffle their oars. The captain's pass helped when they were stopped by Northern guards, and soon after dawn they were near the Confederate stronghold of Columbus.

A steamer sat at anchor a short distance off; hastily Spencer and his companion put handcuffs on the boy's wrists, following their plan. They hailed the steamer, and the captain sent them on to the nearest floating battery. Spencer told a vivid story as to how they had escaped from the Yankees, but wondered if he had convinced his questioners. The captain had his irons removed and kept the two men aboard. While he discussed their case with General Polk, then commanding at Columbus, they "spent three days of idleness and anxiety under a cheerful countenance."

The Confederates were decidedly puzzled over the newcomers and questioned them repeatedly. But the pair had learned their story well, they exchanged no whispered confidences, and never committed the error of asking to be allowed ashore. Some of the Southerners were suspicious, and one officer called them "a couple of damned sharp-looking fellows." Spencer tried to smile at that. "You compliment us, sir," he said, and hoped he didn't look as nervous as he felt.

Transferred to a Confederate gunboat, the boys were ordered below and put under guard. Later, however, they were brought up from the hold and permitted to fraternize with the crew. The men welcomed them with food and grog, and asked dozens of questions. Meanwhile Spencer had succeeded, as he had on the trip when he was a captive in Missouri, in winning the sympathy of officers and crew. He had a respectful manner, a wish to please. Typical of the general reaction was the comment that one slightly tipsy Confederate made to him: "Kellogg, they say you're a spy, but I reckon it's all right. You've got a damned good forehead and a fine open countenance!"

The two "open countenances" convinced most of the crew members, who now urged the boys to ship on the gunboat and fight for the South. Captain Porter had predicted just such offers, and Spencer and Trussel had answered that they'd like to do it, but if they did and the Union caught them, they'd be hanged on sight. When the gunboat moved downriver from

Columbus to the vicinity of Island No. 10, there were further consultations, and then the Confederate officers sent them ashore.

Spencer needed no one to tell him that he and Trussel would remain under surveillance for some time. Promptly they hired themselves out to a captain of an engineering corps as men of all work. One day they labored with carpenters, the next they cleaned sixty-eight-pound mounted guns. Meanwhile they had hours alone and many opportunities for discreet espionage. (On the Southern gunboat they had not missed chances to study the peculiarities of the ship's construction and her four rifled Parrott guns, mounted on a carriage and slide, that Spencer considered superior to anything the Union had.)

Next, Spencer was sent with a surveying crew along the river bank, and he trudged beside two Negro workers, making note of the distance covered. He had a momentary temptation to trick the Confederates by giving figures inaccurately, but he resisted it, and rejoiced that he had. The Southerners rechained the ground, and found he had not erred. . . .

The boys had learned a great deal by then, and the time had come to return to the Union lines. Spencer spoke nervously to Trussel, and urged him to hurry. But his partner, seeing still more information at hand, persuaded him to wait. Trussel went into Columbus with an engineer captain who happily got drunk and left him to himself for two whole days, during which he checked fortifications, guns, and torpedo facilities.

Spencer became alarmed; the time limit set by Captain Porter had by now expired. When Trussel returned from Columbus, they were again ready to leave. This time the drinking water made them both sick, and Trussel fell seriously ill. At the same time, as Spencer had feared, the Federal ships advanced down the Mississippi, and the Confederates hastily evacuated Columbus. Boatload after boatload of Southern men, ammunition, and commissary supplies swept past the two spies. After the Southerners steamed a line of five Union gunboats, transports, and mortar vessels in angry pursuit.

At Island No. 10 shells began to burst on all sides, and Spencer watched from a distance in increasing frenzy. He and Trussel were close to the heart of battle, but on the wrong side! Stretched in his bed in a hut on the river bank, Trussel urged Spencer to escape to the Union lines. Spencer argued that he couldn't desert his friend like that.

The enemy decided the matter for him. As Spencer left the hut to get water for Trussel, a doughty Irish lieutenant collared him and dragged him to the Confederate commander. "Sir," said the lieutenant, "I been watching this one, standin' on the bank all day long, actin' peculiar, lookin' and lookin' toward the Yankees. He *must* be a spy!"

Spencer protested angrily, until the hard-pressed commander made an abrupt gesture and turned him over to the 12th Louisiana Volunteers, part of the land armies in the area. Certainly the suspect could do no harm in their hands.

Separated from his companion, Spencer could only debate miserably what to do next, and again the Confederates made the decision for him. The Louisiana Volunteers were ordered to withdraw, and this they did, keeping their prisoner under close guard as Union mortar shells exploded in the air along the river. When they boarded a vessel for Fort Pillow, Spencer went along. At first the Confederate officers scowled in hostility. No damned Yankee spy was going to pull anything on them!

Then, however, Spencer's winning manner slowly relaxed their doubts. At the fort he began to drink with the men, and play whist and ball. With obvious good will he offered to help in some of the lesser duties; curiously, for a suspected spy, he gave raw recruits pointers in bayonet tactics and swordplay. Meanwhile he "used his eyes" for a comprehensive study of the fort, the breastworks, and the caliber of the guns. He even managed to send an extensive message back to Colonel Porter by a Negro.

Before long one of the Southern officers approached him, saying that Spencer would certainly make a good Confederate, and asking why he didn't join *his* company? The youth recalled Captain Porter's warning, but, as he said later, he pretended to agree. It might give him the chance he wanted so badly to get back to the Northern lines. Yes, he replied, he'd be glad to go to the company's headquarters to enlist. It was over in Corinth, Mississippi, and Spencer took down directions.

The friendly officer conferred with the general in command, who asked his own questions. Obviously the lieutenant spoke with conviction, for the officer ordered Spencer's release and gave him a pass, transportation, and five days' provisions. For the moment, things were looking up again, Spencer thought. Some opportunity to escape would surely present itself, and meanwhile he would follow directions and continue to "use his eyes."

Calmly he rode into Memphis, which he inspected at length before he went to the provost marshal's office. There he had his pass visaed and took a train, as instructed, to reach his destination. On the next lap he used ears as well as eyes. Discovering a general and his aide in the same coach, he maneuvered a seat near them and learned a little more. Halting for the night at the town of Grand Junction, Spencer met a member of a new company, the 1st Louisiana Cavalry Volunteers, and blithely he changed his plans again.

The two men got on famously. This Southerner also asked if Spencer wouldn't join *his* company. Of course he would, said the spy. Pleased that he had discovered an experienced recruit, the Confederate paid all expenses from that point on. At Iuka they entered the company headquarters, and the difficult moment arrived when Spencer was expected to take his place in the Confederate ranks.

The new friend had promised a fifty-dollar bounty. It was not immediately available, and Spencer had an excuse for declining to be mustered in at the moment. Nevertheless, he put on the gray uniform and, in his own words, "I commenced serving without being sworn in at all." Here was the crux of the trouble that would eventually plague him. Most spies, on both sides, managed to avoid donning army dress and marching to the battlefield. . . . The next day Spencer realized that a major battle was beginning, at a place on the Tennessee River called Pittsburg Landing, or Shiloh.

In later years it would be known as the first truly great clash of the Civil War, in which thousands of men were thrown at each other by both sides. The stake was a large one: control of the Cumberland and Tennessee rivers. On the Southern side every available man was needed and Spencer received a double-barreled shotgun, ten rounds of ammunition, and "an ambitious but extremely emaciated horse."

Swinging out of camp on April 5, the Confederates rode forth in high spirits. But for Spencer Kellogg Brown the prospect was less than thrilling. Every few minutes brought him closer to the roar of battle; at any time he might meet his own side at the wrong end of their guns and cannon. Almost exhausted, he dozed in his saddle, wakened from time to time by a sullen boom from Union boats on the river. Late that night the troops rested in a field, and Spencer asked where they were. He learned that the Tennessee River, bordering Federal territory, lay scarcely a mile and a half away.

That was the sort of thing he had been longing to hear. At dawn, as Spencer fed and watered his horse, he discovered that no camp guard had been posted. Tossing his gray coat on a fence, he walked casually into the brush. A few seconds later he was crashing toward the stream. At its edge, wet with perspiration, he stripped and leaped in. The icy water took his breath away; swimming hard, he reached a small island, rested for a few minutes, and then hunted about in the grass. He couldn't swim the rest of the way, but if he could only find something to carry him across . . . He stumbled on an ancient, half-cracked dugout, into which the water poured. It would have to do. Sitting in the water almost to his hips, he rowed frantically until he fell gasping on the opposite shore. Again he could not linger; any border area was risky, and in any case he had news to bring the Union army.

Spencer raced through the woods. Several natives, seeing the naked youth, took him for a "wild man," he said. Finally the boy found a farmer who proved friendly to the Union and offered him bread and bacon, his first food in many hours. By this time Spencer's legs bled from scores of scratches, and flints had cut into his feet. Another farmer provided old clothes and worn shoes, and pointed out the route to Union headquarters.

"Thirteen miles, that way?" Spencer was exhausted and needed help, and finally he persuaded the farmer to ride him there by mule. Appearing in his improvised costume at the town near the Northern battle lines, the boy demanded that someone take him to General Grant. The Yankee officers were dubious, and he had the familiar experience of being put under guard until they decided what to do about him. By then the Battle of Shiloh was in its second day, and it seemed to be going badly for the Union.

More anxious than ever, Spencer begged and argued. He had news he was sure the general would want to hear! Grant's subordinates gave him looks more chilly than the river water. It was obvious that they regarded him as a Southern spy. He could only wait, fuming, until a guard rode him out to Pittsburg Landing, where he waited again. After two hours he was taken to the harassed general.

Spencer talked quickly, persuasively, summarizing what he had seen at Corinth, Island No. 10, Memphis, Fort Pillow, and other points. Most important, perhaps, was the data he could offer about possible re-enforcements. From all he had seen, he would swear that the Southerners were thin in reserves. Of Grant's reaction, Spencer says simply, "My reception was good."

He could not claim that he influenced the result of Shiloh, but he had brought timely information to Grant, to reinforce other intelligence in the general's hands. The Southerners fell back from Shiloh. Both sides had suffered heavy losses, yet the battle had gone to the Union. Spencer learned that Island No. 10, scene of his earlier spying, had fallen; the Confederates abandoned besieged Corinth and Fort Pillow. The spy could now go back to St. Louis. His friend Trussel turned up later at Vicksburg with his own information for Grant. Their mission had ended well.

Such was the story that Spencer wrote to his family. From Missouri he could add the further news that his navy superior had promoted him. Within six weeks he rose again, to fourth mate of the *Essex*. "My captain evidently intends to do well by me," he noted. From then on, he was a protégé of bluff Captain Porter. Now that he was in funds at last, the boy used part of the money to help his family and, as he told Sister Kitty, for another purpose too.

> In the evening I go to see the young lady. I've got such a good one, Kitty–go to see her about four nights in the seven; or to the theatre or varieties concert hall. To tell the truth, Kitty, I have been leading quite a dissipated life.

Naïvely, he added:

> Don't misunderstand me . . . for I don't go to houses of bad repute or drink anything stronger than Catawba wine. My dissipation consists of eating oysters and ice-creams, going to the theatre, and late hours.

Spencer's romance matured while he waited for repairs to be made on the *Essex*. The girl was Mary Manahan, sister-in-law of a fellow officer. "I talk about getting married—don't know yet, but we are having quite a flirtation." Whether the ice creams or the Catawba wine did it, the flirtation fetched up at the altar. For nearly a month Spencer and Mary Brown stayed happily together, and then he had to return to the gunboat.

He had put spying behind him. Talking over his service with superior officers, Spencer received assurances that he had now reverted to his regular navy status. Even if he were captured again, he could be treated only as an ordinary prisoner of war, and not an espionage agent. . . . On the *Essex* he had a part in the gunboat's spectacular duels with the Confederacy's ram *Arkansas*.

Although the *Essex* was ripped and riddled, she churned steadily past the blazing batteries at Vicksburg, clearing the river of her enemies. Spencer performed several acts of bravery under fire, and his navy standing seemed assured. Then, once more, in mid-August of 1862, the young officer went to his superior, Porter, with a request for special service.

At Port Gibson, Mississippi, a Southern garrison continued to defy the Union, and a daring rebel crew was shuttling back and forth to give it regular provisions. Spencer wanted to wipe out their vessel. Though Porter thought it might be an impossible undertaking, the boy insisted he could do it. "I've been in many a tight place and always got away. Let me try."

When the captain agreed, Spencer went out in a transport with forty men and sank the Confederate vessel. Then the jubilant young officer was seized by a wild impulse: wouldn't it be quite a sensation to step on Southern soil again? In a small boat, unmindful of the fact that a guerrilla contingent was watching a short distance off, he landed and walked up and down the shore. Someone called to him; he turned and was seized with four others of his party.

Learning of the incident, Captain Porter was alarmed, and dispatched a gunboat from nearby Baton Rouge in an effort to release the prisoners. It was too late; they had already been taken to Jackson, the Mississippi capital. Porter went to work immediately for an exchange of prisoners of war. The captain was racing against time.

Spencer impressed his captors with his friendliness and, had he stayed in prison, he might eventually have been exchanged without difficulty. He received temporary release on his parole as an officer, however, and was free to wander around the town.

A Confederate engineer, who had been on the river when Spencer made his spying trip, was also in Jackson, and he stopped on the street one day and, pointing to Spencer, asked a friend who *that* was. Shortly afterward the engineer sought out the authorities and swore that Kellogg was the same young fellow who had left the Federal forces, served in the Southern Army, and then run away with information for the Union! Spencer went to prison again, this time as a spy and as a deserter from the Confederacy.

For weeks Spencer's wife and family heard nothing from him. After leaving St. Louis he had sent only one message back to the girl. Rumors reached the Browns that Spencer was captured, and Federal officials sadly confirmed the story. The family wrote frantically to friends, appealed to connections in the North and a few in the South. Captain Porter himself petitioned officers on both sides, and the Union Secretaries of War and Navy made one appeal after another.

The Browns sent dozens of notes to Spencer, asking why he didn't answer their questions or at least let them know how he was? Much later the family learned that their messages had not been delivered. Spencer, too, wrote them repeatedly, and did not know that none of his letters was forwarded.

General Grant moved toward the Mississippi capital and

Spencer and his fellow prisoners were given a flash of hope. But instead of being rescued, they were taken under guard to Montgomery, Alabama, and eventually on a long trip to "Castle Thunder" in Richmond. There another prisoner, Captain J. H. Sherman of Lafayette Baker's detective force, found Spencer a "pale, care-worn, reserved young man."

The Browns came to realize that in Southern eyes their son had committed a deadly offense. He had passed among the Confederates as a secret agent; he had joined their army and fled to the other side. The Union could argue, and it did, that Spencer had never actually enlisted in the Confederate service, and, whatever his earlier status, he had gone back to his own command and terminated his spying. The Federal authorities quoted the first Army manual: in such cases a man could not be held responsible for acts under his original assignment. . . . But the South was determined to make its own interpretation of the rule.

A Mississippi minister had heard of Spencer's troubles and, though a firm Confederate, tried hard to help him. He gave the boy a prayer book, which Spencer studied. On its blank pages the young officer started a diary in which he described first his hopes that he might go free, then the way he reconciled himself slowly to his possible execution.

A trial was scheduled, the date set, but delayed and delayed again. Months passed, seasons changed. Spencer Brown underwent a strong religious experience, and began to accept the situation in which he found himself. Covering pages with reflections and messages, he declared:

"Have passed a day of rest and, I trust by God's blessing, of profit. . . . Another week has gone and (let it be written unto God's praise) with such cheerful content and happiness as I have rarely, if ever, had. . . . Time since Sunday passed in diligent study of Latin, Greek and the Scriptures. . . ."

Now at last Spencer had the opportunity to do some of the studying for which he had yearned. He read everything he could get his hands on, absorbed it, and talked about it to others in the prison. At the same time, closed in from the war and the outer world, he worried about what was happening beyond the walls. Spencer did not know that his wife Mary, struggling against uncertainty and sorrow, had become ill. His twenty-first birthday arrived, and his trial approached. He had written his wife to tell her where to locate a few jewels he had left, and how he wanted his small possessions divided. He thought he owed ten or fifteen dollars to officers on the *Essex;* could the loans be repaid? He hoped Mary would receive various trinkets he had fashioned in prison. And in a final message:

Dear wife: I do earnestly long to see you once more before I die, but we must not complain, for God has done it. . . . We had happy hours together, darling; God grant they be not the last. . . . I have always loved you, dear one, and love you to the last . . .

Spencer was found guilty, and late in the morning of September 26, 1863, a detail of a hundred men marched from "Castle Thunder," with Spencer Kellogg Brown in custody, up Richmond's Main Street. A "vast crowd" of all ages had gathered. During his long confinement Spencer's skin had become paper-white. He appeared "about thirty-three years of age."

The prisoner heard a brief prayer, then, unaccompanied, mounted the scaffold. When a detective followed to fit the rope over his head, Spencer's hat fell, hitting a man below, and he turned and said, "Excuse me, sir." He asked the detective who tied his arms, "Isn't this hard, Captain?"

A Negro ascended to fasten the rope to an upper beam, but the prisoner told him the fall would be hardly a foot long; it would not break his neck. "I don't want to have a botched job of it," he said, and requested the doctor to readjust the length. The change made, a cap placed over his head, Spencer Brown lowered his head to pray. Then, head raised, he spoke in a strong voice: "All ready." A moment later he dropped in the air.

Chapter 11

Grant's Spy in Richmond

By every rule of background, Miss Elizabeth Van Lew should have been among the Confederate women who hurried in and out of Jefferson Davis's "Gray House" on fashionable Clay Street, knitted for the Southern boys, and wept softly to themselves as the Stars and Bars floated past the iron-balconied residences of Richmond.

Miss Van Lew was the daughter of a prominent Richmond citizen. Their house stood on one of the city's most commanding hills, a mansion soaring three and a half stories high. And Elizabeth in her soft Southern voice always spoke of Virginians as "our people."

Yet Miss Van Lew became a freak in Richmond, a woman whose existence was a protest against the beliefs of her class and region. Defying old friends, civil and military authorities, she opposed slavery and war. She poured out money and energy to assist Union soldiers, and gained the hatred of her neighbors. But Elizabeth Van Lew was more than the "fanatic" and "theorist" that most Richmonders considered her. For the four full years of war she operated as a dedicated and resourceful spy, according to several Northern generals, the best one inside the Confederate capital.

Her reputation as a Union sympathizer, though it brought her heavy censure, served as a blind behind which she practiced espionage, directing a band of assistants of assorted ranks and occupations. Miss "Lizzie" was so foolishly and openly attached to the North that most people considered her a silly, hysterical woman. A spy would be expected to be silent or speak the opposite of what he felt. Deviousness was the last thing to be looked for in anyone like Miss Van Lew.

Yet dissimulation, it seems clear, was actually the quality that she possessed above all others. Without it she could not have bribed farmers, used Confederate clerks and attorneys, maintained lasting contact with secret service men, and helped prisoners to escape. At times Miss Lizzie could be acid-tongued, scalding in her contempt; again she was gentle and flattering when it helped her to get what she wanted.

Prim and angular, nervous in movement, she had once been pretty, but by her early forties she had turned into an old maid. She was the same age as her fellow Virginian, Rose Greenhow, but she had no men in her life. Tiny, blondish, with high cheekbones and a sharp nose, Miss Van Lew went about with an "almost unearthly brilliance" in her blue eyes. The opposite of the seductive lady, she accomplished her ends without the help of charm or a lush figure or a coquette's air.

Miss Lizzie served particularly the general whom Southerners regarded with marked dislike, U. S. Grant. After the victorious Union army arrived in Richmond, one of Grant's first visits was to the spinster's home. Proudly, her ringlets bobbing, she received him for tea. Nevertheless, some years later, when a little girl demurred against meeting her, a "Yankee," Elizabeth Van Lew bridled: "I'm not a Yankee." For she maintained at all times that she was only a good Southerner, holding to an old Virginia tradition of opposition to human bondage. *She* had been the loyal one, she said, *they* the traitors. . . .

Some Richmonders insisted the Van Lews had not, after all, come originally from the Old Dominion. Elizabeth's father was from Long Island, a descendant of a colonial Dutch family. Going to Richmond at twenty-six, John Van Lew cast his lot in 1816 with a member of the well-established Adams family. Their commercial firm failed, owing a debt that the daughter recalled as a hundred thousand dollars. With the sense of rectitude strong among the Van Lews, he "honorably paid" his share. Then, starting again as a hardware dealer, Mr. Van Lew prospered magnificently.

On a trip to Philadelphia he met the daughter of that city's late mayor, and brought her back as his bride. Of their three children, Elizabeth was, though least robust, the strongest willed. She was tutored, and given the best of academic and social training, and she soon grew proud of her family's magnificent home on Church Hill, across from the church in which Patrick Henry called for liberty or death. The Adamses had lost the property, and the Van Lews acquired it.

Handsome as the building was, John Van Lew transformed it, adding the superb portico and other embellishments. For years the great of America and some from the Continent visited the house to admire the chandeliered parlors with their walls covered with brocaded silk, mantels of imported marble, the sixteen-foot hallway, the terraced gardens lined with boxwood, and the summerhouse at the edge of the James. Jenny Lind stopped there, when she sang her way across America, and Chief Justice John Marshall, and Edgar Allan Poe, who, it has been claimed, recited in one of the parlors.

From her earliest days Elizabeth was very close to her quiet mother. Then the girl left for school in Philadelphia, and Richmonders maintained that she "imbibed abolitionism" there. It appears, however, that she had always been a serious, introspective child. As she put it in a rather self-pitying analysis: "From the time I knew right from wrong it was my sad privilege to differ in many things from the . . . opinions and principles of my locality." She described herself as "uncompromising, ready to resent what seemed wrong, quick and passionate but not bad tempered or vicious. . . . This has made my life sad and earnest."

When his daughter was twenty-five, Mr. Van Lew died, and his son John, as energetic as he was unspectacular, took over the hardware business with success. Meanwhile the bond between Elizabeth and her mother grew stronger. In the early 1850s, when Fredericka Bremer, the Swedish novelist, visited Richmond, she met Elizabeth, who was then thirty, "a pleasing, pale blonde," who "expressed so much compassion for the sufferings of the slave, that I was immediately attracted to her."

As the 1850s passed, this Richmonder did more than feel compassion for her slaves. She freed all the family servants (Elizabeth dominated her mother in such matters), and most of them stayed on in their jobs. Hearing that the children or relatives of Van Lew slaves were to be sold by other owners, she bought and liberated them as well. And she set down such firm opinions as: "Slave power crushes freedom of speech and of opinion. Slave power degrades labor. Slave power is arrogant, is jealous and intrusive, is cruel, is despotic, not only over the slave but over the community, the state."

Surviving today is an unusual manuscript of hundreds of pages, part diary, part reminiscences, confused yet vivid in many passages. In it Miss Lizzie recalls the days just before the war: "I was a silent and sorrowing spectator of the rise and spread of the secession mania." From the hour of John Brown's raid, "our people were in a palpable state of war." In the general fury, rumors spread that Northern forces were immediately marching on Richmond. "The alarm bells would be rung, the tramp of armed men . . . heard through the night."

About this time Miss Elizabeth started her pro-Northern activities by writing to Federal officials and telling them everything that was happening. In her recollections she pictured the Virginia Secession Convention, and quoted a number of women as asking: "Do you think the state will go out today? For if it does not, I cannot stand it any longer." Upon this she commented: "God help us. Those were sorry days. . . ."

On April 17, 1861, Miss Van Lew first beheld the Confederate banner over Richmond. "Alas for those with loyalty in their hearts." Through tears she watched a torchlight procession, and fell to her knees. "Never did a feeling of more calm determination and high resolve for endurance come over me. . . ." Friends understood her general sentiments, but some of them must have thought Miss Van Lew's attitude would change. A delegation came to ask Elizabeth if she and her mother would make shirts for the troops.

The Van Lew ladies declined, but when they began to receive "personal threats" they agreed reluctantly to take religious books to the camps. If the people of Richmond thought the Van Lews had given in, they were wrong. An uneasy May and June passed. July brought the preparations for the first battle at Manassas. The two women saw the soldiers ride off to the applause and tossed roses of Richmond admirers. Their hearts sank when the South sent the Union Army reeling back. Through Richmond rolled wagons with dispirited Northern prisoners, and resentment against Yankees rose so high that no one dared speak to them.

A day or two later the Van Lews heard stories of suffering in the grim warehouse that was Libby Prison. Miss Lizzie went to Lieutenant Todd, the Confederate prisonkeeper (who was also Mrs. Abraham Lincoln's half-brother) and asked to be a hospital nurse. The lieutenant gasped. She didn't mean she wanted to nurse those men! Why, he knew people who would be glad to "shoot the lot of them."

Miss Van Lew next tried Secretary of the Treasury Memminger, with whom she was acquainted. Ah, he could not hear of such a thing. A class of men like that—they were "not worthy or fit for a lady to visit." She changed her tactics and reminded

Memminger of the time he gave a beautiful discourse on religion. His face beamed; so she had liked it? "I said that love was the fulfilling of the law, and if we wished 'our cause' to succeed, we must begin with charity to the thankless, the unworthy." She won her point and the Secretary gave her a note to Provost Marshal Winder.

Once Miss Lizzie assured a friend: "Oh, I can flatter almost anything out of old Winder; his personal vanity is so great." Now she proved it. With her gaze fixed on his white head, she smiled: "Your hair would adorn the Temple of Janus. It looks out of place here." A few more such remarks, and she had her pass!

From then on Miss Van Lew called regularly at the prisons, until, as one man said, she shopped as much for the prisoners as for her own family. She carried clothes, bedding, medicines. Discovering sick men, she persuaded Confederate doctors to transfer them to hospitals. Some thanked her for their lives. As one of the Union secret service chiefs ultimately declared: "By her attractive manners and full use of money she soon gained control of the rebel prisons. . . ." But before long the Van Lews were in the limelight, when newspapers singled them out.

> Two ladies, mother and daughter, living on Church Hill, have lately attracted public notice by their assiduous attentions to the Yankee prisoners. . . . Whilst every true woman in this community has been busy making articles for our troops, or administering to our sick, these two women have been spending their opulent means in aiding and giving comfort to the miscreants who have invaded our sacred soil, bent on rapine and murder. . . . Out upon all pretexts to humanity! . . . The course of these two females, in providing them with delicacies, bringing them books, stationery and paper, cannot but be regarded as an evidence of sympathy amounting to an endorsement of the cause and conduct of these Northern vandals.

The Van Lews did not take the hint. Instead, they expanded their activities. Learning of Lieutenant Todd's taste for buttermilk and gingerbread, they plied him (shades of Mati Hari!) with these wholesome items. They worked similarly to gain favors from others. And Miss Lizzie's enemies would have been even more indignant had they known she was getting military information from the Union prisoners. The day she first sent secret messages through the lines is not known, but it appears that she soon established contact with Union agents who slipped into Richmond on secret missions. The prisoners understood the meaning of Confederate troop movements, the shifting of regiments near the capital, and they and Miss Lizzie picked up hints from soldiers and guards.

Elizabeth's servants were ready to leave the Van Lew mansion on a minute's notice on innocent-looking errands. The Van Lews had a small vegetable garden out of town—an excuse for the Negroes to go in and out of Richmond. Not many people would poke into the soles of muddy brogans worn by an old colored man on a horse. Few would inspect a servant's basket of eggs, one of which was an empty shell concealing a coded message.

The Confederate attitude toward Miss Lizzie's prison visits varied. A commanding officer once asked her to stop bringing in special meals because it "subverted the consistency of prison rules." Such orders inconvenienced but seldom halted her. During a tense period when she was ordered not to exchange a word with the prisoners, Elizabeth brought books. When the soldiers passed them back to her, the Confederates did not know that tiny pin pricks conveyed military data.

The spinster also slid notes into the "double-bottom" of a dish, originally intended to hold warm water. Advised that a suspicious guard planned a thorough inspection of the dish, Miss Van Lew prepared for him. When he reached for it she gave it up readily; for she had been holding it for some time cradled in her shawl. He let it go with a howl; she had taken care to fill the bottom with boiling water!

In the summer of 1861 the Union seized fifteen Confederates as privateers on the vessel *Savannah*, and threatened to hang them. In retaliation Jefferson Davis ordered the same number of Federal soldiers held as hostages. Miss Lizzie protested and won the right to visit the endangered men, comforting them, bringing food, taking out forbidden letters. At this time the old maid developed a particular friendship for one of the condemned men, a young Colonel Paul Revere of Massachusetts. At one point she connived in his attempted escape. The danger of the mass hanging passed, and Colonel Revere eventually was exchanged, only to die later at Gettysburg.

Each incident meant intensified Confederate bitterness against Miss Van Lew. She did not dare keep a complete journal. "Written only to be burnt was the fate of almost everything which would now be of value. Keeping one's house in order for Government inspection with Salisbury prison in prospective, necessitated this. I always went to bed at night with anything dangerous on paper beside me, so as to be able to destroy it in a moment." Again: "The threats, the scowls, the frowns of an infuriated community—who can write of them? I have had brave men shake their fingers in my face and say terrible things. . . ."

Miss Lizzie once went to Jefferson Davis himself to request protection. Not many spies for one government asked the head of the opposing government for his aid! Mr. Davis's secretary advised her to apply to the mayor, but she had a better thought, which grew out of the housing shortage. Lieutenant Todd was to have a successor as keeper of prisons—a captain with a family. The newcomer had to live somewhere, and Miss Van Lew knew just the place—her big house. While he stayed there with his "interesting family," the Van Lews were left in peace.

It is hard to tell when the next step occurred in her evolution as a spy. Slowly, however, she took on a new, protective coloration. Richmond had long regarded her as a trifle odd. Elizabeth began to accentuate that oddity. As she walked along the street, she mumbled and hummed to herself, head bent to one side, holding imaginary conversations. Richmonders glanced at one another and shook their heads. The prison guards gave her a new name: "Crazy Bet." She lived up to her title, combing her curls less carefully, wearing her oldest clothes and most battered bonnets.

Yet there was nothing crazy in the next exploit credited to Miss Van Lew. Among the slaves she had liberated was slim, intelligent Mary Elizabeth Bowser, then living outside of Richmond. Mary Elizabeth returned at Miss Lizzie's request and became the new house servant for the Jefferson Davises. The Union now had its spy in the household of the Confederate President. The girl apparently brought back some interesting stories. . . . Mary Elizabeth and her former mistress met at intervals after dark near the Van Lew farm. For such trips the older woman varied her Crazy Bet routine and wore a huge poke bonnet, leather leggings, "belt canvas coat." Tucking up her curls, she played the poor country woman driving around in her buggy.

Miss Lizzie enlisted the help of a number of simpler folk, farmers, storekeepers, factory workers, united in their belief in the Union. In the words of General George Sharpe of the Army Intelligence Bureau: "Their [the Van Lews's] position, character and charities gave them a commanding influence, and many families of plain people were decided and encouraged by them to remain true to the flag, and were subsequently able during the war to receive our agents. . . . For a long, long time, she represented all that was left of the power of the United States government in the city of Richmond."

Other Federal spies or scouts arrived in the capital to "take her orders," the intelligence chief added. They usually slipped into the Van Lew house at night, to stay for days in rooms at the back of the mansion. In emergencies they stopped only at the family farm. Miss Lizzie's friends took them frequent messages. One such friend was a seamstress who stitched dispatches into her patterns. Several times the girl was halted by Confederate guards; rough fingers felt the patterns but none of the messages was discovered.

The Union threat against Richmond became ominous in 1862. McClellan came so close that the people of the capital could hear gunfire. "We are in hourly expectation of a battle. . . . We have hatched eight chickens today and have a prospect of rearing and eating them under our 'dear young government'; and so we go, mixing peace with war," wrote Elizabeth.

Miss Lizzie had the happy notion that when McClellan entered Richmond he should be their guest. Using "new matting and pretty curtains, we prepared a chamber." Meanwhile, revealing another side of herself, she went out with friends for a ringside view of the fighting. "The rapid succession of the guns was wonderful. . . . No ball could be as exciting as our ride this evening. Only think of the bright rush of life; the hurry of Death on the battlefield!" Here was a sight that not many other Richmond spinsters would have enjoyed.

McClellan never set eyes on Lizzie Van Lew's pretty room. Robert E. Lee took charge of the Confederate defenses, and Little Mac pulled back. For the saddened Van Lews there were other misfortunes. One day Elizabeth took pity on an undernourished milliner, "friendless and alone." Bringing this Miss McGonigle home, she helped her for months. Overnight the milliner turned on her and paid a call at Confederate headquarters to report her suspicions. Luckily Miss McGonigle knew nothing definite against the Van Lews, but Elizabeth was deeply hurt by this occurrence.

By now the family had taken in other boarders. One such guest, who might have told far more than the milliner, received a note from "W. W. New, Detective, C.S. Police," with a request to appear for testimony against the Van Lews. Her evidence was needed "to conclude the case." Detective New added that if the boarder felt some hesitation in going she would not have to appear before Mrs. Van Lew, nor would her name be mentioned in the case. The lady felt more than delicacy in the matter; she declined to say a word.

Some of the neighbors, however, were not so loyal and the Van Lews were continually trailed by detectives. As Miss Lizzie wrote: "I have turned to speak to a friend and found a detective at my elbow. Strange faces could be seen peeping around the column and pillars of the back portico." The grand jury investigated the old maid and her mother for "trafficking in greenbacks," United States currency, and Elizabeth's mother fell sick when she heard that warrants had been prepared against her.

With the supply of army horses decreasing, few Richmonders were allowed to keep their animals. One day Elizabeth received a tip from a friendly Confederate clerk that soldiers were headed for her home to confiscate her horse. She needed him badly for spy work, so she hid the animal in the smokehouse. A few days later Confederates learned of this and, being warned again, Miss Lizzie led the horse through the house and up the stairs to the library. Straw had been spread, "and he accepted his position and behaved as though he thoroughly understood matters, never stamping loud enough to be heard nor neighing." He was "a good, loyal horse," Elizabeth assures us.

Many townsmen were certain that Crazy Bet hid more than horses. In these later days, as privations increased and men in prisons turned desperate, scores escaped. The Van Lew home was searched several times without result, but people whispered stories of secret passages and hidden rooms. Miss Lizzie's niece told eventually how she saw Aunt Elizabeth glide toward the attic with a plate of food, and tiptoed after her. As the niece peered around a corner the spinster touched a panel. It slid back, and a bearded man reached out hungrily for the food. Years afterward the girl found the concealed chamber beneath the slope of the rear roof.

General Sharpe of the Union Intelligence credited Miss Van Lew with helping in many escapes, including the celebrated exploit in which a sixty-foot tunnel was dug under Libby Prison. The time was a chilly February day in 1864. Elizabeth had been told "there was to be an exit" in the near future, and she prepared "an off, or rather end room." Personal problems intervened and she had left the house when some of the escaping prisoners sought refuge, and the servants turned them away. Other Union sympathizers took them in, communicated with Miss Van Lew, and she went to work to assist them on their perilous journey. . . .

By now she had further systematized her espionage, establishing regular contact with General Ben Butler at Fortress Monroe. Becoming more professional, she received a cipher and hid the key to it in her watch case, which she retained until her death. As an additional safeguard, her niece said, Miss Lizzie would tear cipher messages into two or three pieces and roll them into tiny balls, to be handed over in that shape. Years later the retired spy herself told a Richmond child how she hid papers by unscrewing the top of the andirons in her bedroom.

Crazy Bet's spy organization had also widened. The chief of Federal spies, speaking of her and her mother, said: "They had clerks in the rebel war and navy departments in their confidence." On that point Elizabeth always remained reticent, and such helpers, traitors to the Confederacy, were apparently never exposed. Once, she noted, she did go to General Winder's office with an emergency message from General Butler to a Union agent on the Confederate payroll. Had it fallen into Southern hands, the letter could have destroyed the man and also Crazy Bet.

The old maid acted with cool daring. She entered Winder's quarters, sought out the individual in question, and placed the note directly in his hands. A few feet away were the central offices of the Confederacy's secret service. The man trembled and seemed about to break. Might he betray her, in his terror? Instead he slipped the paper into his pocket and whispered that Miss Lizzie must never come there again. Apparently she did not have to, as the next time he went to *her*.

Late in January of 1864 Elizabeth Van Lew and her friends in Richmond passed on vital information about Confederate plans to move thousands of prisoners. Here was an opportunity for a sudden Northern attack which would free a great many Union soldiers and might even take Richmond. Miss Lizzie called in a few well-placed assistants and then sent a young emissary on a dangerous trip to Butler's headquarters in Virginia. The official war records contain her dispatch, originally in cipher:

> It is intended to remove to Georgia very soon, all the Federal prisoners; butchers and bakers to go at once. They are already notified and selected. Quaker knows this to be true. They are building batteries on Danville road. This from Quaker. Beware of new and rash councils. This I send to you by direction of all your friends. No attempt should be made with less than 30,000 cavalry, from 10,000 to 15,000 infantry to support them. . . . Forces probably could be called in from five to ten days; 25,000 mostly artillery, Stokes's, and Kemper's brigades go to North Carolina. Pickett's is in or around Petersburg. Three regiments of cavalry disbanded by Lee for want of horses. . . .

When Butler received Miss Lizzie's message four days later, he marked it "private and immediate" and forwarded it to Secretary of War Stanton, with an explanation that it came "from a lady in Richmond with whom I am in correspondence." The bearer had carried a token to show he could be trusted. "Now or never is the time to strike," Butler added, and told of his questioning of Miss Van Lew's nervous courier.

The boy had contributed dozens of other military facts, troop movements of which the Van Lew group had learned at the last moment, and other advice from "Quaker" and "Mr. Palmer," two of the Union agents who concealed their identities. All pointed to the belief that "Richmond could be taken easier now than at any other time of the war."

This advice from civilians had its defects, to be sure; they threw figures about carelessly, and there were military factors about which they lacked information. Nevertheless, the Northern officials apparently accepted the truth of the general situation as presented, and accordingly launched a major operation. The Union War Department gave considerable time, attention, and manpower to a cavalry movement to surprise Richmond and free the prisoners. Unfortunately for the enterprise, however, the "secret" project became as confidential as a White House reception. Too many officers' wives, and officers themselves, talked about it.

On February 28 a body of four thousand picked troops swept toward Richmond from the left, under General Judson Kilpatrick and Colonel Ulric Dahlgren. From the right several thousand other Union soldiers would make a feint. Then young Dahlgren was to drive on the Confederate capital in one direction while Kilpatrick knifed in from the other. The blow might be one of the most brilliant of the war; his superiors expected a great deal of the twenty-two-year-old Dahlgren, son of Rear Admiral Dahlgren, and the Army's youngest man of his rank. Having lost a leg shortly after Gettysburg, the boy used a wooden leg and crutch, but could still outride anyone in sight.

The raid started on schedule, then rapidly went to pieces. There were unforeseen obstacles, a Negro guide who could not or would not find a ford across the James, and, not least, Confederate foreknowledge. In badly frightened Richmond, as Miss

Van Lew reported: "every reliable man was called out. There was an awful quiet in the streets; the heavy silence was impressive. . . . At night we could hear the firing of the cannon. . . ." By the time Colonel Dahlgren reached a road only five miles from the city, strengthening resistance made the attack hopeless. As the Union troops retreated in darkness and rain, young Dahlgren himself was killed.

Then began a macabre episode that involved the boy's remains. The body was hastily searched by Confederates, a memorandum taken, a finger cut off for its ring, and the valuable wooden leg was removed. Casually they buried what was left of Dahlgren near a road.

Soon afterward Southern officials made an announcement that sent a wave of fury over Richmond. Dahlgren, they said, had carried orders to burn and sack the city, and kill Jefferson Davis and his Cabinet. Whether or not the documents were authentic has never been determined. Richmond papers described the captured Union soldiers as "assassins, barbarians, thugs . . . redolent of more hellish purposes than were the Goth, the Hun or the Saracen." Kill them all as enemies of humanity! One journal urged a public showing of the Dahlgren corpse as a "monument of infamy" to teach young Confederates to hate such men.

Where Ulric Dahlgren lay interred, no one knew, said the newspapers. "It was a dog's burial, without coffin, winding sheet or service. Friends and relatives in the North need inquire no further." As a matter of fact, the remains had meanwhile been placed in a coffin and transferred to Richmond, and on orders from President Davis workmen reburied Dahlgren late at night and secretly among thousands of other Union graves. But not entirely secretly, because of Elizabeth Van Lew.

She tells us that a Negro she knew was "in the burying ground at night . . . entirely accidentally, or rather providentially"! The man marked the spot of Dahlgren's grave, sought her out, and she took over, managing a remarkable job of plotting, body stealing, and transfer through the Confederate lines. Needing six or seven helpers, she had no trouble enlisting them at once among her Union friends.

Late one night, four men rode to the burial place. Digging up the rude casket, they unscrewed the lid and identified the corpse by the missing right leg. Over rutted back roads they hastened to the farm of W. C. Rowley, where Miss Lizzie waited in a seed house, and once again the boy's remains were examined, but with "gentle hands and tearful eyes," she said. She helped transfer the corpse to a new metal coffin, which would now be put into the earth on Robert Orrick's farm outside town.

First, however, they had to take the box past Confederate pickets. In the morning Farmer Rowley climbed to the seat of his wagon, the coffin on the floor behind him, covered by a dozen closely packed peach trees. Approaching the pickets, the farmer saw that they were examining everything. He was panicky until he recognized the soldier who strolled over to inspect his wagon. He reminded the man of their last meeting. Vaguely the soldier recalled the incident. "But whose trees are these?" Rowley tried to be casual: "They belong to a German in the country." The two acquaintances talked about the unwisdom of planting peach trees at this season. Ah, well, that was the German's worry. The uniformed man sighed: "It would be a pity to disturb those trees, when you've packed them so nice. Go ahead."

With the body safely buried, Elizabeth Van Lew promptly started a cipher report of the exploit on its way to General Butler. Dahlgren's sorrowing father had meanwhile asked that Ulric's remains be returned to him and Jefferson Davis issued orders to grant the request. When Confederate soldiers dug in their own burial grounds and found nothing, Richmond buzzed with a greater mystery than ever. Not until after the war was the matter cleared up.

At least once Miss Lizzie was almost led to betray her connection with Butler. The general had requested an up-to-date report on Richmond's defenses, and she had her cipher message ready, torn in strips and rolled in wads as usual. An expected scout had not arrived and as she walked along the street, wondering how she was going to send her report, a man beside her murmured: "I'm going through tonight," and continued on without pausing.

Perhaps it was the Union agent, who might have some urgent reason for approaching her this way without identifying himself. Quickening her steps, she passed the stranger, and again she heard: "I'm going through the lines tonight." She frowned and made no acknowledgment. The risk was too great. The next day a Southern regiment marched by, and she recognized the man, now in his gray uniform. Belle Boyd had once been trapped in much this fashion; Crazy Bet was more crafty.

From General Sharpe, we learn that as General Grant moved closer to Richmond Miss Van Lew's communications with the Union command reached a new peak. With the distance shortened, she could forward messages almost daily. She used a system of five "stations" or points along the way, from the mansion on Church Hill, to her farm, and beyond. Grant asked repeatedly for "specific information" and she "steadily conveyed it to him," Sharpe explains.

So expert was her transmission belt that flowers from the Van Lew gardens often arrived fresh and dewy on Grant's breakfast table! And Sharpe declared that "the greater portion" of the information passed to the general's army in 1864–65 "in its collection and in a good measure in its transmission, we owed to the intelligence and devotion of Miss E. L. Van Lew."

But at this late date Crazy Bet faced a final threat of exposure. In February of 1865 Union officials believed they had an inspiration when they dispatched to Richmond an Englishman named Pole. Prodigious spying deeds were predicted. On his way Pole met many Union sympathizers. Careful arrangements had been made for him in the city and supposedly he was to meet Miss Lizzie. Her diary described her suspicion and anxiety, which turned to terror when Pole suddenly rushed into Confederate headquarters to sell out his employers.

At least two Union agents went to prison. For hours Elizabeth waited in apprehension, fearing the man had discovered enough to implicate her. Then nothing more happened. She had missed disaster by a thread. Personal deliverance was not long in following. On a Sunday in early April a roar echoed in the Richmond streets; Lee's lines had given way, the Confederates were marching out, and the town had gone mad. Fires crackled in one square and another. "Hundreds of houses had fallen victims to the spreading fire. . . . The constant explosion of shells, the blowing up of the gunboats and of the powder magazines seemed to jar, to shake the earth and lend a mighty language to the scene . . . the burning bridges, the searing flames added a wild grandeur. . . ."

Neighbors borrowed the Van Lew wheelbarrows to save their belongings. The prisons were emptied and scores of Union soldiers were taken out of Richmond. Miss Lizzie had determined to make a grand gesture, whatever its cost. At considerable peril she had ordered a big American flag smuggled through the lines. She and her servants scrambled to the roof and set it to waving its thirty-four stars against the sky. Hers was the first Union flag to be unfurled again in the Confederate capital.

Richmonders glared, and a howling mob gathered. God damn the old devil; burn her place down! Men shoved toward her house, trampled the garden, and Crazy Bet stepped forth to confront them. "I know *you,* and *you* . . ." Her thin face contorted, she screamed their names and pointed them out. "General Grant will be in town in an hour. You do one thing to my home, and all of yours will be burned before noon!" They were convinced and they backed away.

Miss Lizzie had one last assignment for herself. She ran to the Confederate Capitol, to search among the ashes of the archives for secret documents which the Union government might find helpful. She was found there by a special guard dispatched for her protection by General Grant. He had remembered her and the danger she might face on this day. . . .

Soon after his arrival the general paid his formal visit. Mrs. Grant explained later that her husband said they must visit Miss Van Lew, for she had given great service to the Union. They drank tea together and talked politely on the columned porch. "Crazy Bet" was very proud; for the rest of her life she kept Grant's calling card.

Chapter 12

The Day after Thanksgiving

In a simple white house with four narrow wooden columns at the front and log cabins in the yard, there was a nervous stir during November of 1863. As the early morning mists rose from Stewart's Creek at the base of the hilly plateau, the Davises and their younger children were talking of their hopes. Perhaps the situation might change and son Sam would come home, after all, if only for a little while. . . .

Nobody at the Davis farm in the rolling green foothills of middle Tennessee spoke much about Sam's army work. With the Union forces so close around them, it was not a subject to be discussed, even among friends. From Nashville, only fifteen miles away, rumors had arisen of trouble down in Chattanooga, where a great battle could break out at any time. But one or two relatives whispered that Sam and his fellow scouts had been seen somewhere near the farm only a day or two ago.

Sam's mother, her hair slightly grayed, might not have found this good news. She worried over her twenty-one-year-old son, even though his superior was their good friend, Captain Shaw. . . . She had been sorry that Sam agreed to join Shaw's scouting service. Still, they should consider it fortunate that Henry Shaw, and not a complete stranger, had charge of Sam's work. For that, at least, the Davises might be grateful in this Thanksgiving month.

For weeks the Union spy director, General Grenville Dodge, had fretted. For all his energetic efforts, a band of Confederate scouts was moving within Northern lines and gathering alarmingly accurate information. In early November General U. S. Grant's powerful army faced that of the Southerner Bragg at Chattanooga, with the green majesty of Lookout Mountain as a backdrop. A decision was close, and few knew it better than Grenville Dodge.

With his headquarters in the middle area of Tennessee, Dodge worried as each day brought new reports of the damaging presence of the Confederate scouts. They slipped in and out of Nashville, in the open country and along back roads so familiar to these Tennessee natives. Several had been detected among Dodge's own forces.

The Union general gave orders to his own spies and scouts to wipe out the Confederate agents, to arrest anybody who was the least suspicious or who could not offer a clear explanation of his reasons for being there. In particular Dodge wanted to get a shadowy individual whom the Federal Army appeared to know only by the assumed name of E. C. Coleman, sometimes a soldier, more often a civilian—an "herb specialist," this Dr. Coleman. There was a substantial reward out for him, preferably alive, though a dead Coleman would also be acceptable.

Captain Henry Shaw (Coleman), a man of several names and identities, left a trail through Union territory, but it was a thin one, a ghostlike thread. If the Federals could just once identify and lay hands on him! The Davis family of that mid-state farm had been Henry Shaw's friends for years, during his schoolteacher days and his time as a steamboat clerk. Shaw was an outstanding fellow with an imposing physique, tall and robust. His bright blue eyes were keenly observant, his nose was sharp, and he had a small reddish beard. He had considerable self-possession, a look of quiet assurance—an assurance that was to undergo the supreme test of his life. There would be another kind of testing for the Davises.

Young Sam Davis had spent most of his days on the family farm a mile outside Smyrna, Tennessee. The first of eight children, with three older half brothers and a half sister, he had been accustomed to horseback rides and hunting through the woods of the county—the usual life of the country boy. By all accounts, the sixty-three-year-old father was upright, undemonstrative, some said stern; Sam's mother, who was only forty, had a soft and gentle manner, shared to a degree by her eldest son. The boy had always been close to her. When he left to attend Western Military Institute at Nashville, neighbors and friends thought that Sam suffered a special homesickness; as often as he could, he returned to see his mother.

Yet Sam fitted in at the school, adapting to the discipline, liking it. He had started at the Institute when he was eighteen, in 1860; a year later, at the outbreak of war, Sam and his schoolmates marched off to join the Rutherford Rifles, 1st Regiment, Tennessee Volunteer Infantry. As his father ultimately told the proud story of Sam's career, he first tasted fire at Cheat Mountain in western Virginia, under the command of Robert E. Lee. Then, in Stonewall Jackson's brigade, he helped push the Union army across the Potomac during the harsh winter of 1862.

Next Sam was called back to Tennessee with his fellows. Bad times had come to the West; under Johnston and Beauregard the youth had known the violence and tragedy of Shiloh, where he suffered battle wounds. Then, in the days of scant arms and reduced rations, Braxton Bragg had taken command of the Army of Tennessee. Quickly Bragg approved the formation of a new company of scouts to be his "eyes and ears" and find out what the Federals intended to do.

Sam Davis's friend Shaw was recruiting scouts and Sam volunteered. He looked younger than his twenty years, tall, with a lean body, dark brown hair, and a skin well tanned by years in the sun. He had a mustache but, unlike most soldiers, no beard. He was not talkative, and his manner had a suggestion of shyness. But Captain Henry Shaw needed no recommendation; he had seen Sam under fire, and he accepted him at once. For months Sam had served efficiently and quietly, and Shaw's respect had increased with each assignment.

In the fall of 1863, Captain Shaw and his scouts had to try to get all available information about Union operations at Nashville and at Dodge's headquarters in the town of Pulaski, to be dispatched to the battle headquarters of General Bragg. The shadowy Shaw conferred from day to day with his group, gathering their reports, comparing the facts that they brought him.

One agent went into Nashville in country clothes, driving a wagon filled with firewood, and mingling with townspeople and soldiers. Another, in neat civilian dress, attended a dance in a town near Union headquarters, arriving late, listening carefully to the privates' conversation, leaving early before the question was raised of his identity. The adroit Shaw had long ago learned another device, the trick of placing his agents at fixed points along a Union line of march. For forty-eight hours or longer each vantage point—a clump of bushes, a large boulder—would be manned, and a definite count made by trained soldiers.

This time the Confederate scouts had a windfall, in a source of information close to Dodge's own headquarters. According to a native, a good-looking Tennessee girl "beguiled" one of the general's young officers. Another insisted that a Negro porter picked up documents from a table, sought out a Confederate who employed his wife, and gave them over. Whatever the explanation, the papers were accurate, so accurate that the Union general felt utter dismay when he came upon them at a later date.

For Shaw and his scouts a deadline approached; in a few days all of this information must be unified and sent to Bragg, and the men would start for Chattanooga, separately or in small groups. It was their custom to have all documents carried by one of the party. If any of the others were caught, there would be no evidence against them; if the enemies trapped the carrier, only one man would be in danger. For this vital role Shaw picked Sam Davis, who looked like a schoolboy but had shown himself perhaps the most dependable of the lot.

Within twenty-four hours the group would meet again. Meanwhile Sam had great good fortune—permission to go home if he wished. Union soldiers had camped scarcely a mile from the Davis farm, but he could get through on a black night. So on a chill fall evening the boy rode stealthily toward the farmhouse. Tying his horse behind a big rock, he made his way across the lawn and tapped lightly at a window.

His tall father opened the door and Mrs. Davis ran out. Sam took his mother in his arms, shook his father's hand, and a few minutes later explained that he had only a little time, but he had wanted to see them. No, they mustn't wake the youngest girls, sleeping in a trundle bed; they should cover the windows and keep the lights low. Nobody else must know he had come. . . . As he spoke, his mother touched his hand, asked questions, examined him with loving eyes.

Though there would later be confused descriptions of his dress, Sam Davis wore gray, washed-out Confederate trousers, a light nondescript jacket, and, it appeared, hat and top boots from a captured Union uniform. Hard-pressed Southerners frequently used any Yankee garb that fell into their hands. The boy shivered slightly; Mrs. Davis saw that he needed a coat, and she remembered one of Union blue, with cape, that he had once left at the house.

She had prepared it for him, dyeing it a vague brown. Using butternut or white walnut, the only coloring available, she had succeeded in making the garment an in-between shade. "Boy, you've got to take it," she told him. He agreed, and meanwhile his father stared at Sam's broken shoe. "Here, let me fix that one," he urged. As Mr. Davis worked, Sam lay down to rest for an hour or two.

Early in the morning his mother shook him and held the big coat for him. They waved from the door as he rode off. He might not be with them for Thanksgiving, and still they could be thankful. They had seen their boy again, and he was alive and well. . . .

In the home of a friend near Dodge's own quarters at Pulaski, young Sam met his chief. He went early to bed the next night, but Captain Shaw stayed up for hours, working over his reports. Not until dawn did he finish, and then he signaled that he had everything in order. Rising, Sam shook hands, swallowed a half cupful of weak wartime coffee, took the reports, and left.

He made good time, using lightly traveled roads. On November 20, on Lambs' Ferry road in Giles County, men in blue sprang out of ambush and surrounded him. They were members of the 7th Kansas Cavalry, the so-called "Jayhawkers" who had been sent out to catch Shaw's scouts.

Soon afterward a Union officer asked him to take off his shoes. In silence Sam Davis removed them, and from a hollow beneath the sole a Northern soldier drew several sheets of paper, including a letter from "Coleman" to Bragg with full details of Federal troops, locations, intentions. Another soldier entered and displayed what he'd come across in the saddle—a full map and description of Nashville's newest fortifications.

The prisoner said nothing, and he was taken to the well-guarded county jail at Pulaski. Already it held about twenty-five other men, picked up on Dodge's order on varying degrees of suspicion. Sam recognized three of his fellow scouts, among them an older man with a reddish beard and a certain assurance.

The Federals had captured the Confederate they wanted most, for whom they had offered their large reward—the brilliant Captain Shaw himself. But they had no idea of his identity; they had picked him up as one of many civilians who had thus far not explained their presence in the area. The only person on whom evidence had been discovered was Sam himself.

Henry Shaw did not talk or signal to Sam. There was no need; the boy understood that no matter what happened in the days ahead, he was to give no sign that he had ever met him before. General Dodge went over the papers, and he was much disturbed. There was a traitor at his own headquarters, and he had to find who it was! He glared at the name of Coleman, chief of Bragg's scouts, on the letter Sam had carried. The man had signed it only a short time before; he must be nearby, and surely the boy knew where.

General Dodge had the prisoner brought to him. "Davis met me modestly," he recalled afterward. "He was a fine, soldierly-looking young fellow, not over 20. . . . He had a frank, open face and was bright." The general spoke seriously.

"I tried to impress on him the danger he was in, and told him that I knew he was only a messenger, and urged him, on the promise of lenient treatment, to divulge the source of all the information. . . ."

Politely Sam shook his head. "That's something I won't tell, sir."

The general went on. Here the prisoner was, in Federal lines, wearing portions of Union costume, with damaging papers about Federal strength, written from one Confederate official to another. Didn't Sam see how damning that was? Surely he understood enough about Army rules to realize what would happen if he went before a court-martial. Let him help them in finding the man Coleman. . . .

The boy bowed his head; he had nothing more to say. With a sign Dodge summoned the guard. The general still had hope of locating Coleman by his own efforts. When he wrote General Sherman, forwarding a copy of Sam's messages, he noted: "Captain Coleman is pretty well posted. I think we will have him in a day or two."

Two days passed, and the Union soldiers reported failure in their hunt. Meanwhile Sam continued in jail with Coleman and the other scouts a few feet away; none of them betrayed themselves. Years afterward General Dodge disclosed that he placed in the jail "one of our own spies," who assured the prisoners that he was a good Confederate. They sensed the scheme at once, "and we obtained no information of value from them."

The Federal officers talked to Sam at length. The infantry chaplain, James Young of the 81st Ohio, spoke with him for a long time, as did the provost marshal and the leader of Dodge's scouts. They used varying tactics, blustering, threatening, pleading; he told them nothing.

One of the Confederate scouts said afterwards that each time Sam left the jail Captain Shaw watched anxiously, trying to hide his emotion. Would the boy be browbeaten into an admission, or trapped by an accidental answer? . . . Over and over his captors asked Sam: Where was his chief, Coleman? When had he last seen him?

General Dodge, speaking as earnestly as he could, asked him to "give me a chance to save his life." Sam behaved more coolly than the man who had power over him: "I won't tell, General. You're doing your duty as a soldier, and I'll do mine, if I have to die."

Sam was the same age as the sons of many of the officers; with each day he impressed them more favorably. Even under war conditions, it was hard to kill such a boy. The Federals, it seems clear, went to remarkable lengths to provide him with an opportunity to escape. They wanted Coleman badly, of course, and yet there was something more. . . .

Reluctantly Dodge ordered a court-martial in the courthouse. The prisoner was accused of spying, of going within Union lines for the purpose of "secretly gaining information" and taking it to the enemy. A second count called him a "carrier of mails, communications and information" from Union lines to persons in arms against the United States.

Sam Davis faced the older men. He was innocent of spying, he said; but he admitted carrying Southern information. He had a single defense. He had entered only as a military scout, with a Southern pass in his pocket, as they knew; his costume had been that of a Confederate, and he had worn no insignia of the Union. Therefore he should be regarded simply as a prisoner of war.

The grave soldier judges listened with care, taking down the opinions for and against Sam. In their eyes, however, the verdict was obvious—guilty. The sentence was hanging, on November 27, 1863, the day after Thanksgiving. . . .

Through Thanksgiving day the Union officers continued their efforts to persuade Sam to speak. A middle-aged townswoman who knew the Davis family asked permission to see him. When she failed to change his mind, she went to Dodge himself to beg the general somehow to spare the boy. Other people added their appeals. The general said he could not: "A soldier caught in the uniform, or part of the uniform, of his enemy, within his enemy's lines, establishes the fact that he is a spy. . . ."

Still Sam's leader, Captain Shaw, watched developments anxiously. Might Sam break at the last minute? Among the prisoners many were certain that he would.

In spite of the holiday festivity, a number of the staff members felt the weight of the impending execution. On Thanksgiving night the chaplain visited Sam, and they sat together for a long time, talking softly. Then they prayed. Sam asked Chaplain Young if they could sing a hymn. The chaplain nodded, and the condemned youth chose "Land of Promise," a favorite of his mother's.

The music drifted through the jail, and the other prisoners listened. Among them was Shaw, now sad and silent, his eyes on the boy in the dim corner of the building. That night Sam thought again of the family he had left a few days before, and wrote:

Dear Mother: O how painful it is to write you! I have got to die tomorrow—to be hanged by the Federals. Mother, do not grieve for me. I must bid you goodbye for evermore. Mother, I do not fear to die. Give my love to all.

Your dear son.

The day after Thanksgiving was chill and dark, and it did not improve as the hours passed. By 10 A.M. Provost Marshal Armstrong had arrived with a wagon, on it a plain new pine coffin. Sam's eyes turned to the windows at which his fellow Confederates, Shaw and the others, were watching. With his manacled hands, he saluted them, and Henry Shaw's head dropped. . . .

The boy sat on the top of his coffin. The procession moved through the main street of the town, to the muffled roll of drums, and stopped at a ridge just outside town limits. There the XVI Army Corps lined up to form a hollow square before a tree with a scaffold.

After the wagon jolted to a halt, Sam Davis got out and sat on the ground. He faced the provost marshal: "How long do I have, Captain?"

"About fifteen minutes."

The youth's face was impassive. "What's the news from the front?"

"Bragg lost at Lookout Mountain, Sam."

This time the eyes lowered. "I'm sorry. The boys will have to fight the rest of the battles without me."

The marshal started to collect Sam's personal belongings to be forwarded to his mother and sisters, when suddenly the group about the gallows heard a commotion. A man on a horse rode up, a paper in his hand. "Stop the execution, stop!" He was Dodge's chief scout, and he had timed his arrival for the maximum effect on the prisoner.

Jumping off the horse, the scout went to the boy and held out a pardon. Sam could have it, with a safe conduct to the Confederate lines, if he would give the name of his informant. The listeners could not hear all the conversation, but they clearly heard what Sam Davis said when he ended the interview. For the first time he spoke in anger: "Do you think I'd betray a friend?"

He had a last few minutes, and he spent them writing another note to his mother, while the chaplain sang the hymn he had chosen:

> *"On Jordan's stormy banks I stand*
> *And cast a wistful eye*
> *To Canaan's fair and happy land . . ."*

Then Sam turned: "I'm ready." As his body swung, he started on his way to the "land of promise" that he had chosen.

The Davis family held no resentment toward their boy's friend, Henry Shaw. After the war he lived for a time with Sam's half brother and went into business with him; ironically, he died with that other Davis in a steamboat explosion. To those who said that Shaw might have come forward to take the responsibility in the case, the Davises pointed out several facts. Shaw had many assistants; had he spoken they, too, might have been tracked down, and more men would have suffered.

Sam had made his choice, dying so that his friends might live.

In the town of his execution an avenue has been named for Sam Davis, a marker erected to him; a monument has been placed on the grounds of the state capitol in Nashville. The state has purchased the Davis home as a memorial, which is visited annually by thousands. Among those who contributed to the Nashville monument was Union General Dodge.

He had done all he could to save Sam Davis, the general said, "but it was one of the fates of war, which is cruelty itself, and there is no refining it." The statue in Nashville bears the words attributed to the boy: "If I had a thousand lives, I would lose them all here before I would betray my friend or the confidence of my informer." General Dodge, the man who had him hanged, said simply: "He was too brave to die."

Chapter 13

Sister Act

Little Miss Ginnie Moon helped the South's war morale by getting herself engaged to sixteen boys at one time. She justified the risk by means of simple logic: "If they'd died in battle, they'd have died happy, wouldn't they? And if they lived, I didn't give a damn."

Miss Ginnie's sister Lottie made romantic history in another way, because she could not make up her mind. A man, famous years later as a Union general, stood beside Lottie at the altar, and answered firmly as the minister put the questions. But when asked if she took this man for her husband, Miss Lottie Moon paused to reconsider, and shook her head spunkily: "No-sireebob!" And lifting her skirts, Lottie marched out of the church.

The jilted man eventually had his chance for revenge. As a commanding general, Ambrose Burnside had sworn that he would "make an example" of any secesh agent within his lines. Yet when both Moon sisters were brought before him, charged with espionage, the general softened and let them go. As someone said, it paid a girl to jilt Ambrose Burnside.

The two Moons are, as far as I have been able to discover, the South's most authentic sister spy act. They were also distinguished as fervent agents of Dixie who happened to come from Ohio and spent most of their early days along the Western rivers.

Miss Ginnie and Miss Lottie were paradoxes, women of the new day born in the old. They traipsed around in wide skirts and flowered headgear; at the proper times they gazed soulfully at the boys. Yet they also devoted much of their lives to rebellion against custom—specifically, the male dominance in their era. One, Miss Ginnie, became a chain smoker in the 1880s, and stunned her nephew (a Presbyterian minister) by sitting on his gallery and puffing away while his parishioners gaped. Both of them startled their contemporaries by talking about women's rights, attacking fashionable affectation, and calling their neighbors genteel frauds.

Miss Ginnie toted a gun during most of her life—a pretty pearl-handled revolver that she knew very well how to use. In her late seventies she caused a furor when the proprietor of her hotel discovered what everybody else knew, that Miss Ginnie kept the gun tucked away in the old-fashioned black umbrella that accompanied her everywhere. When the hotel manager protested, Miss Ginnie shrugged and told him, in the old-fashioned phrase, that he could kiss her foot, and she hunted up a new hotel.

They were, everybody said, perfect ladies, and at the same time hellers in their own special fashion. The Moon girls came of good family, but that never kept them from being themselves. All of their lives Miss Ginnie and Miss Lottie invited the world to kiss their feet, and they chuckled happily whenever they heard the whisper: "She was a spy, and people said . . ."

The Moon girls shared an air of fragility, for both were small and dark, high-strung, and charming. Born Virginia, Ginnie was the beauty of the pair—long-faced, aristocratic, with big blue eyes, a high forehead, and a small nose. In a favorite family portrait, wearing a tall Spanish comb and dangling earrings, Ginnie looks like the heroine of a novel.

Fifteen years older than Ginnie, Lottie (born Charlotte) was generally described simply as an "interesting" girl. Her apple-round face was not improved by a coiffeur that drew her uncurled hair severely down on the back of her neck. Ophia D. Smith, their Ohio home-town authority on the Moons, said that Lottie had "an 'Ariel' face . . . illuminated by the glow of a scintillating mind." The husband she eventually chose called her, with marked enthusiasm, "the damnedest, smartest, woman in the world."

Despite that intelligence of hers, Lottie achieved twelve simultaneous engagements. Sister Ginnie's total of sixteen fiancés was the result of her margin of additional loveliness. (There was a third Moon girl, who was also a beauty. Mary stayed home, minded her own business, and, as a result, is entirely forgotten.)

Although Ohioans, Lottie and Ginnie came naturally by their interest in the South. Their father, Robert S. Moon, was a native Virginian, of a family dating back to Colonial days. He moved in the early 1830s to Oxford, near Cincinnati, in the southwest corner of Ohio. The Moons established early connections with the strongly Southern town of Memphis on the Mississippi. Anyone who called either of the girls a Yankee did well to step back immediately out of reach.

Robert Moon was a reader, a thinker, a man of gentle and tolerant ways, though some people thought his liberal opinions a bit strong. By contrast his wife was described as "a close-lipped, unbending, orthodox Presbyterian." The two spies-to-be inherited their father's originality, their mother's determination. To the astonishment of neighbors, they read science, heavy biography, and eventually (though for a time in privacy, of course) even Darwin. Their interest was always in the underdog.

The Moon girls had the gift of kindness—the considerate word, the quick smile, the small favor for a friend or even an enemy. And they possessed a quality not essential in spying, but one that would inevitably help—an ability to laugh at the Yankees and at themselves as well.

Born in 1829, Lottie soon demonstrated what a contemporary considered her "great power and originality of character." In her teens she shot a pistol at targets, "took dares" to ride bareback through the streets, and spoke her mind about anything that occurred to her. Like other spies-in-the-making, she became a fair actress. For amateur theatricals or for the simple amusement of friends, Lottie played many parts, and did clever imitations. She also learned a peculiar trick which would stand her in good stead. In Ophia Smith's words, she could "throw her jaw out of place with a cracking sound," assuming an expression of extreme agony.

Lottie did not seem to crack her jaw when the boys were around, and she gave special attention to Ambrose Burnside of Indiana, a big, heavy, kindly youth. Ginnie remembered that when she was four or five years old, Ambrose was "in love with a sister of mine; and when he came to see her I had sat on his lap. He always brought me candy, and I called him Buttons."

According to several accounts, "Buttons" Burnside proposed to the volatile older sister, and asked her to name the good day. Lottie made an answer that Ambrose might well have pondered at length: "Any day's a good day." At literally the last moment, Lottie changed her mind and flounced off at the church, as we have already seen.

This might have seemed calculated to end the man's tolerance for anything that reminded him of the Moons. It did not. The family said that Ambrose Burnside returned to woo Lottie again! He accepted defeat only when that tight-lipped mother sent back his latest letter with a laconic notation on the envelope: "Lottie was married to James Clark last week."

For young attorney, later Judge, Jim Clark, the courtship had been almost as difficult as Burnside's. Another man considered Lottie definitely pledged to him. Some Ohioans insisted that Lottie told the second fellow she would marry *him* on the day she had set for Jim Clark, "if you get there first"! In any case, that gentleman also showed up at the wedding. Jim Clark made up his mind there would be no jilting this time. Just before the couple went into the parlor, the youthful groom shoved a revolver against Lottie's satiny side and declared: "There'll be a wedding today, or a funeral tomorrow." There was a wedding. . . .

Lottie was twenty, her bridegroom twenty-five. The bride did not grow perceptibly quieter, and Jim Clark demonstrated as much energy in getting ahead in his career as he had in trapping his bride. He won two judgeships, then retired to private practice. During a domestic interlude Lottie Moon Clark won prizes for flower growing—surely a claim which could be made by few spies, American or otherwise!

Before long, however, the Clarks and the Moons had far more than prize dahlias to occupy them. When the war came, the two Moon boys went into the Confederate Army. After Father Moon's death, Mrs. Moon had moved down to Memphis, Tennessee, but had sent the peppery young Ginnie to the Oxford Female College. With the start of war, the teachers revealed their "Northern faith," as one of Ginnie's friends put it, and the girl felt a sense of outrage. Stepping into the principal's office, she announced she wanted to go to Memphis. The principal shuddered. Ginnie was only seventeen. How could she think of such a trip?

Ginnie won her freedom, however. She took out her little pistol and calmly shot every star, one by one, out of the American flag that flew over the school grounds! Packed off to her sister and brother-in-law in their nearby Ohio home, she waited her chance to return to Tennessee.

In the Clark residence Ginnie learned a great deal more about pro-Southern activities. This section of Ohio had a small but fervent branch of the Knights of the Golden Circle, one of the wartime undercover organizations with Confederate ties. Judge Clark himself was described, in a mixed phrase, as "the brains of the butternuts" in that area, butternuts being the common word for Dixie partisans.

One day in 1862 the Clarks received an excited caller, Walker Taylor of the Zachary Taylor clan, from over the line in Kentucky. Taylor was traveling under a false name and telling questioners he was here to "buy mules to restock his farm." Instead, he whispered to Lottie, he carried messages from Confederate General Sterling Price which must be taken at once to General Edmund Kirby-Smith in Kentucky. *He* couldn't do it; too many people knew him by now. . . .

"Could anybody carry them?" Lottie asked.

"Oh, yes."

"Then I will." Within a few hours Lottie put her acting skill to a test. From her house there went "a woman, very much bent, an old bonnet tied over her ears and partly concealing her face, toothless and muffled to the ears in a dilapidated shawl." That afternoon the bent figure crossed the Ohio by ferry, and found a transport ready to leave for Lexington—in the precise direction she had to go.

There Lottie turned Irish. "Her husband, poor dear ould man, was . . . dying, in the hospital." Shure, it was little enough to let a poor woman see her darlin' once more. . . . When the officials refused permission, Lottie did not give up. She spied several "fellow Irishmen" and went into her act again, with tears and gestures. To hell with officialdom, said the sentimental boys, and why shouldn't the likes of this good woman be allowed to join her man? They smuggled her aboard.

At Lexington the pathetic creature said good-by with thanks, and walked toward the outskirts of town. What she would do next depended on luck. Hearing hoofbeats, Lottie swung around to face Colonel Thomas Scott, a Southerner whom she had once met. Without bothering to see if anybody were watching, the "old woman" straightened up, hailed him, and thrust the papers into his hand: "Colonel Scott, promise on your life you'll give these to Colonel Kirby-Smith, and nobody else."

Scott stared. Who was this creature?

Lottie repeated that the important thing was to get the documents to the colonel. Then she walked back to Lexington, and when the train for a point near home left that night, the tiny Irishwoman sat mournfully in one of the coaches. Listening, she learned that a warning had just been issued to watch for a "female spy" on the train. A few minutes later Lottie was crying sadly again. In the seat in front of her sat General Leslie Coombs, a former Kentucky governor and a strong Union man. The general turned and Lottie poured out her story of a stricken husband and—a new detail—the hungry children waiting for her.

She was afraid, she sniffled, that with all these war suspicions, somebody would take her for one of those dangerous spies they talked about. . . . General Coombs sympathetically assured her he would look out for her. When the train reached Covington, Kentucky, Coombs himself helped Lottie down, and she rode across the river to safety. Without transportation from that point, she walked home through woods and across fields. Arriving in time for breakfast, she told her story to the delighted butternuts, and young Ginnie, the apprentice spy, listened with even more interest than the others.

One success invited another, and Lottie carried many important messages for the South. Her next major assignment came about because she knew Dr. Stuart Robinson, editor of a Louisville Presbyterian paper. Writing vigorously against the Union, the minister had to escape to Canada, and there he helped in the complex Southern effort to stir uprisings from over the border.

The Canadian Confederates had use for somebody like Lottie Clark. She made the long trip to Toronto, conferred at length with her friends, and devised a plan. Like Pryce Lewis, she would go out as an English subject on her way to Virginia's marvels, in this case to repair her tragically depleted health at the curative springs. The Confederates forged papers, Lottie talked her way through minor difficulties, and arrived eventually at Washington, D.C.

There, under a new name, she asked for a pass into Virginia. She had crossed the ocean, she asserted, in search of some benefit to her health. Come what may, she could not die content until she had tested the Virginia waters. Please, couldn't the authorities help her? Lottie drooped, sighed, put her lace hankerchief to her pale lips. Though obviously no beauty, the tiny lady had a winning manner, persistence, and an accent which, however stagy, must have convinced her auditors.

Lottie had taken care, too, to concoct a story that held together well. Eventually she was questioned by Secretary Stanton, noted for his suspicions. He asked questions about Canada and the Confederates, and the lady told, or seemed to tell, a great deal. Why, yes, she had met a Dr. Robinson in Canada and she knew one or two others whom Stanton named. She volunteered something about each—not enough to hurt, yet enough to impress the Northerners. By one account, Lottie even went along with President Lincoln's party for a review of the Army of the Potomac at Fredericksburg.

Getting her pass for Virginia, the spy rode quietly off. When Stanton finally got wind of the ruse, it was too late. The little agent dispatched long messages to her Southern employers, and she collected more data on her roundabout way toward Cincinnati and her home base. When she reached the Shenandoah Valley, she had her first serious difficulty. Near Winchester, Federal General F. J. Milroy listened politely as Lottie rattled off a few variations on her story. Lacking information about the location and true nature of American resorts, the confused Britisher said she had gone to the wrong place. Now she realized that she wanted to visit not Hot Springs, Virginia, but Hot Springs, Arkansas. Wouldn't the general give her a pass through the lines?

This time, perhaps Lottie had ad-libbed too glibly. General Milroy answered cunningly that since a question of illness was involved, his surgeon would have to decide. The general summoned a pouter pigeon of a doctor, a man clearly anxious to show his abilities. The English lady became more ill than ever. At the army hospital to which he took her she groaned that she could not leave her carriage. "It would be my death to go up the broad steps." The surgeon snapped his fingers, and two helpers lifted the spy in a chair.

Now, Madame, what was her ailment? Rheumatism, sir, she said; it had also affected her heart. With those words Lottie did the best acting of her life, crying at the doctor's touch, going white with the agony of her arthritis. According to Ophia Smith's account, the spy also called on her old knack of dislocating her jaw. The lady's heart fluttered, her joints seemed to creak, and the pompous doctor nodded. Truly a sad case. . . .

Carried downstairs, the patient received a pass to Cincinnati, and started out for that city, not realizing that she would soon be caught in another spy drama involving her sister Ginnie and also her onetime admirer Burnside.

Ginnie Moon had returned to Memphis and for months had been at work in and about the city. The cotton capital remained in Confederate hands until June of 1862, in spite of increasing Union pressure upon it. Ginnie had helped her mother roll bandages and nurse wounded soldiers. Like Belle Boyd, however, young Miss Moon yearned for more lively doings. The Yankees took the forts upriver, and on a warm summer morning, while several thousand Memphians watched from the bluff, the Federal fleet steamed down to the city itself.

The battle lines shifted still again, and Nathan Bedford Forrest's troops began to make daring raids, striking lightning blows at the Northerners. Unverified stories are told of the way the handsome Ginnie rode out from Memphis with information and supplies needed by the Confederates, and of the way, when once arrested, she coquetted herself free. Again, she supposedly made a twilight tryst, snagged the military facts she wanted from her beau, and hurried away to deliver them.

"She needed no pass to get through the Union lines," said the Memphis *Commercial Appeal*. "Her eyes and her way won her permission."

About February of 1863 Ginnie was visiting in Jackson, capital of Mississippi. The Confederate, Sterling Price, had new and vital intelligence for Ohio's Knights of the Golden Circle. It dealt with negotiations for an alliance between Southerners and Western sympathizers, which might bring uprisings against the Union. Hearing of the matter, Ginnie went to the general and asked why she and her mother could not take the message through. With relatives in Ohio, they had an excuse for a trip. "I won't be caught. Let me go," she begged.

Ginnie had never been a girl who could easily be denied, and the general agreed. With an escort of eight soldiers, she went part of the way by government ambulance. At Memphis she picked up her mother, and they made an ostensibly casual journey to her brother-in-law's house near Oxford, Ohio.

Sister Lottie was still away in Canada on her own Confederate duties. Judge Clark took the safely delivered Southern message, conferred with his friends, and prepared an answer—terms under which the Ohio Knights might affiliate strongly with the Southerners. One of the signatures, Ginnie says in the memoir she wrote years later, was that of the Copperhead leader, Vallandigham, that enigmatic figure who might have changed America's destiny.

When Miss Moon and her mother appeared to head back South, they realized the return trip might not be altogether easy. In nearby Cincinnati, Ambrose Burnside, newly appointed head of the Union Department of the Ohio, was making history in his own way, strenuously prosecuting civilian friends of the Confederacy. The burly general was soon to issue an order that created bitterness for years to come. It provided treason trials for all who showed Southern leanings, the death penalty for anyone who helped the Confederacy. Clearly the Moons' old friend was in a harsh mood.

Various Union agents already had their attention trained on Judge Clark and his family. To check on them, the Union now assigned a counterspy, a plausible young Ohioan "whose charm of manner and personal popularity made his entree into any house an easy matter."

The envoy "made himself so agreeable" that the Clarks invited him to spend several days as their guest. The judge expressed his regret that his wife Lottie was absent; she had had to go to Virginia to see relatives, he claimed. The young gallant melted some of the reserve of the untalkative Mrs. Moon and had a brief flirtation with Ginnie, who added him to her string of conquests.

The Union representative found nothing incriminating, for although Clark and his in-laws were true to the South, they were very careful in what they said. Still, the young man noted one interesting thing: the ladies "did nothing but quilt," working from dawn to dusk. Judging by the piles of stuff, they must have been doing it even while they slept. When Ginnie and Mrs. Moon declared themselves ready to return to Memphis by boat from Cincinnati, they asked their new friend to help them get passes.

He did. Union officials sent them papers, but at the same time sent a confidential message to the boat captain that the vessel was not to depart without special orders. Judge Clark smilingly accompanied his mother-in-law and Miss Ginnie to the *Alice Dean*, installed them aboard, and left. Tucked in her bosom Ginnie had the secret dispatch of the Knights of the Golden Circle, wrapped in "oil silk." As we shall see, that wasn't all she was smuggling into the Confederacy. Sweating attendants were muttering over her heavy trunks and bags.

The time for the 5 P.M. departure arrived and passed. Mrs. Moon remained in their stateroom, watching over the trunks. Ginnie was sitting in the cabin when, as she recalled in after years, "I saw a Yankee officer coming through the cabin, looking at the numbers on the doors." He asked the girl to go to her stateroom with him, and when she complied he entered behind her and she heard the lock snap.

He was Captain Harrison Rose of the Cincinnati customhouse, the officer told her, and he had orders to search Miss Moon and bring her to the provost marshal. With a businesslike gesture he showed a note: "Arrest Miss Virginia Moon. She is an active and dangerous rebel in the employ of the Confederate government. Has contraband goods and rebel mail and is the bearer of dispatches."

Scornfully Ginnie gave back the document. "That's a very ridiculous charge." Captain Rose moved nearer. "Anyway, I'm ordered to do what they tell me." Little Ginnie looked up: "*You*, a man, ordered to search *me?* I'll never endure it!"

The captain expected scant trouble on that score. "How can you help it?"

Clearly the man had never heard of Ginnie's prowess. He was standing inside the door across the washstand from her, with Mrs. Moon between them. As Ginnie explains: "There was a slit in my skirt and in my petticoat I had a Colt revolver. I put my hand in and took it out, backed to the door and leveled it at him across the washstand. 'If you make a move to touch me, I'll kill you, so help me God!' "

Captain Rose hesitated, and Ginnie lashed out at him again: "Does General Burnside know of this? I don't think he does. He has been a friend of mine since I was five. . . . You had better be careful what you do or I will report you to him." As she spoke, she informs us, she was thinking hard. She could shoot the fellow and, since the door was locked, get rid of the dangerous dispatch before anyone else broke in.

Fortunately her threats worked. Captain Rose told her she would be searched in the office. Taking the luggage and keys, he went out to summon an orderly. That was his mistake, for Ginnie swiftly locked the door, pulled the paper from her bosom, "dipped it in the water pitcher and in three lumps swallowed it." When he returned Captain Rose found the door unlocked and Ginnie with her hat on. The two women and their escort had trouble in pushing through the heavy crowd on the street, and the annoyed Union officer mumbled to Ginnie: "I suppose you feel like hurrahing for Jeff Davis."

As a matter of fact, Ginnie confides in her memoir, she was so pleased over destroying the dispatch that she did exactly that. "I raised my hand over my head and said in a loud voice, 'Hurrah for Jeff Davis!' " In the provost marshal's office the Union officers, opening a trunk, uncovered a supply of blue-checked gingham. She wanted it for children's aprons, Ginnie told them, though she confesses to us that she "meant it for soldiers' shirts." The men drew out about fifty letters to Southerners, and then—a ball of opium. Captain Andrew Kemper, officer in charge, asked in astonishment: "What are you doing with that?"

"My mother can eat that much in a month," Ginnie retorted. "She requires it." As Captain Kemper "covered his mouth with his hand to hide a smile," Mrs. Moon sat up straight in her chair, even more firm-lipped than usual. Ginnie observed that "she might have been under the influence of it then." A moment later Kemper picked up a heavy quilt, felt it, ripped it open, and found that it was filled with opium, quinine, and morphine, drugs that were sorely needed in the South.

As to what happened next, accounts differ; but apparently a Federal officer started to close the door and Ginnie's hoop skirts got in the way. "He put his hand down to put them aside and found that the dress and petticoats alike were quilted." He called for a housekeeper, who searched the spy, confiscated her costume, and gave her a substitute. According to the next day's paper, Ginnie had been wearing "forty bottles of morphine, seven pounds of opium and a quantity of camphor," some of it "in a huge bustle, or sack, fastened to her person"!

Regretfully Captain Kemper announced he would have to keep the two Confederates as prisoners. Ginnie pertly suggested one or two nearby Federal prisons. Ah, but they were not suitable for ladies, the Yankee told her; perhaps a hotel would be best. Kemper named a fashionable one along the river. Ginnie inquired if General Burnside was due back soon, and where he stayed. Learning that Burnside lodged at the Burnet House, she announced she and her mother would go there or nowhere.

Paroles were handed to them, and the stern Mrs. Moon said she would put her name to nothing at all. Ginnie signed for them both. At the hotel, Captain Rose chivalrously asked her down to dinner. Ginnie answered: "You're my jailer. I have to put up with you." Nevertheless, the meal went pleasantly enough, and Ginnie's charm and humor made Captain Rose still more friendly. With an arch look he held up a telegram. He thought she'd like to know its contents, but he couldn't let her see it. Feeling sure he "would not dare to scuffle with me before all those people," Ginnie snatched it, and learned that General Rosecrans in Nashville was demanding that Miss Moon be forwarded to *him.*

Ginnie lost no time in dispatching her card to Burnside's

office. In the morning the general sent word he would receive her. She recognized old Buttons at once, despite the passage of thirteen or more years, "by his uniform, side whiskers and size." Holding out both hands, Burnside cried: "My child, what have you done this for?"

"Done what?"

The general was sad. "Tried to go South without coming to me for a pass. They wouldn't have dared stop you."

Ginnie gave her friend Buttons a straight look. "General, I have a little honor. I couldn't have asked you for a pass and carried what I did." The general sighed, asked her a few more questions, and then told her he would take the matter out of the hands of the customhouse officials and "try her himself." Delighted, Ginnie thanked him. Meanwhile her spirits were so much restored that she was reproving the Yankees, accusing one official of keeping her intimate garments. "I had not the least idea that my stockings, petticoats or *corsets* could be construed as *government prizes*." She had been left without a change, she observed, while the Union officers must intend to consign her property to the use of their friends!

Since General Burnside was so obviously sympathetic, other officers tried to gain Miss Ginnie's good will. "I was asked down to the parlors every evening to meet some of the staff officers," she recalled with evident pleasure. "The Yankee women in the parlor looked very indignant to see these officers being so polite to a Secesh woman." She was still not yet nineteen.

Even then the forthright girl amused herself with a bit of Union-baiting. One of Burnside's aides told her that Joe Jefferson was playing at a Cincinnati theater. Wouldn't she like to see him? Miss Ginnie considered and said yes, she would. Then would she accompany the captain? Ginnie sighed; that would be breaking her parole, which prohibited her from leaving the hotel without competent military authorization. The captain smiled; he could fix that. The younger man went out and called on General Burnside, who returned with him; Miss Ginnie had authority to see the play.

"Oh, I *can* go?" The blue eyes brightened.

"Yes."

"Then I won't." The light had become a small flame. "My brothers are in front of your bullets daily, and I wouldn't be seen escorted by a Yankee!"

General Burnside bowed: "I'll bid you good evening," he said, and returned to his room.

Soon afterward the general lifted his eyes from his desk to see before him a much agitated lady. With a markedly British accent she explained that she was an Englishwoman journeying from Virginia's springs to the Arkansas waters. Only a few hours ago she had been informed that two other women had been arrested, and now she "hastened to ask protection from such a possible misfortune to herself, and also for a pass to proceed." Warming to her subject, the visitor explained testily that she had hoped for a few days of relaxation in Cincinnati, but "this continued excitement would be the death of her, and worse than the fatigue of travel."

Ambrose Burnside, who had courted Lottie Moon so long that he knew every line of her face, sat silent through the barrage. Then he told the caller, gently: "You've forgotten me. But I still remember with pleasure the hours I used to spend with you in Oxford." Lottie still tried to brazen it out, protesting against these ridiculous accusations. She was only a traveling Englishwoman, ill and hopeful. . . .

The general shook his head, and Lottie realized that her game had failed. Even had she tried her old specialty of jaw-cracking, she could not have fooled Ambrose Burnside. . . . She joined Sister Ginnie and her mother and for weeks they remained under surveillance in Cincinnati or at her home nearby. There are indications that her onetime beau kept Lottie in suspense for a long time, making every effort to frighten her out of her Confederate activities.

The records show that no action was ever taken against Lottie or Ginnie. And yet the official correspondence, discovered in recent years in Ohio, reveals that some of Ginnie's rebel mail presented evidence of earlier writing in invisible ink. Other notes, it was declared, showed that "the fair mail carrier is widely known in . . . Philadelphia, Montreal, Canada; Murfreesboro, Tennessee. They show that she has traveled diligently and has been engaged for some length of time in this way." The report concluded that the "known disloyalty and disloyal connections of these ladies" demanded that a stop be put to their activities.

In spite of everything, charges were dropped against both Moon sisters. The Knights of the Golden Circle eventually proved an ineffectual organization, confused in its purposes, and the movement slowly collapsed. Lottie and Judge Clark left Ohio for New York. For them spying and conspiracies—even the war—had ended. For little Ginnie, however, Yankees were Yankees, and she continued her own form of hostilities. Back in Memphis, she collected marriage proposals again, slipped information to handy Southerners, and otherwise acted as a gadfly to the Union side.

Ginnie had orders to report daily at 10 A.M. to Federal General Hurlburt, the Northern officers hoping this would limit her operations. Obviously it did not, and after three months the general commanded that Miss Ginnie Moon was to get out of the Union lines and stay out! Gathering up her skirts, Ginnie cheerfully shook off the Yankee dust. Her movements for the next seven or eight months are a mystery. Then about the middle of 1864 she turned up at Danville, Virginia, with her sister-in-law.

Ginnie's brother, ill and defeated, had escaped from the United States to the South of France. From there he wrote to ask if his wife, two children, and Ginnie could join him, to sit out the war overseas. The two women obtained passes and worked their way to Newport News—only to be halted by none other than Ben Butler. Unless they took the Union oath, they learned, they could not go on.

Ginnie's sister-in-law felt she had to accept; Ginnie tossed her head and announced that she'd never do it. Afterward she asked her sister-in-law how she could have taken the oath, and the lady answered: "I didn't hear a word that man talked about. I kept saying the multiplication table as hard as I could."

Butler kept Ginnie in custody for a time. Her relatives said she lived on "bread and water," but this report may well be doubted. After a while the general said that if she agreed to the oath, he could still help her join the family group. The general's emissary pointed out that, after all, Miss Ginnie would have to take it before summer, when Butler would be in Richmond.

Miss Ginnie gave him a look. "If Butler's in Richmond, he'll be hanging to a tree!" That settled that. The Union finally permitted Ginnie to go on into Confederate territory, and there she strengthened friendly relationships with someone she had already met, Jefferson Davis. Her family has kept several Davis letters, addressed to "Dear Ginnie" and asking a blessing on her and "my dear friend, your sister."

In spite of Ginnie's help the long war ended. The South had lost, but Ginnie, who lived on for sixty years after Appomattox, never accepted defeat for a moment. . . . The older sister Lottie became a novelist and pioneer woman newspaper correspondent, covering European capitals during the Franco-Prussian war. Ginnie remained for years in about Memphis, rambunctious as ever. She seemed a living anachronism in her rustling silk dresses, her beribboned shirtwaists, starched and stiff, and her tiny hat in the style of earlier days. But the few people who took Ginnie Moon for Whistler's mother had surprises in store for them.

For a time she took in boarders—men only; she wouldn't have women around the house. She became a heroine in a grim yellow fever epidemic of the 1870s. When she reached her own mid-seventies, Ginnie had an idea—Hollywood—and she went there. Standing before the producer Jesse Lasky, she said she wanted to act. "What makes you think you can do it?" Lasky asked. Ginnie folded her small arms: "I'm seventy-five years old, and I've acted all of them." The producer nodded: "You'll do."

She did, taking parts with Pola Negri, Douglas Fairbanks, and Mary Miles Minter. At seventy-six, she donned padded jacket and helmet for a seaplane flight. In her later years, tired and a bit bored, she took herself to Greenwich Village. Delighting in the atmosphere, she chain-smoked, mixed her own juleps, and talked by the hour, with scorn and spirit, to the younger residents who crowded around her. Riding on Riverside Drive with a party of Northern friends, she once glanced at Grant's Tomb. "Damn him," she said.

As one of her final deeds, the little woman who some called wild "tamed" an alley cat and made him her companion. In September of 1926 an artist neighbor found the eighty-one-year-old Miss Ginnie stretched on the floor, her hand extended toward the door, the cat beside her. She had stopped fighting at last. . . .

Acknowledgments

In 1947, doing research in Richmond for a book on Mrs. Jefferson Davis, I came on a story telling how Miss Elizabeth Van Lew, the Union spy, had "planted" one of her agents in the residence of the Confederate President. That afternoon I asked Mrs. Ralph Catterall of the Valentine Museum for a book or other material on civilian spies of the war. There was no volume dealing primarily with the nonmilitary agents, she assured me, and only diffuse and widely scattered data on the subject. "There *should* be a book about them," Mrs. Catterall added.

Later that year, and several times afterward, I discussed the matter with the late Dr. Douglas Southall Freeman, distinguished biographer of Robert E. Lee. Dr. Freeman contributed a number of suggestions of individuals, incidents, and sources of information. Since that time, in Richmond, Washington, New Orleans, New York, and other cities I have taken time from other duties to gather material on the espionage of 1861–65. Then for the past year and a half I have worked intensively in the writing of this book.

The search has led to some unexpected sources of data—descendants or connections of the spies; letters, memoirs, and recollections left by the figures in these pages; the accounts of contemporaries and documents from official agencies which often confirm stories told by the agents or their friends. As usual, one source led to the next; a visit to one city indicated a trip to another. The material fills several desks and ranges from daguerreotypes to private notes, from government citations to thick albums of magazine and newspaper clippings to the barely illegible scrawls of sick, hard-pressed men and women. In some cases, by happy accident, my inquiries encouraged families to find in trunks and dusty boxes papers that they had not known they possessed.

As usual, libraries of all sizes proved to be repositories of printed or manuscript information and the means of reaching other individuals or agencies. Without the generous help of librarians in all parts of the country much of the information could not have been gathered. All told, some hundred librarians and several hundred individuals gave assistance.

Last summer in London I used the magnificent collections of the British Museum and the Public Records Office, and in Paris, the remarkable facilities of the Bibliothèque Nationale. Through the aid of the expert staffs of each institution I was able to trace the progress of British-born spies involved in difficulties during the war, and also of Southern agents who went later to England and the Continent.

Dr. T. Harry Williams of Louisiana State University first called my attention to a little-known collection of Rose Greenhow letters at Duke University. Miss Mattie Russell, curator of manuscripts, made available the full set, giving fresh light on Mrs. Greenhow's acts and feelings during her later days in America and in England.

Mrs. Melia Davis Sinnott of the Sam Davis Home at Smyrna, Tenn., sent me hundreds of pages of data on the career of that war figure, and suggested other persons who made further contributions.

Mr. Paul North Rice, reference librarian of the New York Public Library, and Mr. Robert W. Hill, in charge of the manuscripts, made possible a full study there, including, by use of microfilm copies, the scores of items in the library's Van Lew Manuscript Collection. Mr. Sylvester Vigilante, formerly of the American History Room, and his assistant, F. I. Avellino, answered dozens of queries on various occasions.

In the National Archives at Washington, through the help of W. Neil Franklin, chief of the General Reference Section, Mr. Richard G. Wood, and others of that agency, I was able to examine and obtain copies of portions of *Captured Confederate Correspondence*, originally taken by the State and War departments, documents dealing with hearings of prisoners before the Dix-Pierrepont Commission, and the great variety of papers taken from Rose Greenhow's house. In the National Archives I was also permitted to go through the Baker-Turner Papers relating to the work of Union detectives on the trail of Southern spies and other offenders.

In the manuscript division of the Library of Congress the chief, Mr. David Mearns, as always provided quick and courteous assistance in the use of the Hamilton Fish Collection and others with data relating to espionage.

Mrs. Merrill Parrish Hudson of Memphis and Mrs. E. S. Hathaway of New Orleans first suggested the striking Moon sisters of Ohio. Mrs. Ophia D. Smith of Oxford, Ohio, who has given long study to the subject, helped in many ways, as did Mrs. Gladys Sepin, librarian of the Lane Public Library, Hamilton, Ohio; Mrs. P. G. Dearing of Alexandria, Va., and Mrs. Mary Autry Higgins of San Antonio, family members who sent me extensive papers and recollections; Mrs. Viva Jones of Coronado, Cal.; R. H. Allen, Rembert Moon, Mrs. Catharine Van Court Myrick, Mr. George Person, Sr., all of Memphis; Jesse Cunningham, librarian of the Cossit Library, Memphis; and Eldon Roark, the able and gifted columnist of the Memphis *Press Scimitar*.

Dr. Harriet H. Shoen of New York City on several occasions gave me the benefit of her long study of wartime espionage, answering numerous queries and clarifying disputed points.

Over a period of years India Thomas, house regent of the Confederate Museum in Richmond, and her assistant, Eleanor Brockenbrough, helped in tracking down manuscripts, letters, and other material, providing pictures, and, not least important, suggesting sources.

I am indebted also to the late Clayton Torrence, director and corresponding secretary of the Virginia Historical Society Library, and John Melville Jennings, the president director; Randolph Church, librarian of the Virginia State Library; Mrs. Ralph Catterall and Mrs. G. S. Sydnor, Jr., of the Valentine Museum; and Virginius Dabney, editor of the Richmond *Times-Dispatch.* Clifford Dowdey, Virginia's distinguished novelist, and Frances Dowdey as usual helped in many ways.

Particular thanks for swift and expert aid are due, too, to Ethel L. Hutchins, head of the Reference Department of the Public Library of Cincinnati and Hamilton County, Ohio; Mrs. Irene McCreery, head of the Local History and Genealogy Division, and Herbert M. Sewell, librarian of the Toledo Public Library; Mrs. Marie Banhead Owen, director of the Alabama Department of History and Archives, Montgomery; Wayne Andrew, curator of manuscripts at the New York Historical Society; Ruth Abrams of the Michigan State and Local History Division, Grand Rapids Public Library; and Dr. Roy P. Basler, head of the Division of General Reference and Bibliography, Library of Congress.

Louis T. Moore, chairman-secretary of the New Hanover Historical Commission, Wilmington, N.C., went to special effort to provide data from his own extensive collection, and to assist in other ways. Mary Lemuel Boykin, curator of the New Hanover County (Va.) Museum, provided a photostat of a Rose Greenhow address book.

Allan Nevins, professor of history at Columbia University, again gave me the benefit of his years of experience in research, as did Dumas Malone of the Columbia History Department; Dr. Bell Irvin Wiley of the Department of History, Emory University; and Dr. E. Merton Coulter, professor of history, University of Georgia.

Mrs. Wallace Brown, Oshkosh, and Mrs. George A. Frye, Chicago, members of the family of Pauline Cushman, made courteous response to inquiries regarding that war figure.

Robert Meyer, Jr., of Festival Information Service, New

York City, did yeoman service in helping track down data in that city. Mrs. Ralph Pulitzer (Margaret Leech), author of *Reveille in Washington,* as on other occasions generously clarified a number of disputed points. Van Dyke MacBride of Newark loaned photostats of spy letters. W. M. (Billy) Steele, veteran newspaperman, recalled a story of his father when the latter was one of Belle Boyd's military escorts. Stanley Horn, the Tennessee Confederate authority, kindly loaned a little-known letter relating to Rose Greenhow's exploits.

John Bakeless, Seymour, Conn., an old hand in such matters, sent a series of letters that guided my hand at several points. Mrs. Rhoda Christmas of Croome, Prince Georges County, Md., helped locate connections of Walter Bowie. Among others who helped were:

Judge Walter W. Faw, W. S. McGann, and Marshall Morgan, of Franklin, Tenn.; Mrs. Florence H. Barber of St. Petersburg, Fla.; Mrs. Fidelia Anding of the Anding Bookstore, New Orleans; Raymond Emerson, Boston; Mrs. Edythe Capreol, literary editor of the Beaumont (Tex.) *Journal;* Alfred Leland Crabb of Nashville; Bill Fountain of the Fountain Library, Columbus, Ohio; Louise Guyol of New Orleans; Mrs. Margaret Dixon and Charles East of the Baton Rouge *Morning Advocate;* Robert Selph Henry, the Confederate authority of Alexandria, Va.

Mrs. Arthur W. Chase, Washington, D.C.; James Keith, secretary of the Historical Society of Fairfax County, Va.; Edwin S. Friendly, vice-president of the New York *World Telegram and Sun;* Jean Selby, Vicksburg; Mrs. Glendy Culligan, feature editor of the Washington *Post-Times-Herald;* Hudson Grunewald, Sunday editor of the Washington *Star;* Ralph F. Rhodes, Savannah; Mrs. Rosalie S. Magruder, Bluff Point, Yates County, N.Y.; Jerry Schmal, Chicago; Mr. Frank X. Tolbert of the Dallas *Morning News.*

Mrs. Medora Perkerson, Atlanta; Mrs. Cazenove Lee, Washington, D.C.; Mr. and Mrs. Claude A. Mahoney, Fairfax, Va.; Charles Clagett, Baltimore; Walter Chandler, Memphis; Mrs.

Ferguson Cary, Alexandria, Va.; J. Winston Coleman, Jr., Lexington, Ky.; Mrs. Corinne Bailey, Jackson, Miss.; Mrs. Ferdinand C. Latrobe, Baltimore.

Dan S. Robison, state librarian and archivist, and Mrs. Gertrude Morton Parsley, reference librarian, Nashville; Mary A. Schaeffer, librarian, Kingston City Library, Kingston, N.Y.; Harland A. Carpenter, director of libraries, and Florence E. Kniffen, head of the Reference Department, Wilmington Institute Free Library, Wilmington, Del.; Dennis A. Dooley, librarian, Commonwealth of Massachusetts State Library, Boston.

James H. Pickering, director, Charlottesville-Albemarle Public Library; Helen M. Talbert, senior librarian, Roswell P. Flower Memorial Library, Watertown, Mass.; Charlotte D. Conover, librarian, New Hampshire Historical Society, Concord, N.H.; Claude R. Cook, curator, Iowa State Department of History and Archives, Des Moines.

Virginia L. Close, reference librarian, Dartmouth College, Hanover, N.H.; Mrs. Augusta B. Richardson, director, Northeast Regional Library, Corinth, Miss.; Mrs. Mildred P. McKay, state librarian, Concord, N.H.; Margaret G. Hickman, principal librarian, Periodical Department, Los Angeles Public Library.

Martha L. Ellison, head of reference department, Lawson McGhee Library, Knoxville; Louis M. Nourse, librarian, and Mildred Boatman, head of Reference Department, St. Louis Public Library; Robin R. B. Murray, St. John Free Public Library, St. John, N.B., Can.; Allan R. Ottley, librarian, California Section, California State Library, Sacramento; Clara E. Follette, librarian and museum director, Vermont Historical Society, Montpelier.

Mrs. Dorothy Thomas Cullen, curator and librarian, Filson Club, Louisville; Laura E. Howard, librarian, War Memorial Library, Franklin, Tenn.; Elizabeth C. Litsinger, head of Maryland Department, Enoch Pratt Free Library, Baltimore; C. Vernon Eddy, librarian, Handley Library, Winchester, Va.; Ethel A. L. Lacy, curator, Washingtoniana Division, Public Library,

District of Columbia; Dorothy E. Ryan, head of circulation, Library of the University of Tennessee.

Clifford K. Shipton, librarian of the American Antiquarian Society, Worcester, Mass.; James T. Babb, librarian, and Dorothy W. Bridgwater, assistant reference librarian, Yale University Library; Mrs. Lucille T. Dickerson, librarian, Jones Memorial Library, Lynchburg, Va.

Alice Cynthia Dodge, librarian, Utica Public Library; Clarence E. Miller, librarian, St. Louis Mercantile Library Association; E. E. Seebach, chief of circulation, Milwaukee Public Library; Mrs. Alice P. Hook, librarian, Historical and Philosophic Society of Ohio, Cincinnati; Kenneth J. Boyer, Bowdoin College Library, Brunswick, Me.; Esther Norman, acting librarian, Public Library of Kansas City.

Charles Van Ravenswaay, director of the Missouri Historical Society, St. Louis; Charles W. Sargent, curator, Kansas Historical Collections, University of Kansas; Mrs. Louise S. Parker, librarian, Des Moines Art Center; L. M. Allison, associate librarian, Mt. Allison Memorial Library, Sackville, N.B., Can.; Edgar W. King, librarian, Miami University, Oxford, Ohio; Betty Y. Bell, reference librarian, Nashville Public Library; Ida Padelford, Sondley Reference Library, Asheville, N.C.; Fred Shelley, librarian, Maryland Historical Library, Baltimore.

Mary Isabel Fry, reference librarian, Henry E. Huntington Library and Art Center, San Marino, Cal.; Robert L. Peterson, librarian, Newspaper Collection, Library of the University of Texas; Floyd C. Shoemaker, State Historical Society of Missouri, Columbia; R. Gerald McMurtry, editor in chief, *Lincoln Herald*, Lincoln Memorial University, Harrogate, Tenn.; Mrs. E. C. Harris, librarian, Reference Department, Mobile Public Library.

Mrs. Littleton Fitzgerald, Richmond; Dr. Robert D. Meade, Lynchburg, Va.; Louis Koppel, Dr. Gerald Capers, and Mrs. Yvonne le Mercier Duquesnay, New Orleans; the late Ruth Wallgren, Philadelphia; Mrs. Maud O'Bryan Ronstrom, want ad columnist of the *Times-Picayune States*, New Orleans; W. A.

Klein, Randall Butler, Ellen Prowell, William H. Ratcliff, W. C. Robinson, Herbert J. Broussard, John Morgan, R. B. Moodie, Albert Craigie, and T. P. McLaughlin of New Orleans; E. L. Fugler, Baton Rouge; Mrs. Vivian Sims and J. P. Rousseau, Clermont Harbor, Miss.; Mrs. Ethel Moore Mullins, Meadville, Miss.

Sarah A. McAllister, Centreville, Miss.; Mrs. H. S. Giere, Hammond, La.; Mrs. Thomas W. Walsh, Baton Rouge; Dorothy Blackman, New Orleans; Mrs. Charles O'Neal, Jackson, Miss.

Dr. William McCain, director, and Charlotte Capers, assistant director, Mississippi Department of Archives and History, Jackson; Ben Mathews, director, Mrs. Rosa Oliver, librarian, and Mrs. Frances Bryson Moore, Louisiana State Museum, Baton Rouge.

Dr. Garland Taylor, librarian of the Howard-Tilton Memorial Library of Tulane University, New Orleans; Marguerite Renshaw, formerly reference librarian, and Mrs. Evangeline Thurber, Mrs. Dorothy Lawton, Martha Ann Peters, Diane Duvic, Robert Greenwood, and Mrs. Beatricia Ford, former members of the staff.

V. L. Bedsole, archivist of Louisiana State University; Mrs. Ruth Campbell, late librarian of the Louisiana Room, Louisiana State University, and Lucy B. Foote, her successor.

John Hall Jacobs, librarian, George King Logan, assistant librarian, Ruth Renaud, Margaret Ruckert, Gladys Peyronnin, Lily Mouton, Marian Mason, Mrs. Alice V. Westfeldt, Mrs. Ellen R. Tilger, and Mrs. Bernice Zibilich, of the New Orleans Public Library.

James W. Dyson, librarian of Loyola University, New Orleans.

And Mrs. Florence Kane Reynolds, Anna Marie Kane, and Mavis McIntosh.

Bibliography

ADAMS, HENRY. *The Education of Henry Adams.* New York: 1918.

ALER, F. V. *History of Martinsburg.* Hagerstown, Md.: 1889.

ANDREWS, MATTHEW PAGE. *The Women of the South in War Times.* Baltimore: 1920.

ASHBY, GEORGE F. *Major General Grenville M. Dodge.* New York: 1947.

ASHBY, THOMAS A. *The Valley Campaigns.* New York: 1914.

AVARY, MYRTA L. *A Virginia Girl in the Civil War.* New York: 1903.

AVIRETT, JAMES B. *The Memoirs of General Turner Ashby and His Compeers.* Baltimore: 1867.

BAKER, LAFAYETTE C. *History of the United States Secret Service.* Philadelphia: 1889.

BANCROFT, FREDERIC. *The Life of Willim H. Seward.* New York and London: 1900.

BARTON, GEORGE. *The World's Greatest Military Spies and Secret Service Agents.* Boston: 1917.

BATES, DAVID H. *Lincoln in the Telegraph Office.* New York: 1907.

BATES, SAMUEL P., and B. SINGERLEY. *History of the Pennsylvania Volunteers, 1861–65.* 5 vols. Harrisburg, Pa.: 1869–71.

BEALE, G. W. *A Lieutenant of Cavalry in Lee's Army.* Boston: 1918.

BEATTY, JOHN. *Memoirs of a Volunteer.* New York: 1946.

BEMIS, SAMUEL F., and GRACE GARDNER GRIFFIN. *Guide to the Diplomatic History of the United States, 1775–1921.* Washington: 1935.

BEYMER, WILLIAM G. *On Hazardous Service.* New York: 1912.

BLACK, ROBERT. *The Railroads of the Confederacy.* Chapel Hill: 1952.

BLACKFORD, SUSAN LEIGH, comp. *Memoirs of Life In and Out of the Army of Virginia.* 2 vols. Lynchburg, Va.: 1894–96.

BLAINE, JAMES G. *Twenty Years of Congress.* 2 vols. Norwich, Conn.: 1884–86.

BONHAM, MILLEDGE L., JR. *The British Consuls in the Confederacy.* New York: 1911.

BOUDRYE, L. N. *Historic Records of the Fifth New York Cavalry.* Albany, N.Y.: 1865.

BOYD, BELLE. *Belle Boyd in Camp and Prison.* New York: 1865.

BOYD, SCOTT LEE. *The Boyd Family.* Santa Barbara, Cal.: 1935.

BOYD, WILLIAM P. *History of the Boyd Family and Descendants.* Rochester, N.Y.: 1912.

BRADFORD, GAMALIEL. *Confederate Portraits.* Boston and New York: 1914.

BRADLEE, F. B. C. *Blockade Running During the Civil War.* Salem, Mass.: 1925.

BREMER, FREDRIKA. *The Homes of the New World.* 2 vols. New York: 1853.

BROCK, SALLY. *Richmond During the War.* New York: 1867.

BROCKETT, L. P. *The Camp, the Battle Field and the Hospital.* Philadelphia and Chicago: 1866.

—— and M. C. VAUGHAN. *Woman's Work in the Civil War.* New York: 1867.

BROOKS, NOAH. *Washington in Lincoln's Time.* New York: 1888.

BRYAN, GEORGE S. *The Spy in America.* Philadelphia: 1943.

BRYAN, WILHELMUS B. *A History of the National Capital.* 2 vols. New York: 1914–16.

BUCHANAN, JAMES. *Mr. Buchanan's Administration on the Eve of Rebellion.* New York: 1866.

BULLOCH, J. D. *Secret Service of the Confederate States in Europe.* 2 vols. New York: 1884.

BUTLER, BENJAMIN F. *Autobiography and Personal Reminiscences of Major-General Benjamin F. Butler.* Boston: 1892.

CALLAHAN, E. W., ed. *List of Officers of the Navy of the United States, 1775–1900.* New York: 1901.

CARPENTER, FRANCIS B. *Six Months at the White House.* New York: 1866.

CASTLEMAN, JOHN B. *On Active Service.* Louisville: 1927.

CATTON, BRUCE. *Mr. Lincoln's Army*. New York: 1951.

—— *A Stillness at Appomattox*. New York: 1953.

CHAMBERLIN, THOMAS. *History of the 150th Regiment, Pennsylvania Volunteers*. Philadelphia: 1895.

CHAMBERS, ROBERT. *Secret Service Operator 13*. New York: 1934.

CHASE, SALMON P. "Diary and Correspondence," *Annual Report of the American Historical Association*. 2 vols. 1903.

CHESNUT, MARY BOYKIN. *A Diary from Dixie*. Ed. by Ben Ames Williams. Boston: 1949.

CIST, HENRY M. *The Army of the Cumberland*. New York: 1882.

CLARK, ALLEN C. *Abraham Lincoln in the National Capital*. Washington: 1925.

CLAY, MRS. CLEMENT C. *A Belle of the Fifties*. New York: 1905.

COIT, MARGARET L. *John C. Calhoun*. Boston: 1950.

COLMAN, EDNA. *Seventy Five Years of White House Gossip*. New York: 1925.

"CONFEDERATE, A." *The Grayjackets*. Richmond: 1867.

COOKE, JOHN ESTEN. *Wearing of the Gray*. New York: 1867.

COOLIDGE, LOUIS A. *Ulysses S. Grant*. New York and Boston: 1917.

COULTER, E. MERTON. *The Confederate States of America, 1861–65*, Vol. 7, *A History of the South*. Baton Rouge: 1950.

CURTIS, GEORGE T. *Life of James Buchanan*. 2 vols. New York: 1883.

CUTHBERT, NORMA B. *Lincoln and the Baltimore Plot, 1861*. San Marino, Cal.: 1949.

DAHLGREN, MADELINE V. *Memoirs of John A. Dahlgren*. Boston: 1882.

DANA, CHARLES A. *Lincoln and His Cabinet*. New York: 1899.

—— *Recollections of the Civil War*. New York: 1883.

DANDRIDGE, DANSKE. *Historic Shepherdstown*. Charlottesville, Va.: 1910.

DANIEL, JOHN M. *The Richmond Examiner During the War*. New York: 1868.

DE LEON, T. C. *Belles, Beaux and Brains of the Sixties*. New York: 1909.

—— *Four Years in Rebel Capitals*. Mobile: 1890.

DICEY, EDWARD. *Six Months in the Federal States*. 2 vols. London: 1863.

Dictionary of American Biography. New York: 1928–37.

DIX, MORGAN. *Memoirs of John A. Dix*. New York: 1883.

DODD, WILLIAM E. *Jefferson Davis*. Philadelphia: 1907.

—— *Statesmen of the Old South*. New York: 1911.

DODGE, GRENVILLE M. *The Battle of Atlanta and other Campaigns, Addresses, etc*. Council Bluffs, Iowa: 1911.

DONALD, DAVIS, ed. *Divided We Fought*. New York: 1952.

DORRIS, JONATHAN T. *Pardon and Amnesty under Lincoln and Johnson*. Chapel Hill: 1953.

DOSTER, WILLIAM E. *Lincoln and Episodes of the Civil War*. New York: 1915.

DOUGLAS, HENRY KYD. *I Rode with Stonewall*. Chapel Hill: 1940.

DOWDEY, CLIFFORD. *Experiment in Rebellion*. New York: 1946.

—— *Bugles Blow No More*. Boston: 1937.

DOWNS, EDWARD C. *Four Years a Scout and Spy*. Zanesville, Ohio: 1866.

EATON, CLEMENT. *A History of the Southern Confederacy*. New York: 1954.

ECKER, GRACE D. *A Portrait of Old George Town*. Richmond: 1933.

EDMONDS, S. EMMA E. *Nurse and Spy in the Union Army*. Philadelphia: 1865.

EGGLESTON, GEORGE C. *A Rebel's Recollections*. New York: 1875.

ELLETT, ELIZABETH. *The Court Circles of the Republic*. New York: 1869.

ELLIS, JOHN B. *The Sights and Secrets of the National Capital*. New York: 1869.

ELY, ALFRED. *Journal of Alfred Ely*. Ed. by Charles Lanman. New York: 1862.

Famous Adventures and Prison Escapes of the Civil War. New York: 1893.

FISKE, JOHN. *The Mississippi Valley in the Civil War*. Boston and New York: 1900.

FREEMAN, DOUGLAS S. *A Calendar of Confederate Papers*. Richmond: 1908.

—— *Lee's Lieutenants*. 3 vols. New York: 1942–44.

—— *R. E. Lee, a Biography*. 4 vols. New York: 1937.

GEER, J. J. *Beyond the Lines*. Philadelphia: 1863.

Genealogy of the Cutts Family in America. Albany, N.Y.: 1892.

GILMOR, HARRY. *Four Years in the Saddle*. New York: 1866.

GLAZIER, WILLARD. *The Capture, the Prison Pen and the Escape.*

GOLLOMB, JOSEPH. *Spies.* London: 1928.

GOULD, JOHN M. *History of the First—Tenth—29th Maine Regiment.* Portland, Me.: 1871.

GRANT, U. S. *Personal Memoirs.* 2 vols. New York: 1885–86.

GRAY, WOOD. *The Hidden Civil War.* New York: 1942.

GREELEY, HORACE. *The American Conflict.* 2 vols. Hartford, Conn.: 1869.

GREENHOW, ROSE O'NEAL. *My Imprisonment and the First Year of Abolition Rule at Washington.* London: 1863.

HARPER, ROBERT S. *Lincoln and the Press.* New York: 1951.

HARRISON, MRS. BURTON. *Recollections Grave and Gay.* New York: 1911.

HARROLD, JOHN C. *Libby, Andersonville, Florence.* Philadelphia: 1870.

HART, CHARLES S. *George Washington's Son of Israel and Other Forgotten Heroes of History.* Philadelphia and London: 1937.

HEADLEY, JOHN W. *Confederate Operations in Canada.* New York: 1906.

HEITMANN, FRANCIS B. *Historical Register and Dictionary of the United States Army.* Washington: 1903.

HENDERSON, G. F. R. *Stonewall Jackson.* London and New York: 1898.

HENRY, R. S. *The Story of the Confederacy.* Indianapolis: 1931.

HERGESHEIMER, JOSEPH. *Swords and Roses.* New York: 1929.

HESSELTINE, W. B. *Civil War Prisons.* Columbus, Ohio: 1930.

History and Biographical Cyclopedia of Butler County, Ohio. Cincinnati: 1882.

HOPLEY, CATHERINE. *Life in the South.* London: 1863.

HORAN, JAMES D. *Desperate Women.* New York: 1953.

—— and HOWARD SWIGGETT. *The Pinkerton Story.* New York: 1951.

HORN, STANLEY. *The Army of Tennessee.* Indianapolis: 1941.

—— *The Robert E. Lee Reader.* Indianapolis: 1941.

HUMPHREYS, ANDREW A. *The Virginia Campaign of '64 and '65.* New York: 1883.

HUMPHREYS, DAVID. *Heroes and Spies of the Civil War.* New York and Washington: 1903.

JARECKA, LOUISE L. "Virginia Moon, Unreconstructed Rebel," *Delphian Quarterly,* XXX (1947), January.

JOHNS, GEORGE S. *Philip Henson, the Southern Union Spy*. St. Louis: 1887.

JOHNSON, R. U., and C. C. BUEL, eds. *Battles and Leaders of the Civil War*. 4 vols. New York: 1888.

JOHNSTON, R. M. *Bull Run; Its Strategy and Tactics*. New York and Boston: 1913.

JOINVILLE, PRINCE DE. *The Army of the Potomac*. New York: 1862.

JONES, JOHN B. *A Rebel War Clerk's Diary*. Ed. by Howard Swiggett. New York: 1935.

JONES, VIRGIL C. *Ranger Mosby*. Chapel Hill: 1944.

KAISER, RUBY A. *Famous Ohio Ladies, 1803–1953*. Columbus, Ohio: 1953.

KEYES, E. D. *Fifty Years' Observation of Men and Events*. New York: 1884.

KING, HORATIO. *Turning on the Light*. Philadelphia: 1895.

KOOP, THEODORE. *Weapon of Silence*. Chicago: 1946.

LAMON, WARD HILL. *Recollections of Abraham Lincoln, 1847–65*. Chicago: 1895.

LAWRENCE, GEORGE A. *Border and Bastille*. New York: 1863.

LEECH, MARGARET. *Reveille in Washington, 1860–1865*. New York: 1941.

LEECH, SAMUEL V. *The Raid of John Brown on Harper's Ferry*. New York: 1909.

LITTLE, JOHN P. *History of Richmond*. Richmond: 1933.

LOMAX, VIRGINIA. *The Old Capitol and Its Inmates*. New York: 1867.

LONN, ELLA. *Desertion During the Civil War*. New York: 1928.

—— *Foreigners in the Confederacy*. Chapel Hill: 1940.

LOSSING, BENSON J. *The Pictorial Field Book of the Civil War*. 3 vols. New York: 1874–81.

MC DONALD, CORNELIA. *A Diary with Reminiscences of the War and Refugee Life in the Shenandoah Valley, 1860–65*. Nashville: 1935.

MC ELROY, ROBERT. *Jefferson Davis, the Unreal and the Real*. 2 vols. New York: 1937.

MC GINNIS, RALPH J. *History of Oxford, Ohio*. Oxford: 1930.

MC GUIRE, MRS. JUDITH W. *Diary of a Southern Refugee*. New York: 1867.

MAHONY, DENNIS A. *The Prisoner of State.* New York: 1863.
MALIN, J. C. *John Brown and the Legend of Fifty Six.* Philadelphia: 1942.
MARSHALL, JOHN A. *The American Bastille.* Philadelphia: 1872.
MAURICE, MAJOR GEN. SIR FREDERICK. *Statesmen and Soldiers of the Civil War.* Boston: 1926.
MAURY, GEN. DABNEY H. *Recollections of a Virginian.* New York: 1894.
MEADE, ROBERT D. *Judah P. Benjamin.* Toronto: 1943.
MEREDITH, ROY. *Mr. Lincoln's Camera Man, Matthew Brady.* New York: 1946.
MERRILL, SAMUEL H. *Campaigns of the First Maine Cavalry and First District of Columbia Cavalry.* Portland, Me.: 1866.
MIERS, EARL S. *The General Who Marched to Hell: William Tecumseh Sherman.* New York: 1951.
MILLER, F. T. *The Photographic History of the Civil War.* 10 vols. New York: 1912.
MILTON, GEORGE FORT. *The Age of Hate; Andrew Johnson and the Radicals.* New York: 1930.
—— *Abraham Lincoln and the Fifth Column.* New York: 1942.
MOORE, FRANK. *The Civil War in Song and Story.* New York: 1882.
—— *The Rebellion Record.* 12 vols. New York: 1864–68.
MORDECAI, S. *Richmond in Bygone Days.* Richmond: 1856.
MORTON, O. F. *The History of Winchester in Virginia.* Strasburg, Va.: 1925.
MOSBY, JOHN S. *The Memoirs of Col. John S. Mosby.* Ed. by Charles Wells Russell. Boston: 1917.
—— *Mosby's War Reminiscences, and Stuart's Cavalry Campaigns.* New York: 1887.
MYERS, WILLIAM S. *General George Brinton McClellan.* New York and London: 1934.

NEELY, RUTH, ed. *Women of Ohio.* n.d.
NEVINS, ALLAN. *Frémont, Pathmarker of the West.* London: 1939.
—— *Ordeal of the Union.* 2 vols. New York: 1947.
NICOLAY, HELEN. *Our Capital on the Potomac.* New York and London: 1924.
NICOLAY, JOHN G., and JOHN HAY. *Abraham Lincoln, a History.* 10 vols. New York and London: 1914.

O'CONNOR, RICHARD. *Sheridan the Inevitable.* Indianapolis: 1953.

Official Records of the War of the Rebellion. 128 vols. Washington, D.C.: 1880–1901.

OWEN, W. M. *In Camp and Battle with the Washington Artillery.* Boston: 1885.

OWSLEY, FRANK L. *King Cotton Diplomacy: Foreign Relations of the Confederate States of America.* Chicago: 1931.

—— *State Rights in the Confederacy.* Chicago: 1925.

PEMBER, PHOEBE Y. *A Southern Woman's Story.* New York: 1879.

PERKINS, JACOB R. *Trails, Rails and War: the Life of General G. M. Dodge.* Indianapolis: 1929.

PIKE, JAMES. *The Scout and Ranger.* Cincinnati: 1865.

PINKERTON, ALLAN. *History and Evidence of the Passage of Abraham Lincoln from Harrisburg, Pa., to Washington, D.C.* New York: 1907.

—— *The Spy of the Rebellion.* New York: 1883.

PITTENGER, W. *The Secret Service.* Philadelphia: 1882.

PLUM, WILLIAM R. *The Military Telegraph During the Civil War in the United States.* 2 vols. Chicago: 1882.

POLLARD, EDWARD A. *Observations in the North.* Richmond: 1865.

POORE, BEN: PERLEY. *The Life and Public Services of Ambrose E. Burnside.* Providence, R.I.: 1882.

PORTER, DAVID D. *Incidents and Anecdotes of the Civil War.* New York: 1885.

PORTER, HORACE. *Campaigning with Grant.* New York: 1897.

PRATT, FLETCHER. *Secret and Urgent: The Story of Codes and Ciphers.* Indianapolis: 1939.

PRYOR, MRS. ROGER A. *Reminiscences of Peace and War.* New York: 1905.

PUTNAM, MRS. S. A. *Richmond During the War.* New York: 1867.

QUARLES, BENJAMIN. *The Negro in the Civil War.* Boston: 1953.

RANDALL, J. G. *The Civil War and Reconstruction.* Boston and New York: 1937. "The Newspaper Problem in Its Bearing upon Military Secrecy during the Civil War," *American Historical Review*, XXIII (1918), January.

READER, FRANK S. *History of the Fifth West Virginia Cavalry.* New Brighton, Pa.: 1890.

RHODES, JAMES FORD. *History of the United States from the Compromise of 1850.* 8 vols. New York: 1902–10.

RICHARDSON, ALBERT D. *The Secret Service, the Field, the Dungeon and the Escape.* Hartford, Conn: 1865.

RICHARDSON, WILLIAM T. *Historic Pulaski.* Nashville: 1911.

RIDLEY, B. L. *Battles and Sketches of the Army of Tennessee.* Mexico, Mo.: 1906.

ROBINSON, WILLIAM M., JR. *The Confederate Privateers.* New Haven: 1928.

—— *Justice in Gray: A History of the Judicial System of the Confederate States of America.* Cambridge, Mass.: 1941.

ROBSON, JOHN S. *How a One-Legged Rebel Lives.* Durham, N.C.: 1898.

ROSEBAULT, CHARLES J. *When Dana Was the Sun.* New York: 1931.

ROSS, FITZGERALD. *A Visit to the Cities and Camps of the Confederate States.* Edinburgh and London: 1865.

ROWAN, RICHARD W. *The Pinkertons.* Boston: 1931.

—— *The Story of Secret Service.* New York: 1938.

SALA, GEORGE AUGUSTUS. *My Diary in America in the Midst of War.* London: 1865.

SAMPSON, ANNA E. *Kith and Kin.* Richmond: 1922.

SANDBURG, CARL. *Abraham Lincoln: The War Years.* 4 vols. New York: 1939.

SARMIENTO, F. L. *Pauline Cushman, Union Spy and Scout.* New York: 1865.

SAWYER, FRANK. *A Military History of the Eighth Regiment, Ohio Volunteer Infantry.* Cleveland: 1881.

SCHARF, JOHN T. *History of the Confederate States Navy.* New York: 1887.

SCOTT, JOHN. *Partisan Life with Colonel John S. Mosby.* New York: 1867.

SCOTT, MARY WINGFIELD. *Houses of Old Richmond.* Richmond: 1941.

SHERIDAN, P. H. *Personal Memoirs.* 2 vols. New York: 1888.

SHOEN, HARRIET H. "Pryce Lewis, Spy for the Union," *Davis and Elkins Historical Magazine*, II (1949), March and May.

SIGAUD, LOUIS A. *Belle Boyd, Confederate Spy.* Richmond: 1945.

—— "Mrs. Greenhow and the Rebel Spy Ring," *Maryland Historical Magazine*, September, 1946.

SILVER, J. W. "Propaganda in the Confederacy," *Journal of Southern History*, XI (1945), November.

SIMKINS, F. B. and J. W. PATTON. *The Women of the Confederacy*. Richmond: 1936.

SINGER, KURT. *Three Thousand Years of Espionage*. New York: 1948.

SMITH, EDWARD C. *The Borderland in the Civil War*. New York: 1927.

SMITH, GEORGE. *Spencer Kellogg Brown*. New York: 1903.

SMITH, OPHIA D. *Old Oxford Houses and the People Who Lived in Them*. Oxford, Ohio: 1941.

STEVENS, W. O. *The Shenandoah and Its Byways*. New York: 1941.

STODDARD, WILLIAM O. *Inside the White House in War Times*. New York: 1890.

STONE, CHARLES P. "Washington on the Eve of the War," *Century Magazine*, XXVI (1883), July.

—— "Washington in 1861," *Magazine of American History*, XII (1884), July.

SWIGGETT, HOWARD. *The Rebel Raider*. Indianapolis: 1934.

SWINTON, WILLIAM A. *History of the Seventh Regiment, State of New York National Guard*. New York and Boston: 1870.

TATE, ALLEN. *Stonewall Jackson*. New York: 1928.

TATUM, G. L. *Disloyalty in the Confederacy*. Chapel Hill: 1934.

TAYLOR, CHARLES E. "The Signal and the Secret Service of the Confederate States," *North Carolina Booklet*, II, No. 11. Hamlet, N.C.: 1903.

TAYLOR, RICHARD. *Destruction and Reconstruction*. New York: 1897.

TAYLOR, THOMAS E. *Running the Blockade*. London: 1896.

THOMASON, J. W., JR. *Jeb Stuart*. New York: 1930.

TOWNSEND, GEORGE A. *Campaigns of a Non-Combatant*. New York: 1866.

TURNER, GEORGE D. *Victory Rode the Rails: The Strategic Place of the Railroads in the Civil War*. Indianapolis: 1953.

UNDERWOOD, JOHN L. *The Women of the Confederacy*. New York: 1906.

VOSKA, E. V., AND WILL IRWIN. *Spy and Counterspy*. New York: 1940.

WALLING, GEORGE W. *Recollections of a New York Chief of Police.* New York: 1887.

WEISBERGER, BERNARD A. *Reporters for the Union.* Boston: 1953.

WESLEY, C. H. *The Collapse of the Confederacy.* Washington: 1937.

WHITLEY, EDYTHE J. F. *Sam Davis, Confederate Hero, 1842–63.* Smyrna, Tenn.: 1947.

WILLIAMS, CAROLINE. *The City on Seven Hills.* Cincinnati: 1938.

WILLIAMS, KENNETH P. *Lincoln Finds a General.* New York: 1949.

WILLIAMS, T. HARRY. *Lincoln and His Generals.* New York: 1952.

WILLIAMSON, JAMES J. *Mosby's Rangers.* New York: 1909.

—— *Prison Life in the Old Capitol.* West Orange, N.J.: 1911.

WILLIS, CARRIE H., and ETTA B. WALTER. *Legends of the Skyline Drive and of the Great Valley of Virginia.* Richmond: 1937.

WILSON, JAMES H. *The Life of Charles A. Dana.* New York: 1907.

WILSTACH, PAUL. *Potomac Landings.* Indianapolis: 1932.

WILTSE, CHARLES M. *John C. Calhoun.* 3 vols. Indianapolis: 1944–51.

WINSTON, R. W. *High Stakes and Hair Trigger! The Life of Jefferson Davis.* New York: 1930.

WISE, B. H. *Life of Henry A. Wise of Virginia.* New York: 1899.

WISE, JOHN S. *The End of an Era.* Boston and New York: 1902.

WOLSELEY, VISCOUNT. *Story of a Soldier's Life.* Philadelphia: 1903.

WOOD, LEONORA W. *Belle Boyd, Famous Spy of the Confederate States Army.* Keyser, W. Va.: 1940.

WOOLWORTH, SOLOMON. *The Mississippi Scout.* Chicago: 1868.

WRIGHT, RICHARDSON L. *Forgotten Ladies.* Philadelphia: 1928.

Index